Praise for *Soul Ri...*

"Take a dose of *How Stella Got Her Groove Ba...* of *Zen and the Art of Motorcycle Maintenance* and you get a taste of *Soul Rider*. Literature is full of stories about people taking to the road to find themselves, but this journey is unique and insightful, full of adventure and discovery.

—David Fisher, author of twenty-two *New York Times* bestsellers

"Carolyn Fox was one of the first women in modern history to venture out on her motorcycle on a (mid)life-changing solo journey. Her stories of freedom and liberation will inspire others to do the same for generations to come."

—Genevieve Schmitt, Founder/Editor of WomenRidersNow.com

"*Soul Rider* offers the unique perspective of a single woman traversing America on a motorcycle—all the while conquering her fears, discovering the richness of life, and finding those things that matter most. A great read!"

—Kay Allenbaugh, author of the
Chocolate for a Woman's Soul book series

"While this story will keep you invested, wondering what will happen next, it's more than just entertaining; it's important. There simply aren't enough role models like Carolyn Fox in our world, a woman who shows us how to aim straight for our fears—and run them over."

—Holly Lorincz, author of *The Stonecutter's Daughter*

"Learning to ride a motorcycle at midlife requires great courage. But that just prepares you for the external and internal journeys they'll take you on. In *Soul Rider*, author Carolyn Fox illustrates how you can overcome your fears to discover places of peace, power, and joy, where you can craft a new story for your life."

—Liz Jansen, author of *Women, Motorcycles and the Road to Empowerment*, and *Life Lessons from Motorcycles*

"*Soul Rider* is a lesson in how stepping out of your comfort zone and conquering your fear can lead you to the life that you are meant to live. Readers of any age will be inspired to make every one of their remaining days on Earth truly count."

—Annette White, author of *Bucket List Adventures: 10 Incredible Journeys to Experience Before You Die* (Skyhorse)

"Many people wrestle with their demons all their lives; in *Soul Rider*, Carolyn Fox rides a Harley to take on the darkness of her grief and reach the healing light of forgiveness. Her story is a road map to those stuck in life and needing a lift."

—Bill Johnson, author of *A Story is a Promise & The Spirit of Storytelling*

"In this inspiring memoir, Carolyn Fox takes every woman who has longed to reconnect intimately with herself on an unbelievable ride— across country and across the terrifying and miraculous landscape of the Self. This book reminds all of us that when we have the courage to answer the call of our Soul, profound healing and transformation will surely follow."

—Dawn Thompson, Portland Women Writers

"Carolyn Fox shows us that the world opens up when we step outside our comfort zones. The unexpected happens—sometimes good, sometimes not, but always, we grow. Fox's drive is inspiring and her prose beautiful."

—Ali Shaw, Executive Editor, Indigo Editing & Publications

SOUL RIDER

SOUL RIDER

FACING FEAR AND FINDING REDEMPTION ON A HARLEY

CAROLYN FOX

Skyhorse Publishing

Skyhorse Publishing books may be purchased in bulk at special discounts for sales promotion, corporate gifts, fund-raising, or educational purposes. Special editions can also be created to specifications. For details, contact the Special Sales Department, Skyhorse Publishing, 307 West 36th Street, 11th Floor, New York, NY 10018 or info@skyhorsepublishing.com.

Skyhorse® and Skyhorse Publishing® are registered trademarks of Skyhorse Publishing, Inc.®, a Delaware corporation.

Visit our website at www.skyhorsepublishing.com.

10 9 8 7 6 5 4 3 2 1

Library of Congress Cataloging-in-Publication Data is available on file.

Cover design by Rain Saukas
Cover photo credit : Author's collection

Print ISBN: 978-1-5107-1912-5
Ebook ISBN: 978-1-5107-1913-2

Printed in the United States of America

Dedication

For my children, Elizabeth, Brian, and Travis
And for Dennis Foster

Author's Note

When I began this journey, I carried a small tape recorder and recorded my thoughts and experiences as I traveled. I collected brochures, general information where it was available in various formats, and took hundreds of photographs. Returning home, those tapes were transcribed, resulting in over two hundred pages of notes. Kampgrounds of America (KOA) sponsored me. Upon my return, they offered copies of the newspaper articles and video tapes of the televised interviews, which they'd been tracking. I have changed most, but not all of the names of people in this book. I met many marvelous and fascinating characters on the road, but many times, my interaction was brief. On occasion, I changed some identifying characteristics to protect others' privacy.

Acknowledgments

I want to take a moment and thank the people who have helped and encouraged me on my publishing journey. This has indeed been a long process and I could not have done it without the help of so many people.

When I first started writing twenty years ago, I thought I would just tell the story of my physical ride, add stories from the road, throw in a few jokes, and that would be that. Simple. That was back in my very naïve days, before, as they like to say, "Life got in the way."

I attended the 2014 Willamette Writers Conference in Portland, Oregon, and pitched my story to a dozen agents. There were lots of nice rejection letters, but no offers. Agent Chip MacGregor, MacGregor Literary, liked the story, but wrote and said that after four months of "kicking it around, publishers couldn't quite get over the hump with it."

More editors, more rewrites, and finally I was done. Everything was a go—I was all set to self-publish! Then one morning I woke up and said to my husband, Dennis Foster, something is wrong with the book. I hired Holly Lorincz of Lorincz Literary Services (literaryconsulting.com). Her suggestions changed everything. She encouraged me to talk about the true nature of my trip, which was my twenty-two-year personal struggle to reconcile my egregious behavior after the death of our infant daughter. I had not discussed the magnitude of that experience with anyone, not even with my wonderful mother, Daisy. Thank you, Holly, for encouraging me to return to a place I never wanted to go, but needed to.

I resubmitted the rewrite to Chip, and he became my agent. Thank you, Chip, for not giving up on me!

Thank you to everyone who contributed to this process. You have no idea how much I have enjoyed working with you. Your expertise and input has been invaluable. I would like to give a special thanks to: Kay Allenbaugh, Genevieve Schmitt, Liz Jansen, Bill Johnson, Dawn Thompson, Ali McCart Shaw, Marie Prys, Elizabeth Lyons, Buzz Buzzelli, Sheila Maraigh, Suzanne Copitzky, Carol Elizabeth, Diana Martin, Joy Farmer, and Gail Porter.

Many thanks to Kampgrounds of America (KOA) for allowing me to stay at your campgrounds in exchange for media coverage. KOA was a welcome sight when I was cold, wet, and exhausted. And for assigning Annette Murray, your Communication Specialist, to keep track of me. She was a saint!

Thank you Serge A. McCabe Verriele Photography, for the terrific shot of me on my red FXE Shovelhead and allowing Skyhorse Publishing, Inc., to photoshop. They merged it into their beautiful cover.

Several of my stories embedded in these pages first appeared in *Thunder Press* newspaper. Thank you Cristy Pazera for not objecting to their inclusion in the book.

There are many more people who made suggestions or gave me ideas. Please know I considered all of your thoughts and always appreciated your feedback.

And an extra thanks to Mike Lewis, my Skyhorse Publishing editor! He's been wonderful to work with.

For you Harley riders who notice details: Yes, on my trip I rode a 1989 Springer. I upgraded my red FXE shortly before leaving town. Thank you to all my Harley-Davidson friends, riding has been an adventure of a lifetime.

And to my best Harley-Davidson riding buddy, my husband, Dennis Foster: Thank you. You changed my life forever.

I wish all of you the very best in life!

Contents

Prologue

HAUNTING CRIES

For years now I have heard the crying of a small child, a painful, agonizing wail that is remarkably similar to the sounds I hear coming from me.

Over time, I have come to visualize a long, dark hallway with open doors on both sides. The scene reminds me of what a reflection looks like if you hold one mirror up to another. The doors appear endless, each becoming smaller and smaller in the distance. This is what I always see when I'm drawn to this hallway.

From behind the open doors, I can hear the wailing. I take a deep breath and slowly walk down the hallway, closing one door after another. Maybe this time, if I can close them all, the crying will stop.

I roll on the Harley's throttle to increase the speed and listen intently to the roar of the engine, praying it will drown out the cries, or at least ease my guilt.

It doesn't.

Chapter 1

DANCING WITH THE WIND

A large truck roars up beside me, its long trailer hovering inches from my left shoulder.

The truck's engine emits a high-pitched whine, but the sound quickly succumbs to the howl of the heavy tires crushing the soaked pavement. As the trucker edges past me, I see rows of chains dangling from hooks beneath the bed. The chains swish back and forth, their clank and clatter barely audible, yet only a foot from my head.

Sturdy mud flaps block the wet road rubble slung from the wheels. The flaps are decorated with the silver silhouette of a shapely woman. She barely flinches when pelted with the trapped road debris. As the last wheels scream past, a stream of excess sludge sprays high into the air, and the nasty, gooey mud plasters the left side of my leather pants and jacket. The semi speeds on, leaving me slimed, and exhausted from the burst of terror.

I flip up the visor of my splattered helmet so the rain can hit my face—feels like tiny needle pricks jab at my cheeks and mix with my tears. For the past several hours, my emotions have peaked and fallen, a ride of elation and despair.

When I first struck out on my own, euphoria surged through me.

Here I am, a pioneer, a highway adventurer, a discrete entity separate from my children, my parents, and my boyfriend, Robert. A warrior going forth into the unknown, a professional free from the responsibilities of my legal practice, free from the ties that bind, the securities of the predictable. Now, just as quickly, the surge of euphoria, the exaltation of *doing it*, has melted away. The label of *warrior* sounds so grand, so cavalier, so brave. Why, then, do I feel weak? I know I chose this, but right now, I'm wallowing in my self-imposed misery.

The stinging rain helps. The pain redirects my focus and reminds me of the purpose of this trip: my need to address loneliness—and somehow—see if I can find a way to quiet my devastated soul.

I flip the visor back down. My feelings are on the upswing again, and the rain has thinned the grime on my leathers. After several more hours on the road, the sun clears the rain, warms the wind, and perks up my spirits.

Finally, the rain stops and I switch to my lighter helmet, a half-shell model that clearly shows my face, braided hair, and red lipstick. Now my fellow travelers can easily identify the gender of the person riding the Harley-Davidson motorcycle. Their reactions to a female traveling alone are astounding. They point, stare, smile, wave, honk, and genuinely express their delight.

In particular, women's reactions are more pronounced, more enthusiastic. One of their own is "out there," riding on a machine traditionally thought of as belonging in man's domain. A woman leans out of her car window and shouts, "Go, girl!" Children, too, are fascinated. A small girl, her chin barely above the window ledge, watches me, her tiny fingers posed in a tentative wave. I smile and wave at her. Suddenly, her face beams and her rosebud mouth bursts into a happy smile, her little fingers wiggling in a reciprocal wave.

Men acknowledge me, too. An elderly gentleman reclining in the rear seat of a tired, old Cadillac, sits up, presses his hand against the bill of a worn baseball cap, and snaps off a smart salute.

Get this! Some guy in a passing car is taking my picture. No kidding. I wonder if he saw me on television or read about me in the newspaper. Several days before I left Roseburg, Oregon, in June 1994, a reporter from KPIC, Channel 4, interviewed me about my trip, and the piece played on the evening news. That same day, a reporter from the *News-Review*, Roseburg's major newspaper, also interviewed me.

The following morning, a photo of me astride my Harley graced the front page. It showed me riding down Roseburg's main thoroughfare. The wind caught and grasped my red hair, and the long, black fringe on my leather gloves fluttered in the breeze. An article accompanied the picture and happened to mention my mother's name.

Mom's phone started ringing, and overnight I became a mini-celebrity in town. The calls kept coming, and that was when I realized that many of my family's friends and acquaintances—my mother's church group, the members of her garden club, Dad's cronies, the regulars at my brother Jim's restaurant, my brother Gary's cohorts—would track my adventures via my parents and extended family. Whether we like it or not, our successes or failures vicariously reflect on those we love. This trip's outcome would affect my family's lives and I felt the pressure to succeed ratchet up a notch. What I said and how I behaved on this adventure mattered.

I smile and wave at the man with the camera. Optimism washes over me. The people in the cars are friendly and happy. I do not have anything to worry about. This trip will be easy, a lark.

***

Everything changes after I cross into California.

The wind's velocity has increased with a vengeance, continues to pummel the bike, and I veer unexpectedly into the fast lane. I'm riding in the right lane of the I-5 freeway, struggling to keep the bike near the white fog line, but the wind's relentless. Since the cars in the fast lane approach so rapidly, any sudden slide into their lane further heightens the danger and they swerve to miss me.

Another powerful blast of wind hits the right side of the bike and again effortlessly forces it sideways into the fast lane of traffic. I fight to control the motorcycle's movements, and this struggle wears on my nerves and body.

My new motorcycle, a 1989 Springer, is larger, heavier, and more powerful than my previous model, but it is loaded to the max. The forty pounds of camping and personal gear form a three-by-three mass that extends from the passenger seat to the end of the chrome luggage rack attached above the rear fender. Below the luggage rack, two saddlebags are stuffed full.

The saddlebags are propped out against a metal frame, one on each side, and hang over the rear wheel. The tent rests on top of the right saddlebag; the sleeping bag sits on top of the left one. Due to the girth and height of the load, this mass catches the wind like a sail and accentuates the slide sideways into the fast lane.

In an attempt to manhandle the motorcycle, I tense, grasp the handlebars in a death grip, and brace for the next blast of wind.

As it hits, I tighten my grip even more and try to focus on the highway and the traffic that speeds by. With each sporadic blast of wind, I become more exhausted from my concerted efforts to regain control of the bike and move it back toward the fog line.

The smart thing to do is stop for the night, but my corporate sponsors, Kampgrounds of America (KOA), have arranged for a radio interview this evening, and I hate to disappoint anyone, especially on the first day. On the other hand, if I'm this exhausted, or I kill myself, what is the point?

As my fatigue mounts, a strange thing happens; this continual swaying between the lanes strikes me as a dance. A dance—not a battle. I begin to relax. The wind hits the side of the bike, and it slides toward the left lane. I follow, roll on the throttle, and then glide back toward the fog line on the right side of the highway. A smooth cadence soon follows: a slide left, a glide right. This movement reminds me of the way an elephant walks, its rear weight slowly, yet methodically, shifting from side to side. I correct the slide quicker and, although the bike continues to travel from left to right, the graceful movement is confined to the right lane. Back and forth the bike sways. I follow, a willing partner waltzing in the arms of the wind. How fantastic! I'm dancing with the wind!

My perceived problem arose because I wanted to lead and control the movements of the bike. In a dance with the force of the wind, you cannot lead. You must follow. With this realization, tension vanishes; I smile and follow the wind's lead.

Some obstacles are beyond our control and, if we mean to press forward, it is up to us to make the necessary mental corrections. Sometimes we lead; sometimes we follow. To follow does not necessarily mean to acquiesce. Rather, a minor mental adjustment to a particular set of circumstances becomes necessary, and we rearrange our thinking to accommodate the need. We can become the leader again when the opportunity better fits the situation.

This mental adjustment changes how I feel about the wind and the ride, and exhilaration replaces tension. Together we share a dance mixed with danger, freedom, and delight.

Unbelievably, I have romanced the wind.

* * *

"You are the greatest thing to hit the KOA in a long time, and we intend to give you the VIP treatment."

The Mount Shasta KOA manager reaches for my hand before I have a chance to switch off my motorcycle. His statement surprises me; I certainly did not expect that comment, or that attitude. Nevertheless, I'm honored and flattered that the franchisees are extending to me the same enthusiasm that has been displayed by the corporate headquarters.

"After you have a chance to unpack and settle in, we have made arrangements for you to meet with a DJ from KWHO Country and then, and I hope you don't mind, I thought we could have dinner together." The manager's broad smile is warm and welcoming.

"That sounds wonderful, and I would love to have dinner with you," I respond, still shaking his hand. "If you give me about an hour, I should be ready to go."

Looks like I'm off and running. I check in and head for my campsite to set up my tent and unpack.

The Mount Shasta KOA is one of more than five hundred KOA campgrounds located in the United States, Canada, Mexico, and Japan. Today, with more than seventy-five thousand sites, KOA is North America's largest system of open-to-the public, privately owned, full-service overnight and destination campgrounds. I approached the KOA corporate office prior to my trip because I had stayed at KOAs in the past, and felt like it would be a safe place to camp.

Our agreement was that the KOA would arrange for the television, newspaper, and radio interviews and reimburse me for camp space. In return, my job was to show up on time, and give a woman's perspective of what it was like to travel across America alone. The expectation was my journey would generate positive public relations for the KOA, while encouraging women to stay at their campgrounds, and my overall costs would be substantially lower.

After setting up camp, I meet with a disk jockey from KWHO Country and perform my first radio interview. Questions and answers flow smoothly, a nimble, pleasurable, banter: *What made you decide to ride through all fifty states alone? Do you think it's safe for a fifty-year-old woman to be traveling by herself on a motorcycle? Aren't you afraid?*

These are questions I had struggled to answer before my decision to close my law office and began this journey, but I do not tell him that. Instead my answers are witty, clever, superficial, and, before I know it, our chat is over. I thoroughly enjoyed every minute of it. So far, the media interviews are a kick and easy to conduct. I feel completely at ease.

Dinner, too, exceeds my expectations. My first dinner on the road, and it is with an interesting executive, our conversation lively and fun. Maybe my concerns about loneliness on the road are completely unnecessary. After all, I have had the royal treatment, shared time with a radio personality, and been wined and dined by an entertaining man.

If all the KOA stops are this much fun, I may travel indefinitely.

* * *

I'm lying here cocooned in my sleeping bag, freaked out.

Now that my glamorous evening is over, the reality of the months spent on the hard ground begins to take on new meaning and I do not like it. I have never spent the night by myself in a tent, and it is scary. The sleeping bag encases me, tucked tightly around my body, its warm embrace a feeble barrier to ward off fear.

Thank heavens the Mount Shasta KOA camping sites are relatively close to each other; no one is too far away. Still, everything feels unfamiliar and each sound amplifies and contrasts with the sharp still of the night. The smell of charred campfires, combined with an odd array of cooked food, hangs in the air. Is this my new reality for the next several months? Alone in my tent, and frightened? What else did I expect? I'm not sure.

The decision to ride through all fifty states did not come easily, for first I had to admit to a personal weakness, a flaw. Then— and far more important to me—I had to decide if I was able to face a hidden, penetrating pain: an unspoken guilt concealed deep within me. I did not want to divulge that truth to anyone, especially not to myself. For years it was easier to hide behind the cloak of denial than to admit reality.

It is unnerving to think about confronting hidden demons, fears, and failings. What will become of me, if I cannot master them? Will I continue to live a weakened life? Or will my life be far worse than it is now? Will I regret going on this quest, and wish I had stayed home?

One fear was the approaching reality that I would face old age alone, and in all likelihood, lonely. Since I had never spent much time by myself, this looming anxiety caught me off-guard.

I had been single with custody of the boys for the last ten years. Recently my adult sons, Brian, 21, and Travis, 20, had moved out to begin their own life's journey and the idea of living the rest of my life alone was nerve-racking. I did not understand *why* this frightened me so much; I just knew that it did.

Admitting this secret apprehension embarrassed me because it sounded so weak, even cowardly, and I told no one. Brave people attack cancer, fight in wars, overcome major catastrophes, and face their own deaths.

Parents talk about the *empty-nest* syndrome when their adult children leave home, however, I assumed they were talking about missing their kids. Certainly, I would miss my boys, so their conversations seemed reasonable, and I did not bother to think it through. The idea that these parents might struggle with the issue of *loneliness* was not something I considered, and I felt unique in my fears.

So I lied.

I told everyone that I was going to ride through all fifty states to celebrate my fiftieth birthday. That happened to be true, but not entirely truthful. A lie by omission. People now thought of me as bold, cavalier, fearless, perhaps reckless, or crazy. No one knew or understood the depth of my anxiety. And I was not about to tell them.

Nor was I going to share a deeper, unrelenting pain that pierced my heart. A wound so jagged that it would not allow forgiveness, and because my behavior was so unconscionable, so heartless, that I did not deserve redemption. I prayed that this journey might grant me serenity, but after so many years of guilt, I do not know how it is possible.

As I lie here in my sleeping bag, I did not expect to feel so alone in my quest to attack loneliness, or so stressed. Common sense dictates that isolation surely includes feelings of being secluded. But with all the preparation to leave, I had pushed the thought of actually being by myself out of my mind, as though distancing it would ease the truth of my circumstances. Now that luxury has passed. Fear and loneliness lurk in the darkness, preparing to lunge at me—their hot, heavy essence a heartbeat away.

They did not have long to wait.

My first nighttime panic attack is triggered by a strange sound clawing and scratching at the outside of my tent. I awaken, frozen with fear. Perhaps some large animal or unscrupulous person intends to attack me. The noise continues for some time, then stops, only to begin again as I start to relax.

For a while I lie there, immobilized in the hope that whatever threat looms will leave if I do not make a sound. The scratching continues, intermittent but persistent. I need sleep, as my first day on the road has sapped my physical strength. I tell myself that once I'm outside the tent, if everything falls apart, I can scream for help and make a run for the office.

Peering outside, I cautiously venture around the side of the tent. My heart is pounding, my heavy boot in my hand, I confront the culprit: a small branch that occasionally catches the wind and rubs the side of the tent. *Oh, this is just great. A twig has terrorized me.*

I imagine a crazed, uncontrollable screaming woman with arms flaying, charging into the office, only to have the management discover a small twig has sent her into a maniacal frenzy. That would certainly instill confidence in the KOA executives who trusted my judgment.

Fear of the unknown can ravage the mind. Throw in a dark night, strange environment, and some weird sounds, and the imagination goes on a tirade. It probably has to do with all the scary movies we have seen over the years, or, perhaps, our innate primeval awareness becomes heightened as a means of protection. Whatever the origin, I must make a concerted effort to control this head game or the trip will end before it begins.

Settling back into the confines of my sleeping bag, I recall the day's events. My emotions are raw, my nerves shot. Still, it was fun interacting with the people traveling on the freeway, doing the radio interview, and meeting with the KOA personnel. But, without question, what I enjoyed the most was dancing with the wind on the road. The memory of the dance's sway finally lulls me back to sleep.

I do not know if I slept for moments or hours, but the loud, long scream of a train whistle startles me awake and I bolt upright from my sleeping bag. A train roars past, virtually at my feet. The ground trembles from the impact and I can feel the vibration from the train's power in my chest, like the low base of a stereo system. The engineer blasts the whistle again, its deep, throaty cry a warning to any who dare challenge the right of way of this monstrosity that rampages deep into the night.

The engine must be towing a hundred cars or more. As the long train rumbles past, the whistle blasts in regular intervals, its husky shriek becoming softer and softer as the train distances itself from my tent. The ground below me continues to pulsate from the rhythmic weight of each passing car. I tuck back into my sleeping bag and feel the soothing, metrical beat. Finally, the last car passes and the earth no longer shudders. The clanking of the cars softens until only the murmur of a faded whistle sounds in the distance, a pale testimony of power and intensity. Then silence.

I have always liked trains, the way their ominous power combines with the sensation of tranquility. That first shrill shriek of the whistle startles and frightens. Then the soothing, metallic clatter of metal-against-metal calms and relaxes—a contradiction of sounds and emotions. Had I anticipated its arrival, this train would not have distressed me. But with all the excitement of my first day and night on the road, I had not noticed the railroad tracks, and it never occurred to me a train would pass so close to this campground.

As I lie here in the renewed quiet of the night, my thoughts drift to the similarity between trains and the emotional impact relationships have on us. Relationships often roar into our lives, a combination of excitement, intensity, and passion. The startling blast of passion's emotional whistle awakens dreams, rekindles hope that love awaits, and rejuvenates a hunger for that mysterious bond of lifelong commitment. We may resolve to proceed slowly in the hopes that this relationship will bring the desired elements of longevity, permanence, and endurance. But, often, like the train that travels into the alien night, we are thrust headlong into uncontrollable desire or carried away like cargo transported to some vague destination.

If we are fortunate enough to find the elusive permanence we seek, the nature and quality of the relationship may change over time. Passion's intensity lessens and leaves us with a soft rhythmic quality, a consistent rumble that soothes us into an acceptance and appreciation for each other. In time, or perhaps with the advent of old age, only the recollection of the initial intense passion remains, a faded whistle that beckons only to our memories.

I want an intensely passionate mate but also a partner who can see past the physical fireworks and accept the limitations that most assuredly loom beyond the next bend. A guy I can grow old with. A man who does not immediately request a refund the moment his ticket's punched. Someone who values commitment the way I do, and understands that, while old age brings difficulties, it also may bring unabashed contentment. That does not seem like so much to ask for in a man, does it?

I'm not sure if I have met that man yet. I'm not convinced my boyfriend, Robert, will stick with me if the going gets tough. He is not there for his ailing mother, and that lack of allegiance is disturbing. Does the fear of loneliness bind me to him? Or is it my wishful hope that our future might include devotion and steadfastness?

What if my present relationship is the only one I'm destined to have? If I recklessly cast this one aside, will I have offended the love gods, never to enjoy love's caress again? Much as that thought distresses me, I do not think relationships are cast in concrete.

I believe love can grow in the strangest places, blossom at any time, or flower at any age. Do not abandon hope or believe you are trapped in a faulty relationship. Who knows, if a present relationship does not work or if love has yet to call your name, perhaps you might discover what I did at five in the morning.

Along came another train.

Chapter 2

CHASING ELUSIVE LOVE

Yesterday was physically and emotionally draining.

Going forward, I must pay more attention to my personal limitations and not risk another test of my inadequate coping abilities so early in the trip, or it will be over.

I'm riding back to Sacramento, California, my next KOA stop. Yep, back. About an hour ago, I deliberately smoked right past the KOA turnoff. Although I have never stopped in Sacramento, let alone the Sacramento KOA, this fact does not keep me from smirking at the directions on the map. No way will the KOA be *there*. The diminutive dot on the map did not *feel* like the right location. Therefore, I determined the directions and the road signs were not correct and let out a hearty "Ha!" as I smugly sailed right past the KOA turnoff, convinced that its location belonged somewhere up the road another twenty miles or so. It was nowhere to be found.

I spend the next hour irritated as I accept the inevitable and retrace my steps. The KOA is located in precisely the map's designated place: a pleasant, orderly campground topped with palm trees and a soft, grassy site, an ideal location for pitching a tent. As much as I hate the thought of releasing some control back to the mysterious makers of maps and road signs, tomorrow I intend to do just that.

No media interviews are scheduled in Sacramento, so the task of setting up the large, unwieldy tent begins. This tent had belonged to Robert, who *sold* it to me prior to this trip. Although I helped him set it up and take it down, he orchestrated every move. And since a year has passed, the process feels awkward to me.

When the tent belonged to Robert, we had rules—strict, explicit rules.

"Carolyn, take off your boots before you enter the tent, straighten the floor before placing anything on it, and don't lean gear against the sides. Remember, when you pack the tent, fold it *exactly* the way I showed you, and then house it neatly in the tent bag."

"Yes, master," I responded, my voice edgy and argumentative.

Robert demanded that each step be accomplished with meticulous precision. My attempts at perfection never met his standard, regardless of how hard I tried. I continually thought *I'm such a klutz.* Or, *Why can't I do this right? I'm such an idiot.*

Now that the tent belongs to me, I still feel like a klutz, but in a different way. I can learn the formula to perfect this unfamiliar procedure, and I'm entitled to give myself a break while mastering the learning curve. By the time I return home, I expect to be a competent, seasoned veteran.

I like owning my own tent and no longer feel obligated to abide by the rules set by Robert. Function appeals to me far more than precision, so this morning, rather than fold it, I stuffed the tent into its bag, thus saving time and energy. That business about the boots especially bugs me. Why not wear my boots inside the tent? A sturdy fabric covered the floor. What would it hurt to walk on it? After erecting the tent last night, I stomped in and out as I pleased, carried gear inside, and propped it against the sides of the tent.

"Look, Robert, I have my boots on. What do you think of that?" I said aloud, although no one heard me. I trudged back and forth numerous times, sometimes with no specific purpose and only because it was the principle of the thing. I went forward in a relaxed, comfortable style that suited my needs, without the burden of continually glancing over my shoulder for another's approval.

I find it interesting that I feel there must be something wrong with me if I do not meet the expectations of others. Self-imposed criticism damages the spirit and degrades us. Precision or the lack thereof does not have a value of right or wrong. The choice is personal and I do not need to blame myself if I prefer one approach to another. I'll march to my own beat and feel good about the sound.

Speaking of marching, here is a pearl—do not stomp around inside the tent with your boots on. Dirt and sand cling to the bottom of your boots until, like a thousand fleas deserting a drowning dog, they spring off and attach themselves to every-thing you own; their favorite place will be the inside of the sleeping bag. This makes for a gritty night's sleep.

Once settled into my sleeping bag, tiny grains of sand rolled around like serrated marbles beneath my skin. They poked and irritated, magnifying themselves, until it felt like I was sleeping on constantly shifting boulders. Sometimes arrogance yields to the learning curve, so my belief is this: if you make a mistake, buck up and admit it.

However, when it comes to Robert, it aggravates the hell out of me to admit it.

* * *

The timing could not have been better when Robert arrived in my life two years ago.

After being single for eight years, I had discovered that love is an elusive creature. My attempts at romance included boyfriends, a couple of longer-term relationships, and a few one night stands. I also kissed a number of frogs—none of whom turned out to be the prince I was waiting for.

It always seems so simple in the movies. Eyes lock across a crowded room, pulses race, and juices flow. Love grasps the heart, the star-struck couple marries, and they live happily ever after.

Interesting, isn't it, how love works in real life? What appears to be an absolute slam dunk somehow misses the mark, bounces erratically about for a bit, then dribbles off the court uneventfully. Some shots at love are an embarrassment at best. Other attempts repeat a previous encounter: the exhilaration of the start, the honeymoon phase, the reality of combining two strong-willed adults, children or pets, the decision to accommodate or not—to settle for less or not—and then the eventual fizzle.

Love may be the elusive gold ring, but with love, hope shines eternal. Hope shores us up, gives us a little nudge, and encourages us to give love one more shot. When he arrived, Robert appeared to be the prince I was waiting for.

Robert was a mature, responsible man and shared my passion for motorcycles. He had recently moved to Oregon from New Mexico to care for his elderly mother, was a retired college professor, and had raised a well-adjusted, married son. I considered this a great start. We enjoyed mutual interests and lively conversations. He was well-read, articulate, and bright. We liked one another right away. Robert enjoyed and respected my boys, and they felt the same way about him.

Our relationship had all the elements of success. A love slam dunk. Robert joined the Sunset HOG Chapter, a motorcycle organization, and we both became actively involved with the members. We rode often with our friends, and our lives were full and happy. After three months together, we both believed the gods had blessed us and that we had found that elusive love match. We spent a lot of time together, our commitment to each other sound.

The first hint of turmoil between Robert and me turned out to be our conversational styles. My take on Deborah Tannen's book *That's Not What I Meant! How Conversational Style Makes or Breaks Relationships* is that women are more *hint* based. We do not come right out and say what we mean. We beat around the bush in a frustrated attempt to encourage a man to pick up on our unsaid or subliminal messages and thereby allow him to relate to us on a more personal level. We feel that to spell things out would be condescending and unnecessary.

Intimacy is our foremost goal, while clarity of purpose is irrelevant. When it comes to men, we purr, "If you loved me, you would *know* what I mean." That makes perfect sense, doesn't it?

Men, on the other hand, are more apt to be *informational*. They are like Joe Fridays of the old TV series *Dragnet*. They emphatically state, "Just the facts, ma'am." Blurt it out. Call it like it is. No sugar coating. Give me that detailed data and those divine statistics. When it comes to women, men roar, "If you loved me, you would *say* what you mean."

Good grief! Why would we do that? That is like imposing ourselves upon them. This deprives men of the ability to be chivalrous or to receive our innermost hidden thoughts. It makes women sound crude. And besides, other women knows exactly what we mean when we hint. How come guys do not get it?

A typical conversation between Robert and me went like this:

My phone rings. "Carolyn, I'm going to the Harley meeting tonight. Are you?"

"I don't know. It's snowing and I don't have snow tires on the car, and I don't want to drive in the snow without them." Long pause. This gives Robert the opportunity to offer me a ride since we live only a few miles apart; he has snow tires, and he intends to go to the meeting. No response.

Analysis by me: *Well that was a big hint. Only an idiot wouldn't pick up on a big hint like that. Obviously, I want to go to the meeting. I go to every meeting. Therefore, since he didn't offer, he must have other plans. Maybe he wants to go alone, or has plans afterward, or maybe he doesn't want to go with* me.

The conversation shifts to other meaningless topics, but I'm mad that he did not offer to come and get me. He knows perfectly well I want to go to the meeting. I become more and more aggravated. He hears the agitation in my voice but cannot understand why I'm angry.

Finally, because I have no idea what he really thinks, I'm forced to beg, "Robert, would it be a problem if you came and got me?"

"Oh no, not at all. I'd be happy to come and get you. I'll be right there. Why didn't you just *say* you wanted me to come and get you? I don't understand you. You're a bright, intelligent, outspoken woman. Why don't you just *tell* me what you want?"

He has to be kidding. Is he brain-dead or something? What is there to say? How much clearer can I be? I told him I did not want to drive in the snow. How am I supposed to get to the meeting if I will not drive in the snow? Good Lord! A child could understand what was implied. If he cared, he would have offered to come and get me when I said I would not drive in the snow. His behavior is deliberately thoughtless. Now I do not care if I go to the damn meeting or not.

His insensitivity drove me crazy. My lack of candor made him nuts.

This repetitive communication fiasco took its toll on our relationship. We broke up, then reconciled several times. We tried to accommodate each other, our continual miscommunications a constant frustration. I felt guarded when talking to Robert. Why did I always have to be precise in my speech? It felt unnatural. We were two strong-willed people, set in our ways. Yet, we both wanted this relationship to work. We needed a break and decided on a road trip together.

Robert wanted to visit his relatives in Arizona and introduce me to his extended family. I rearranged my heavy legal schedule and planned an extended vacation for the summer of 1993. Our ride would last three weeks and encompass eight of the southwestern states. We would travel a total distance of 4,500 miles.

The trip was a nightmare from the start.

Robert led, and worried incessantly when I fell behind or failed to keep up on my older Shovelhead. He had ridden for many years, his pace fast and steady. I fatigued quickly and needed to stop often. Within a few days, we did not have to worry about our conversational styles—we had stopped speaking.

Shovelheads are notorious for their vibration. Everything jiggled loose, and I had to continually tighten nuts, bolts, and cables. Parts fell off. Things had to be adjusted. At one point, my motorcycle had to be towed four hundred miles to Las Vegas to replace a sheared pin. Robert whined about my faulty bike and poor riding skills. He understood the conditions when we left, though, so his complaints aggravated me. To expect something different when we were a thousand miles from home was ridiculous.

To add insult to injury, Robert and I camped. Since the tent belonged to Robert, he set the rules and barked out orders like a drill sergeant. This did not sit well with my kind, gentle nature. I rebelled like a madwoman.

Our road trip had become a death march.

Robert felt he had a moral obligation to return me safely home. I insisted I did not need him, and I had the money and wherewithal to rent a U-Haul and trailer the bike and myself home. We fought, reconciled, fought some more—but continued on nonetheless.

Our original plan included a side trip to see the beautiful redwood trees in California, so we made the detour off I-5 to Highway 101. We were near Garberville, California, only a few days from home, when our trip nearly ended in tragedy. The night before, we had the mother lode of all fights. We were so aggravated with one another that we rented separate rooms in a motel that night. Our feelings still raged the next morning.

We rode down a rural, winding, heavily traveled highway. Low on fuel, I inadvertently passed a small gas station, then decided to turn around and go back to fill the gas tank. Once on the shoulder of this narrow highway, I waited for traffic to thin. With little room between a ditch and the highway, my motorcycle sat only inches outside of the white fog line. It was a terrible place to stop. The road curved sharply behind me, and the traffic approaching from the rear was impossible to see. I had not paid attention when I pulled off the road because I was still so mad over our fight.

Robert rode another hundred feet ahead, turned around in a driveway, pulled forward perpendicular to the highway, and waited to cross. Without warning, I felt a strong rush of wind and heard a tremendous roar. I glanced to my left as a huge logging truck piled high with logs swept past, almost grazing my shoulder. I could smell the fresh-cut timber and saw small pieces of bark flying off the logs. I froze, startled at the closeness of that speeding logging truck. It was traveling too fast on this narrow road.

What occurred next seemed like it took a lifetime, but it happened in seconds.

I looked up and saw Robert sitting square in the middle of the logging truck's lane. He must have pulled forward onto the highway, seen the truck round the corner, and known he could not make it across. Up a small incline and beyond Robert, I saw a car headed toward us in the oncoming lane. The car had nearly reached Robert, and I could see a woman driver and three small children in the car.

Robert never moved. He gripped the handlebars, dropped his head, and waited for the full impact of that enormous truck to crush him. The trucker had a choice: hit Robert or collide with the car that held the woman and children.

I have thought about this incident many times since it happened. The picture is still clear in my mind, and the image always makes me cry. I will never understand how that trucker managed to do what he did.

With the smooth grace of an ice dancer, the trucker swung that massive truck filled with logs into the oncoming lane. He missed Robert by inches. Then, with that same smooth grace and only a split second before impact with the car full of children, the trucker slipped his enormous truck back into his lane, and they all passed safely.

I doubt that move could be repeated in a million years. I have gone back to that spot in the road and marveled at the ability of the driver to maneuver his huge truck in such a restricted space. I will always believe that the hand of God touched them all.

The entire incident was so horrific that I started to cry. I stopped at the first motel but continued to sob. Everyone should have been killed, and it was our fault. Arguments and lack of concentration have no place on motorcycles. Focus is critical, and we had lost ours. A tragedy had been narrowly averted, no thanks to us. That did it. I would leave in the morning, alone. The relationship was over. We were through.

The next morning Robert's motorcycle would not start.

I felt obligated to stay with him until it ran properly. By the time we returned to Portland, we had calmed down. The trip had been too much for both of us, our expectations unrealistic, so we agreed to try harder in our relationship. It is difficult to find a romantic match, and we did have many things in common.

Robert hated Oregon's rain and the long, dark winters. He complained about the weather constantly. He loved living in hot New Mexico, and we began to think about a change of scenery. I was sure that if we moved to a different state, love's spark would reignite.

We simply needed a bright, sunny location, and all of our problems would fade away.

Chapter 3

THE LONE ARCHER

Many people are accomplished travelers, but I'm not one of them.

Over the years, I have dreamed about visiting exciting and beautiful places, but the opportunity to travel rarely presented itself. For some time, I have wanted to tour California's rugged Yosemite National Park, and today I have the chance.

The rain has vanished, and the wind is nonexistent. I feel rested and more comfortable with this bike, so I leave the I-5 freeway and head east on Highway 120 toward the park. The distant mountain peaks now emerge closer, as the dry, desert ground surrenders its grasp to lush backwoods.

Established in 1890, Yosemite encompasses almost 1,200 square miles of scenic wild lands, 95 percent of which are considered a wilderness area. Tucked inside a portion of the central Sierra Nevada mountain range that stretches along California's eastern flank, the park ranges from two thousand feet above sea level to spectacular mountains reaching heights of more than thirteen thousand feet. A brochure describes the pristine alpine wilderness of Yosemite that includes over 1,400 flowering species of plants, thirty-seven tree species, eighty different mammals, and 247 varieties of birds. Everything smells clean, and the scent of fresh foliage abounds.

I stop at Bridalveil Fall, a place the Ahwahneechee Indians named *Pohono*, "Spirit of the Puffing Wind." The wind swirls about the cliff, often lifting the falling water and blowing it from side to side as it delicately free-falls. Although this waterfall appears small when seen against the vast surrounding canyon wall, it actually stretches to the height of a sixty-two-story building.

The park has three major attractions: alpine wilderness, three groves of giant sequoias, and the glacially carved Yosemite Valley with impressive waterfalls, cliffs, and unusual rock formations. Perhaps the most famous of the rock formations is El Capitan, the massive granite monolith standing guard near the valley entrance and believed to be the largest single block of exposed granite in the world. A sign says the summit rises 3,593 feet above the Merced River. Rock climbers from around the world challenge their abilities on the face of El Capitan, and I spot small human dots as they attempt the difficult and hazardous ascent.

I prepare to spend some time near El Capitan when a warning in the park brochure catches my eye: *Weather can change rapidly during all seasons of the year. Elevation plays a major role in temperature and precipitation.*

I should cross the high mountain pass while the weather is warm and mild. Already I have had a long day and I'm tired. Evening approaches, and I still must find a place to spend the night.

But, captivated by Yosemite's beauty, I linger.

What began as a beautiful, tranquil ride into the park turns sour as I commence my climb toward the top of the mountain. The wind, seductively calm at the base of the mountain, increases in force and strength the higher I climb. Strong blasts crash into the left side of the bike, and the front wheel hops several inches sideways as though startled by the impact. Another blast smashes into the bike. The wheel jumps again, and my teeth clatter as the front wheel thuds back onto the highway. No way will I dance with the wind today. My full attention rivets on the task of maintaining control.

The surrounding temperature drops dramatically. Sharp cold air seizes the back of my throat, restricting each quickly inhaled breath. With a few deep gulps, the frigid air dives deep into my lungs, then loiters, smoldering with a fiery intensity. My nose, cheeks, and forehead tingle from the cold, a prickly irritation that soon itches like poison oak welts. I ache to rub life back into my chilled features, but I dare not let go of the handlebars.

As I scale higher and higher toward the crest, the security of the valley slips away. The narrow two-lane highway snakes toward the summit, a continuation of hairpin turns and heavy traffic. Guardrails are sparse, and my side of the highway often flanks the exposed abyss. Fierce gusts of wind edge me closer and closer to the sheer drop on my right, and I visualize my unobstructed plunge to the bottom, thousands of feet below. Stressed, I drop my speed to twenty miles per hour, move back to the left, and hug the centerline. Oncoming traffic swerves erratically to miss me and the cars behind me crawl to a snail's pace.

My body aches, and my arms tremble from the fight to rein in the bike. I have grossly misjudged my physical abilities. Although tired when I began the ascent, I had no idea my stamina would disappear this quickly. This was a critical error in judging my endurance. If I do not immediately learn to pace myself, I'm going to be killed.

Utterly exhausted, I reach the summit. Pulling off near a lookout, I switch off the ignition, lower the kickstand, and climb off the bike. Weakened with fatigue, my legs buckle and I slump to the ground. My heart races, and I force myself to breathe in slow, measured breaths. A weathered stone retaining wall separates the highway from the cliff's edge and, after staggering over, I cling to the rock barrier.

What am I doing here? Am I nuts to take on an undertaking like this? What if I'm seriously injured or permanently disabled? Surely another way exists to address my fears. If I'm doomed to live life alone, I might as well stay at home and be safe.

Yet the view is fantastic, a panoramic spectacle framed with jutting, purple-hued mountains that rise majestically from the faded green valley floor. Dark olive-colored fir trees shoot sporadically from the white rocky hillside, their jagged silhouettes spiked into a cobalt sky. I scan the horizon, a solitary shade in a painter's palette. I'm heavy, sad, misplaced.

In the narrow parking space across the highway, a car stops and small children clad in T-shirts and shorts bound out to frolic in the snow packs that lay hidden in shadowed crevices. The children hoot and snicker while pitching handfuls of snow at their approaching parents. They certainly give the impression that they are a successful family unit. Within a few minutes, they gleefully pile back into the car, and I remain alone by the ledge.

Once I was a happily married wife and mother. We, too, cavorted in the snow, laughing and throwing snowballs as we built snowmen in New Jersey. What went wrong? What turned those contented times into discord and divorce? What caused the brightness to grow fainter and then vanish?

Pulling the rubber band from my braided hair, I shake it loose as the tree shadows lengthen. I cannot stay here. The wind whines an eerie, sinister howl. I should turn around and head back home. I would have to eat a little crow for sure, but God knows I have done that before. Everyone would forgive me; they already said this trip was impossible. I'll just say they were right. I'm familiar with the highway now and know what to expect. Within two hours, I will find a motel, a safe haven, a retreat.

The wind lessens, then swirls about the cliff and catches my hair, blowing it gently from side to side. Behind the wind's unsympathetic, ominous moan, I hear a low poignant murmur. A sound. Haunting, yet familiar. Something beckons. Is it *Pohono*, the Spirit of the Puffing Wind, whispering my name?

Unexpectedly, a tremendous blast of wind slams into my chest. I lose my grip on the retaining wall and stagger backward, stunned by its force. I gasp to catch my breath. *Jesus, Carolyn. Go home!*

The wind shrieks at me, its dominance ruthless and unforgiving.

***

The sun has barely shown itself as I sit in some small café in Bishop, California.

While waiting for breakfast, I have a chance to think about my treacherous ride over the Yosemite pass last night. My decision to continue on happened inadvertently by the appearance of an unexpected guardian. From my observation point, I had watched a large truck twist its way toward the top of the mountain.

When the trucker finally reached the crest and began his descent, I pulled in directly behind him, my motorcycle tucked tight near the rear of his truck. The truck sheltered me from the full force of the wind and from the oncoming traffic. Flooded with relief by this unexpected good fortune, I shadowed the trucker through the narrow, winding highway.

As we continued downhill, I was astounded to see a vast green basin and a large body of water stretch out far below me. The highway eventually meandered through a lovely, tiny town nestled securely in the lush, green valley. Someone had named the town *Paradise.*

Isn't that the way it goes? Just when life seems impossible, desolate, and overwhelming, when we think we cannot carry on, a patch of green appears and entices us with a glimpse of paradise.

I spent last night in a motel. My nerves were shot, my energy depleted, and I did not have the strength to pitch my tent. Today, I plan to ride through Death Valley, and since I do not care to repeat yesterday's fiasco, I will start earlier and be off the road well before dark.

Breakfast smells delicious. The special includes a large thick slice of honey-cured ham, two eggs, home-fried potatoes, toast, and coffee, all for $3.99. While the ham sizzles, whiffs of flavor drift toward my table. In the kitchen, the cook gossips with the waitress while potatoes simmer on the grill.

The walls of this tiny dining area hold a mishmash of old pictures, prints, pottery, cookware, and artificial plants, all coated with a thin residue of grease. A large bulletin board features a picture of the local baseball team, upcoming events, newspaper clippings, and photos of adults, children, and animals.

The front door opens and then slams shut with a loud *bang*, the small brass bell above it ringing frantically. Three middle-aged men walk in, the first a large man in worn bib overalls and dusty, weather-beaten work boots. His voice is boisterous and agitated. His two cronies, virtually mute and acquiescent, follow close behind him.

"He cut his hair," the first man storms. "You should see it. It's shaved on the sides damn near to the top of his head. What's left on the top now sticks out and hangs above his ears. It looks stupid." His voice vibrates against the shrinking walls. When neither friend responds to his outburst, he continues to rage.

"I know he did it deliberately to spite me. I was up at three o'clock last night pacing back and forth in the bedroom. I bet my blood pressure has gone completely out of sight."

Before the men can sit down, the waitress hurries over to refill my coffee cup. The inside of the cup, stained dark brown from frequent use, accepts the piping hot liquid. While filling my cup, she glances at me, widens her eyes, and raises one eyebrow before hustling back toward the safety of the kitchen.

Although no one else is in the café and adequate seating surrounds us, the three men choose the table inches from mine. The mismatched wooden chairs screech against the discolored gray linoleum floor as they gather around a small square table covered with a faded plastic tablecloth.

This father, probably a local farmer, is extremely irate, it seems, with his teenage son. I glance at the photo of baseball players on the bulletin board and wonder if one of these youthful, cocky faces belongs to his boy.

I have my back to the men, so I cannot see their facial expressions. The companions mumble a few reassuring words, express sympathy, and commiserate with their friend. They clearly agree it was disrespectful for the boy not to follow the customs and traditions set by his father.

The father's irritation with his son is none of my business, but the man is so aggravated and disappointed in the boy that I think a word or two of encouragement cannot hurt. After breakfast, I pay my bill, walk over to him, touch his shoulder, and then pat his back lightly.

"Excuse me, but I couldn't help but overhear your conversation. I wanted to tell you that my youngest son has exactly the same haircut as your boy and my oldest son is backpacking around Europe. I don't agree with their choices sometimes, but I like to think they get their fierce, independent spirit from their mother. Maybe your son gets that independent streak from you."

"Nope," he answers, obviously disgusted with my intrusion. "I've always been really conservative. This is completely out of the ordinary for him."

"Well, who knows? Maybe it's time for both of you to do something more unusual or adventuresome in your lives. We can learn a lot from our children if we take the time to listen and pay attention to them." I watch his teeth clench and unclench, the muscles bulging around his jaw, but he does not answer. Instead, he sits up a little straighter, tightens his shoulders, and stares at his empty coffee cup.

My unsolicited and apparently unwelcomed opinion obviously incenses him further. This is a good lesson—not everyone is interested in advice from a stranger.

I decide to keep my mouth shut and leave, before he decides to pummel me.

* * *

As I head toward Death Valley, the moisture of the luxurious forestlands is sucked away by parched, arid winds, which blow sparse, twisted brush.

Nevertheless, I find the desert beautiful. Occasionally, flowers peek through the dry ground, set off against a backdrop of mountains receding into a blue-and-purple haze. But I cannot stay focused on the diversity of the region. My mind keeps returning to the café. Something about that father's irritation with his son chips away at me. Why was he intolerant of his son's expression of independence?

My parents preached the importance of raising well-adjusted, self-sufficient, responsible children with the expectation that we would grow into well-adjusted, self-sufficient, responsible adults. Once we had become accountable for ourselves, then we, in theory, would do the same for our children. Each subsequent generation would follow this tradition of teaching responsibility and independence. I thought the idea sounded marvelous, so I bought into this tradition lock, stock, and barrel.

For the last ten years I have had custody of the boys and raised them with little input from their father. Of course I wanted my sons to live strong, independent lives, untied in time from their mother's apron strings.

All I had to do was my part and—*presto!*—off they would go as perfect, independent, self-sufficient adults. I visualized a job well done, slapping the dust from my hands as I sent them off to conquer the world.

I even read books on how to set my children free. In particular, I remember the analogy in Kahlil Gibran's book, *The Prophet*. Gibran says that we are the bows, our children the arrows. We are to launch them forward toward the future, "For life goes not backward nor tarries with yesterday."

I envisioned my boys as strong, straight, fiery arrows, blasted forth from my eager bow. I would draw the string backward, hold it taut against my cheek, point it toward the heavens, and then, in one glorious moment, with one magnanimous gesture, I would release my grip and willingly propel them forward toward their fates. They would streak across the black, star-filled night, their flames igniting earth's dismal void, their flight unstoppable, their destiny inescapable.

It did not work out quite like that.

Actually, I gave them a tentative launch, maybe a foot or two. Then, when they landed with a resounding, trembling *splat*, I quickly scurried over to grab them up, brush them off, and tuck them securely back into the quiver that I religiously carried on my back. And so it went, a blastoff here, a send-off there. But always, they returned to their rightful spot; to the safety and security of my quiver. They returned to me.

Now I have sent them on their final flights. They are independent, free, and self-sufficient, and I stand here alone, bow in hand, empty quiver strapped to my back. I have done what I was taught to do—I have set them free. Hurray for me! Hurray for good ol' Mom!

And here, I have regretfully discovered, is where Gibran's grandiose insight falls apart. Because never once does he mention what is to become of *me* now that my job of child-rearing has ended. Nor does he say what is to become of the quiver, the one that after years of devotion and duty has molded and shaped itself to fit my back. The one that has become such an intrinsic part of me, a part so familiar that I feel naked without it. What do I do with the quiver? Cast it aside, as though it never existed? Carry it on my back, in case one day I may need to use it again? Hang it on the wall, a shrine to the good old days? Weep into it? What exactly is the lone archer supposed to do with the empty quiver?

Maybe the father in the café understands what I do not. Maybe he fears that the more independent his son becomes, the sooner the boy will leave home. And maybe that father, like me, does not relish the idea of being left alone, wondering what happened. Wondering what went wrong.

When I taught my children independence and self-reliance, in essence I taught them to leave home, but more specifically, I taught them to leave *me*. Now my question becomes: why, after all my hard work, after all my years of struggle and sacrifice, after my boys have reached the stage in life when they are a pleasure to be around, would I possibly want them to leave? Because society dictates that I should cast them out? If this is true, then why does their leaving feel so wrong, so lonely? Why does my heart ache with longing to have them back?

Why do I feel like their new life will bring me death?

As I ride deep into the desert, a low, guttural sound slowly rises up from the depths of me. A sob, harsh and rasping, reaches a fervent, fanatical volume—the cumulative ache of generations before me—and explodes into the empty vastness of the desert.

Chapter 4

ANCIENT SENTRIES BECKON

D eath Valley—to put it as succinctly as possible—is one hot son of a bitch.

The heat rises from my motorcycle's engine and combines with the blasting furnace of unrelenting, scalding air that lunges at me from all directions. I increase my speed in the hope that the accelerated movement will cool the air and make my breathing easier. No such luck.

I breathe in short, labored gasps, gulping in the blistering, arid air, alternating my breathing from my mouth to my nose. Both ways hurt. The inside of my nose has become dry and scorched, my throat parched. I glance at my watch; it is only ten thirty in the morning, and already the temperature must be well into the nineties. Whatever moisture I had in my body has been sucked away, dehydration's task easily accomplished.

Death Valley, the arid desert in southeastern California, is one of the hottest places in the world. I have read that the first white people to enter the valley consisted of two small groups of emigrants traveling to the California gold fields. In late 1849, they entered Furnace Creek Wash while looking for a shortcut to the mother lode. They became lost, depleted their food supply, and were forced to endure severe hardships before they could escape from the desert. One of the eighteen survivors of an ill-fated party of thirty gave the valley its morbid name.

The AAA Guide to Death Valley pamphlet warns that temperatures can reach over 120 degrees during the summer months, with ground temperatures often 50 percent higher. Even though I was concerned about the searing heat, I wanted to visit Death Valley and hear the *singing sand*. I had the notion that its song might reach deep into my soul and whisper the secrets of the universe to me.

The Eureka Dunes in Death Valley lie in the remote Eureka Valley and cover an area only three miles long and one mile wide, yet they are the tallest sand dunes in California, possibly in all of North America. A climb to the summit is difficult because the slopes are steep and the sand loose. However, at the top, I'm told the sweeping view rewards the hardy, those who have the chance to experience one of the strangest phenomena to be found in the desert: singing sand.

Evidently, when the sand avalanches down the steepest face of the highest dune, a sound like the bass note of a pipe organ or the distant drone of an airplane can be heard emanating from the sand. If the dune is at all damp, though, no sound will be made. Why this occurs is not fully understood, but it may be because of the friction created when the smooth grains of dry sand rub against one another.

My enthusiasm has, once again, overtaken my common sense. I doubt if I could hike a hundred feet in this heat, let alone to the top of a sand dune. The singing and the mysterious secrets the sounds might reveal will have to wait. My immediate concern is to escape this oppressive heat.

Stopping at the visitor's center, I stand as close as possible to the air conditioner and then fill my two water bottles. I buy extra Gatorade to replenish electrolytes before receiving clear directions on how to exit the park. No one would last long in this scalding valley, and I cannot afford to get lost.

I'm only in the visitor's center a few minutes, yet everything on my motorcycle is red-hot to the touch. The leather seat burns my butt and thighs, the reflective chrome glares into my eyes, and my black saddlebags are too hot to open without gloves. Mine is the only motorcycle in the parking lot. It looks like everyone else has had the good judgment to cross Death Valley in the protective security of a climate-controlled car.

The desolate landscape blends into hues of brown, taupe, fawn, and mushroom interspersed with pale green clumps of sage, usually two or three feet high. There appears to be little life in this drab place—some cactus—but not much. The bare and rugged mountains rise as a distant, deep haze and melt into the sharp, blue sky. There are no clouds to offer the welcome reprieve of an occasional shadow to ride through.

I pass a sign that reads, ELEVATION ZERO. I want to stop and take a picture of my motorcycle in front of the sign, but I can feel the heat sapping my strength and there are no safe havens between here and the end of the park. The heat radiates off the pavement ahead of me, creating ghostlike apparitions that shimmer and then vanish as I'm swept through their illusive path.

My emotions flatten; I'm sweating profusely. I should have crossed earlier in the day, but I never suspected the heat would be this relentless. Again, poor judgment on my part. After riding for twenty minutes, I need water and stop in the middle of the road and shut off the engine. It does not matter that I have parked here, because no one is on this road. The only sound I hear is the *tink, tink, tink* of the engine, a metallic sound made as the metal contracts and the engine cools.

I easily guzzle a liter of Gatorade and some water. Removing my heavy leather jacket and helmet, I walk away from the bike. Away from the sound and security of the engine. If I cannot hear the singing sand, maybe the desert will share its secrets with me in another way.

I'm devoid of all human contact and there are no sounds of life. As I close my eyes, the earth falls silent. Silent. Is this what it is like to be completely and totally alone? I let the emptiness permeate me, wash over and through me. I attempt to understand what this means as I try to come to grips with the idea of life lived in the solitary confinement of my existence. I pray for wisdom, but the answers do not come. Within minutes, my skin turns bright red, so I hurry back to the bike, put on my jacket and helmet, and ride on toward the coolness of the mountains.

Fatigued, I mindlessly follow a solitary line of sparsely spaced, weathered telephone poles, the only indication of man's unsuccessful attempt to civilize this uninhabitable, desolate region. Each pole has a single crossbar and two sad drooping lines.

Like ancient sentries, they beckon, one after another, silently summoning me forward to atone for the sins of my past.

* * *

Have you ever visited a place so peaceful that the very stillness of it resonated deep within you?

A place so tranquil that you wondered why you have not known of its existence before, for surely a place like this should have drawn you to it? And once having found this place, did you question your sanity for leaving, when you knew, deep within you, that if you stayed long enough, this place would bring you peace of mind?

I found a place like that in Utah. The first time I experienced Bryce Canyon's mysterious atmosphere, I felt compelled to return, *driven* to return. I was not sure when, or what circumstances would surround my future visit, but without question, I was meant to stand before this giant amphitheater with its thousands of multicolored red rock pinnacles again. I would let the peace wash over me; attempt to release the fear and guilt that seized me; and see if somehow, I could figure out how to find my way.

Bryce Canyon National Park in southwestern Utah was established as a national monument in 1923 and is located on the eastern rim of the Paunsaugunt Plateau. It is famous for these unusual, awe-inspiring multicolored rock formations and its canyons that are 1,000 feet deep. Erosion has sculpted the canyon walls into thousands of towering spires, fins, pinnacles, and mazes.

These brown, red, orange, yellow, and white pinnacles of limestone, sandstone, and mudstone shoot toward the sky in fanciful formations. Someone dubbed these jutting pillars of rock *hoodoos*, meaning, "to cast a spell," and indeed they do. Folklore has it that the local Paiute Indians explained the colorful hoodoos as legend people who were turned to stone by Coyote.

Last summer, Robert and I visited Bryce Canyon. He, too, had felt its emotional, spiritual impact and wanted to share the experience with me. We were both baffled by the fact that a canyon, an austere grouping of unusual rock formations, could have such a powerful effect on our emotions. Why this canyon but not another? Why these rocks but not others?

Today, I return to Bryce Canyon by myself, and the experience is oddly satisfying. This feeling of fulfillment surprises me because I thought returning would be depressing. But I can relish the time spent here and immerse myself in Bryce's beauty without the distraction of Robert's schedule or his input.

I move toward the canyon's edge and notice many of the people gathered near the precipice are remarkably quiet, and parents hush their children. This place casts a reverent spell and they, too, seem mesmerized by this sacred site. From this overlook, a sign says I could see over a hundred miles on clear days, and in winter, my view is only restricted by the curvature of the earth.

After Robert and I left last year, I regretted that we never watched the sun set on these marvelous stones or waited for the stars to light the black night. Thanks to being a nearly pollution-free area and the fact that there are few large light sources nearby, Bryce Canyon creates unparalleled opportunities for stargazing. I plan to spend the day and evening here to experience these two awesome sights. But first, I want to hike to the bottom of the canyon and walk among the towering pinnacles.

This will be a leisurely, relaxing stroll.

* * *

I have discovered in my vast experience that life is willing to teach me a few good lessons if I bother to pay attention and remember them.

For instance, long ago I learned that going downhill requires far less effort than going back up. It seems to me I would recall that reality, especially before I go skipping off on my next adventure, loaded down with heavy riding boots, camera, ample snacks, extra water, and a backpack stuffed full of warm clothes in case the temperature should abruptly drop below the nineties. But oh, no. Also, I did not remember the caution that I read earlier, the one about this canyon being 1,000 feet deep.

But I will remember it quite clearly when I begin the long, slow, painful trudge back toward the top.

When I reach the bottom of the canyon, I meet the nicest family. The parents, probably in their late thirties, are hiking with three active children. I share my stockpile of snacks and enjoy their easy company as we crane our necks to stare at the fascinating towering hoodoos. We watch big, fat, shiny black birds, often perched all in a row, on the sparse limbs of Ponderosa pines, spruces, and fir trees. We laugh and exchange names and stories as we hike along the canyon floor.

This is fun. I'm enjoying being part of a family again. What a great day I'm having! What a wonderful adventure! I giggle, tickled with a zest for life, joyful at seeing the pinnacles up close and personal, and blathering like a merry fool. Then all at once, my euphoria comes to a screeching halt. No more laughing. No more silly giggles. Joy and merriment have vanished with the rounding of a corner.

It is time to start uphill.

Within a few minutes, it becomes painfully obvious to my new friends that they have a dead weight on their hands. The children bolt uphill, young goats frolicking on winged feet. The parents hang back, not sure what to do with me. A sense of duty slows their pace, but the glances between them give away their unease. What if they have to stay with me all day? All night? Have they innocently become trapped on the canyon floor with a middle-aged woman whose feet have turned to anvils?

I wave them on. It seems like the decent thing to do. They certainly do not owe their entire vacation to me simply because fate has mischievously flung them across my path. I plod onward, upward. I'm not used to hiking, especially uphill, and with this heat I make it about ten feet before my lungs rebel, scream for mercy, and beg me to slow my snail's pace. My arms grow longer, the knuckles of my fingers nearly dragging the ground as I revert to an earlier primate form, hunched over by my heavy backpack, and lean into the incline.

My hair, soaked with sweat, clings to my throbbing face, and my head droops. My entire line of vision is now focused on my bulky, leaden, dust-stained boots. I watch, fixated, as my laboring feet shuffle forward in wobbly baby steps, a hobbled gait that leaves two distinct, continuous grooves in the dirt. Why in God's name did I not take the time to change into my lightweight tennis shoes? I was excited to reach the bottom, and it did not seem to matter as I bolted downhill. It matters now.

My new friends yell at me from somewhere above as they zigzag across the face of the canyon. "Come on, Carolyn!" "You can do it!" "Keep going!" "Carolyn, Carolyn!" My name echoes off the canyon walls, their words growing softer as the distance between us widens.

People pass me on their cheerful way toward the bottom. Then they pass me on their way back toward the top, sympathetic eyes stealing a peek at the wretched, dazed, wheezing creature staggering forward. Everyone passes me, young and old alike. A few people ask me if I'll be all right, and I give them a weak thumbs-up. Speaking is entirely out of the question. I need to save my energy for something far more compelling—like breathing.

It is getting late, and eventually, I'm the last one on the path still lumbering toward the top. I'm not prepared to spend the night on this trail. Although loaded down, I did not bring enough water or my flashlight. If I cannot reach the top before nightfall, I will not be able to see the narrow path and could slip and fall off the edge, tumbling head over heels to the bottom of the ravine. No one would find me until the next day or maybe not at all. I must keep forcing myself forward while there is daylight.

Still, there is something comforting about this tranquil, spiritual canyon, and my thoughts return to my last days with Robert before I left on my trip. Our two-year relationship had been chaotic at best, but we decided that ours was a good match. The boys had recently moved out; both were happily settled into apartments and moving forward with jobs, girlfriends, and college.

I had closed the law office, and most of my personal things were in storage; extra boxes with *New Mexico* written on the side were stored at Robert's house. I moved in with Robert and his aging mother, Margaret. The stay with Robert quickly deteriorated to a state of constant stress. Life with his elderly mother frustrated Robert and he did not know how to handle her mental health issues. I really liked Margaret. Although age had begun to steal her mind, her sweet disposition remained, a tribute to the strength of character that remained deep within her.

I stayed with the two of them for the month before I was to leave on this trip, while Robert continued to brood. Depression and moodiness hovered over him like a dark cloud, bleak and cheerless. I'm not sure what caused his descent into depression, but the stress of it drained both of us. Robert needed my emotional and physical support, and it is not my nature to abandon someone who needs me, so I remained at the house until he felt better. Shortly before I left, Robert arranged for his sister to move to Portland and take over the care of their mother.

One evening before I fell asleep, with Robert's dark form on the other side of the bed, I had an unusual premonition.

Troubled about the magnitude of my upcoming trip, I felt a presence near me. I know lots of people do not believe in spirits or guardian angels, but I do. I believe these guardians offer comfort, assistance, and protection if we need their help. My mother instilled in me the beliefs of life after death, reincarnation, and the progression of the soul. We believe death ends only the physical body, while the soul continues its journey toward divine knowledge and perfection. The belief that we live, die, and are forever dead is as foreign to me as the continuation of the soul may be to others.

It is difficult to express what I mean by a presence. I did not physically hear or see anyone, yet I felt that something external waited to join me, if I chose to allow the company. The best way I can describe it is to compare the experience to listening to the radio. We know that if we turn on the radio, we can hear music. We see no one and no one stands near us, yet if we choose, we can turn up the dial and surround ourselves with unseen sound that profoundly alters our senses. The choice always remains ours. Turn on the radio or leave it off. Whatever we choose does not change the fact that the music still plays, in the ethos. If we choose not to listen, it nevertheless continues to play for others to hear.

My impression of this spiritual presence was a woman named *Ada*. I felt she had come to accompany me on my trip, overseeing my travels and safety. I have no idea why the name Ada came to mind. I did not know anyone named Ada previously, nor had I read or heard the name. Ada waited unobtrusively for me to choose to accept her offer of guardianship.

I chose to turn the radio on.

Relief inundated me. Whatever the trip might bring, I had a guardian angel by my side. I did not believe she doubled as a companion or that she would eradicate my feelings of loneliness, but only that she would be here if I needed her. That night I slept better than I had in months.

Ada is not with me now as I slowly plod forward out of the ravine, and I cannot help but wonder why.

I have managed to put myself in several dangerous situations since leaving Roseburg, and some forewarning would have been nice. Is she really going to be here if I need her, or was my sense of her presence merely a fabrication of my imagination, a security blanket without substance?

The people along the rim who earlier had looked like ants revert to human forms again. I stretch out on the ground near my motorcycle and, oblivious to those around me, sleep soundly for several hours. As night approaches, I wake and move to the edge of the canyon to watch the sunset and wait for the stars to illuminate the black sky.

I wonder if the atoms are different here or if they perhaps intermingle with a person's body in an unusual way. A strange feeling of peace washes over me and I'm content to absorb the tranquility. If I stayed here long enough, I think I could find inner peace. Knowing this, why do I feel compelled to hurry off to some other place? What calls me?

I pack my bike and head back to my campground nearly thirty miles away. Originally, I had planned to always be off the road well before dark. The danger at night increases substantially, especially when looking through the visor of my helmet and a bug-splattered windshield. The motorcycle's headlight beam is minimal and only shows a small portion of the highway directly in front of the bike.

I knew when I came to the canyon today that I would have to ride back at night, but with the stars out, I thought there would be more natural light. This winding canyon is darker than I expected. The small, narrow road has tight turns and limited visibility. It is late, the area is remote, and I have yet to come across another car. A road sign says it is common to encounter deer in this area. Since no one is on the road, I decide it is safer to ride on the centerline of the highway. This way, I can see the headlights of any oncoming cars and watch for deer on either side of the road.

It is peaceful out here; I'm relaxed and happy that I made the decision to stay longer. I approach a tight right-hand curve when I hear a loud, demanding voice scream, "*Carolyn!*" The piercing voice startles me and instinctively, I jerk my motorcycle handlebars hard to the right and move tight against my side of the canyon wall.

On the centerline, a car without the headlights on roars around the corner and streaks past me, exactly where I was riding. It misses me by inches. I hear the screams of young people coming from their open windows. *Jesus Christ!* My heart is pounding, and I pull off the road and stop. I need to regain my composure, control my breathing, and settle my nerves.

The car continues on, the driver not even bothering to stop and check on me. My guess is the kids were out for a joyride and thought it would be fun to drive with the headlights out. My brother, Gary, and I had done that sort of thing when we were teenagers, but *shit*, I could have been killed.

My hands are trembling and it takes a few minutes before I remember the voice that screamed my name. I know: to say I heard a voice sounds outlandish, but, nevertheless, I heard its warning, loud and clear.

Was it Ada's voice that saved me?

Chapter 5

A DEATH IN THE FAMILY

I have agonized for days about whether or not to return to the Grand Canyon.

Now here I am on the North Rim. The ride in was a surprise with tall trees and meadows rather than the dry desert of the South Rim. The trees are different shades of green; the sky is bright blue with big intermittent puffs of white clouds; no high mountains are in the distance. This region, with its twisted pines, reminds me of some areas in eastern Oregon. A wave of loneliness sweeps over me; I want to see my sons.

As I pull up near the Grand Canyon Lodge, glimpses of the canyon appear. It is massive, wide, and seems bottomless. A short distance away is an overlook protected by a waist-high wire fence and metal rail. The ravine is enormous and looks like someone has taken a monstrous plow and gouged deep, uneven grooves into the earth. As far as I can see, massive rock shelves sit one behind the other like children's building blocks, their vast beauty breathtaking. Somewhere far below is the Colorado River.

Twenty-two years ago, I traveled to the South Rim of the Grand Canyon with my mother and father in their camper. We had spent the night parked near the rim, and Mom and I got up early to watch the sun rise over this spectacular canyon. As the canyon slowly came to life with its deep shadows and multicolor peaks and valleys, my mother quietly moved closer to my side, took my hand in hers, and held it tight against her chest. That simple act of compassion remains one of my fondest and most endearing memories, because it was death that brought me there.

My first child, Elizabeth, was born on February 6, 1972, and lived one day.

She was a beautiful baby with lots of black hair, long legs, and a perfect china-doll face. But from the time she was born, Elizabeth was dying. Born six weeks premature and weighing only four pounds, she had underdeveloped lungs. Each time she exhaled or cried, a portion of her tiny lungs fused together. As less oxygen entered her lungs, each breath became more labored than the one before—an unhurried death by suffocation.

It broke my heart to watch her gasping for air and to hear her agonizing cry.

And her father? On this day, of all days, Joe was out of town and did not return until the next morning. All night, I stood outside the nursery, alone, hour after hour, willing Elizabeth to breathe and begging God to let her live. I watched helplessly as my beautiful baby daughter died a slow and agonizing death.

Within a few days of her death, I flew to Arizona and spent several weeks with my parents. My folks, already on vacation, traveled in a small camper fitted on the back of their pickup. It was a tight squeeze for all of us. My dad had to sleep inside the truck while mom and I slept on a small bed located over the cab of the pickup. They never once complained.

They tried their best to show me Arizona, but they knew I was struggling, both mentally and physically. When we reached the Grand Canyon, I remember being struck with the contrast of the canyon's awesome beauty and my overwhelming grief. I sobbed uncontrollably.

Looking back, I find it peculiar that I chose to spend this time grieving with my parents rather than with my husband, Joe. It was a momentous and telling event.

I just did not acknowledge the signs.

* * *

"Carolyn, is that you?"

I'm standing outside the Grand Canyon Lodge and putting on my riding gear when someone calls to me.

It is Jill, a friend of Joe's and mine from when we lived in Springfield, Oregon. We had spent a lot of time together with her and her husband as young married couples and often rafted Oregon's rivers. We were buddies before our divorces, but afterward, as is common with a divorce, we went our separate ways. It has probably been fifteen years since we have seen one another. I meet Jill's new husband, and we have a chance to catch up on each other's lives.

Here I was feeling sorry for myself, and along comes a friend from the past. I'm happy to have her company for an hour or so, and I feel much better when I leave the Grand Canyon behind.

It is getting late. After another fifty miles on the road, a remote motel appears. It is a classic tourist trap, and I'm its weary prey. But I'm tired, and there is no place to pitch my tent, so a room is my only choice. It is small, no television, no air-conditioning, the heater does not work, and the only sink is in the bedroom. The shower and toilet are in one tiny, open space. If I'm sitting on the toilet and lean slightly forward, I can rest my head on the wall in front of me, or I can turn sideways and put my feet under the shower.

But at least I can take a shower, so this will not be so bad. However, the tiles in the shower slant downward at a steep angle, and it is necessary to brace myself against the back wall before turning on the water. The water temperature is not constant and continually switches from freezing to scalding. I stay to one side, wait for the steam to clear, and quickly put my foot in and out of the water. When the temperature starts to switch, I dart in, quickly wash, and dart back out.

A plunger for the toilet sits beside it, ever ready for an onslaught of unexpected problems. The way the bathroom floor slants, any overflow will go into the shower drain. That is a wonderful thought. I do not care to deal with any catastrophes tonight, so I will wait to flush until tomorrow morning. Actually, none of this really matters to me. All I want is to go to bed. I'm exhausted from the ride and the memories. I want my sons. I leave a message on Travis's phone and will be relieved when Brian returns from Europe.

I'm beat but cannot sleep. My thoughts drift back to the earlier days of my marriage, Elizabeth, the boys, and the complications surrounding their births.

There was one crisis after another, and those emergencies changed everything.

* * *

Joe and I married in 1966—Joe was twenty-three, and I was twenty-two. In the early years, we were young and happy.

Joe was a handsome guy with a baby face, dark hair, and brown eyes. A natural salesman, he was always ready with a smile and had lots of friends. He was a member of the 304th Air Rescue Squadron in Portland and his unit trained and supported rescue operations.

We met casually in 1962 during my freshman year at Southern Oregon College. The following year we both transferred to the University of Oregon, then ran into one another and started dating.

Joe quit college his junior year and went to work for AT&T as a Yellow Pages salesman. I graduated from the University of Oregon in 1966, and we married that summer. Joe's passion for life suited me well, as we both had gregarious, outgoing personalities. A tomboy at heart, I loved physical activities and we liked to raft the rivers and surround ourselves with good friends.

Financially, Joe was successful; he was smart and quickly moved into management. As he progressed up the corporate ladder, AT&T moved him from city to city within Oregon. In a three-year period, we moved five times and, while this worked well for Joe, it negatively affected my career opportunities. My jobs as a caseworker for the State of Oregon and then as a policewoman for the City of Salem both ended abruptly when Joe was transferred, and that frustrated me.

We were married for six years when we settled in Springfield, Oregon, and started our family. Elizabeth's birth and the repercussions of her death profoundly affected our marriage and my life, the extent of which I would not fully understand until years later.

After Elizabeth's death, I changed doctors. My new doctor, a neonatal specialist, told me the reason Elizabeth was born early was because my uterus was weak, and that I might never be able to carry a baby to full term. This news was devastating because I had always wanted children.

I was racked with guilt and felt it was my fault Elizabeth had been born early. The doctor explained that there was nothing I could have done to prevent her premature birth, but my physical weakness, Elizabeth's death, and the horrific aftermath continued to torment me.

In the early 1970s, it was common for premature babies to die because their immature lungs did not produce a substance called *surfactant* until around the thirty-seventh week of pregnancy. Surfactant is a liquid produced naturally in the lungs that helps newborn babies keep their tiny air sacs open so they can breathe air normally.

A full-term pregnancy is considered forty weeks; Elizabeth was born at thirty-four weeks. Several years after Elizabeth's death, surfactant was artificially produced and is now given to preterm babies if the doctor suspects they cannot make enough of the substance on their own. This is one reason why many of today's low-weight preemies are able to survive.

When I became pregnant with Brian six months later, my doctor was candid.

"One of two things will happen. If your uterus is still weak, the baby will be born too early. That means it's unlikely that the baby will survive. Or, if we're lucky, you may carry the baby an extra two weeks. If the baby is only four weeks early, we may have a chance of saving it."

For eight months my nerves were on edge. I wished away those months of my life and counted off each week of my pregnancy: twelve weeks, twenty-five weeks, thirty weeks, thirty-four, thirty-five, thirty-six weeks. I did not do anything that might jar the baby and was stressed all the time, which was not healthy for either of us.

The doctor was right with his prognosis; Brian was born four weeks early and weighed five pounds and fourteen ounces. His lungs were strong, but he could not keep his body temperature up. The minute the nurse took him out of the incubator and brought him to me, his temperature dropped, and they had to hustle him back to the nursery. It would take several hours for his body temperature to become normal again.

When Elizabeth was born, she had been too fragile to be removed from the incubator; I never had a chance to hold or touch her. As much as I wanted to hold Brian, I insisted they leave him in the incubator where he had a better chance of surviving. Once again I would spend hours standing by the window in a feeble attempt to guard him. When the nurse removed Brian to feed or bathe him, I would frantically watch until he was securely tucked back into his incubator.

As I stood there, the nurses would come and tell me I needed to stay in bed and rest, but it was impossible, and eventually they left me alone. Brian stayed an extra week in the hospital and weighed five pounds when we brought him home. His little fingers looked like matchsticks, and his head was about the size of an orange. He had big blue eyes and blond hair.

Several days after we brought Brian home, our good friend, Dan, came over to see us. The three of us were peering over the crib at Brian, whose wide-eyed gaze seemed to be peering at Dan's blue eyes and blond hair. Joe spoke first.

"Damn it, Dan, that baby looks more like you than he does me." We had a good laugh over that. In time, though, I would come to realize that Joe was not kidding. He told that joke again and again. Brian did not look like Joe, but then, he did not look like me, either.

The more Joe made that comment and meant it, the more aggravated I became. First it was insulting to me, but more importantly, I considered it highly offensive to Brian. I demanded we take a paternity test, but Joe refused to participate. For years, and probably to this day, Joe has never believed Brian was his child. To compensate, Joe would say, "Well, it doesn't matter, I will love him anyway."

Whether Joe loved Brian more or less, I will never know. What I do know is that his insecurity took a toll on our marriage. If Joe thought I was screwing around with our friend, then I could not help but wonder if he thought that because he was screwing around on me. Perhaps he wanted to shift the blame.

Joe's irrational behavior caused an insidious, downward spiral and was one of the contributing factors to the divorce that ended our eighteen-year marriage. A simple paternity test cost two hundred dollars and would have settled the matter, but Joe refused to spend the money. When it came to spending money, there was something peculiar about Joe's reasoning.

It was an unjustifiable idiosyncrasy that would destroy us.

* * *

I saw my youngest son, Travis, in a dream several years before he was born.

We were in the doorway of a child's bedroom, and I was kneeling in front of a sweet little boy. He was about two or three and had big brown eyes and dark hair. I was buttoning up his yellow shirt, and we were at eye level. He looked straight at me, and I knew I would see him again. I was so surprised when Elizabeth and Brian were born because neither of them resembled the dark-eyed little boy I had seen in my dream.

When I became pregnant with Travis, Brian was three months old. Immediately there were complications with Travis; I started bleeding, and the doctor feared I was having a miscarriage. After a number of tests, he discovered that I had placenta previa, a problem in pregnancy in which the placenta is in the lower part of the womb instead of on top, where it belongs. The doctor explained that as the baby grows inside the mother, if the placenta is near the bottom of the womb, the baby's weight can unexpectedly cause the placenta to rupture. This could lead to the premature birth of the baby or excessive bleeding in the mother, sometimes causing death for one or both.

The doctor explained that it was critical I did not lift anything over five pounds. The doctor limited my activities, and I had to stay within fifteen minutes' drive of the hospital. In the meantime, Brian was growing quickly and was already a big baby. I was not in any condition to lift him.

Since Joe was working during the day, my Aunt Lucille invited Brian and me to stay at her house so she could help with Brian. Joe would drop us off in the morning and pick us up at night. It was a lot for Lucille to offer, but she and I had always been close and she was happy to have us, and I was happy to be there.

The weekly countdown began again, and I worried constantly about Travis being born prematurely, but, thankfully, he was a full-term baby. He was born quickly and without any complications.

Travis's problems started two months later. Plagued with chronic diarrhea, he was continually nauseous and lost weight. He was so sick that I was afraid he would die in his sleep.

We had a rocking chair and I would sit up all night with him so he could sleep upright and breathe easier. I would cradle his little butt in my hand, his body close to my chest, and rock. In the morning, there was lively fourteen-month-old Brian, who had endless energy during the day, while I was continually exhausted and scared.

I took Travis to various doctors, but no one could figure out what was wrong with him. I found many of the doctors condescending. "Babies have diarrhea," they would say, as if my baby's symptoms were nothing, and I was wasting their time with my ridiculous concerns. They sent me home, almost herding me out their doors, but I knew something was wrong.

We saw yet another specialist; Joe was at work, so only the two of us went. After a thorough exam, the doctor's opinion was that Travis had cystic fibrosis, a genetic disorder that affects the respiratory and digestive systems. I remember that discussion clearly.

"Cystic fibrosis? I think of that as a killer of children." I was dumbfounded at the diagnosis and could barely get the words out.

"Well, it does limit their lifespan."

"To what?"

"About ten or twelve years."

"Ten or twelve years? Yes, I'd say that limits their lifespan." I was instantly livid that the doctor sounded so causal when he told me. Travis was sitting on my lap and I held him tighter and could feel my heart pounding against his thin back.

"However, we won't know for sure unless he has a sweat test, and that's very hard on babies. They have to be totally wrapped in cellophane to make them sweat, and then we test the sweat. There's a new procedure coming out, but it's about three months away. I want to wait."

Every time I looked at Travis, I started crying. I never told Joe about the diagnosis because he was stressed at work and I believed the terrible news would put too much pressure on him, so I carried that burden alone.

When the new test came out three months later, I told Joe what the doctor had said about Travis, and he was glad I had not told him.

The test was simple but could only be done in Portland, Oregon, three hours north of where we lived. Joe chose not to go with us, so my mom drove up to Springfield and went with me. The doctor taped a small suction cup to Travis's arm, and then we waited most of the day. At last the nurse removed the cup, and then they tested the sweat. The test was negative; Travis did not have cystic fibrosis.

It is enlightening in retrospect to realize how dysfunctional our relationship was at that point. I should have told Joe about Travis's diagnosis, and Joe should have gone with us to Portland. We were a family, but somehow we lacked the desire or ability to support one another.

Travis was two when he was finally diagnosed with giardia, an intestinal infection caused by a parasite that causes diarrhea, nausea, abdominal pain, and fatigue, and is found in food or tainted water. No doctor considered giardia because it was virtually unheard of for an infant in our area to have been exposed to it. For two long, grueling years, Travis was continually sick and I was constantly afraid he might die. Then, Travis was prescribed the proper medication, and in two weeks, the parasites were destroyed.

The damage to Travis's intestines remained, as did my feelings of resentment toward my husband. Even though I contributed to the unrest in our house by not speaking up, I did not like being left physically and emotionally alone to resolve the critical problems with the boys. It was during this time that I had a conversation with Joe. I was exhausted, scared, and angry.

"Joe, you've always been number one in this family. You've seen to that. But that's over now. I'm number one from now on. Without me, the boys might die. They're number two and three, and you're number four." I was serious. Brian and Travis continued to be my top priority and focus, while my affection and behavior toward Joe waned.

This did not increase his attention or sense of responsibility.

In time, Joe would figure out how to rectify his intolerable change in status.

Chapter 6

COLLECTING PASSENGERS

I confess: I am the queen of vanity.

This morning, I'm in a Colorado KOA bathroom, jostling for sink and shower time with several dozen other women. Women of various ages are standing in line waiting to use the bathroom, shower, put on their makeup, and wash and dry their hair so they can present themselves to the world. It takes forever waiting for my turn. Nevertheless, I wait.

Vanity is a huge aggravation and a lot of work. From the time I was a teenager, I would not have dreamed of stepping out the door without layers upon layers of makeup and my hair coiffed and sprayed stiff. Even camping or floating the river: no exception. I refused to leave the tent without my full regalia: complete makeup, perfect hair, painted nails, and a color-coordinated outfit. My fellow rafters would lift their eyebrows, roll their eyes, and look at me like I was some sort of extraterrestrial being.

The first time I saw a tiny vein on the back of my leg, a precursor to varicose veins, I began wearing long pants to disguise my imperfection. This was a strange reaction, because overall I'm blessed with great genes. I'm height-weight proportionate and attractive, and, like my parents, look about ten years younger than my real age. It made no sense for many years.

Now I know the media contributes endlessly to this obsession with beauty and perfection, especially for women. One cannot turn on the television, watch a movie, or open a magazine without being bombarded with advertisements for beauty products, always presented by young, beautiful women.

When I go out in the hot sun and ride with the dirt and wind in my face, my efforts will have been for nothing. But here I am, programmed like a robot, committed to my daily routine, so I can at least start out looking presentable. This may change because I'm losing time and must travel several hundred miles each day. Instead of being lined up in the bathroom, I should already be on the bike.

Initially, I thought this gathering of women would be fun. We could chat about our trips and exchange adventures, but I quickly learned that it is serious business in the women's bathroom. There is little conversation; the stress level is high, the pressure mounting to whip ourselves into shape. I can feel the tension, theirs and mine. The pursuit of vanity is a driving compulsion.

I like to think I'm making some headway. As I approach fifty, my varicose veins have taken a backseat to comfort. It is hot out here, and in the spirit of getting over my ridiculous need for perfection, I buy a pair of shorts to wear while hanging out around my tent. If people want to judge me based on the way the back of my legs look, so be it. I'm also getting age spots. I mean, honest-to-God age spots—little round brown spots— that appear without warning on my body, face, and hands that bring home the reality of aging.

As I leave the restroom, an older woman, perhaps seventy, passes me wearing shorts and a tank top. She appears to be completely comfortable with her wrinkles and loose skin, which jiggles when she moves. Good for her. I hope I feel that way when I'm seventy, but I worry this may not be true.

For the present, my immediate beauty dilemma is solving my vision problem. I swear, the day I turned forty my eyesight went south, and I had to buy reading glasses. While I can see perfectly objects in the distance, I cannot read a thing without my glasses. This is a major problem since I'm constantly looking at a map.

A sensible person would have bought a pair of bifocal glasses to wear all the time. But because I believe I look better without glasses, reasonable behavior went out the window. See how this vanity thing works? After dragging my glasses in and out of a small pouch strapped to my handlebars twenty times a day, I finally cut a couple of holes in the fabric case and slipped my belt through it. Very clever, I thought, until I went to use the facilities and my glasses slid off my belt and landed with a splash into the toilet.

It is getting late, and there are many miles to cover before dark. Why did I stay for so long in the bathroom this morning? My chest muscles constrict and my shoulders tighten.

I need to keep moving—though I am driven to return to a place and time no one would willingly choose to go.

* * *

A tremendous storm heads toward me: the lightning flashes, and detonating thunder blasts follow.

I barely have time to unload my bike and set up my tent before it starts pouring. I'm thankful my clothes did not get wet because it takes too long for them to dry inside the tent. The rain and booming thunder are relaxing; the noise does not scare me and I find the sound of the pounding rain on the top of my tent calming.

I stretch out on my sleeping bag in the Durango, Colorado, KOA. I'm carrying a tape recorder with me and in the evenings I try to recap each day. What I'm finding, however, is that I'm tired at night and lack the energy or desire to ramble on. Tomorrow, I plan to tuck the tape recorder in my leather jacket pocket, and then, when stopping, I can record my feelings, thoughts, and experiences as they happen.

Earlier today, as I was repacking the bike, a young woman, maybe seventeen years old, saw my Oregon license plate and asked about my trip. I mentioned that yesterday I crossed the Navajo Indian reservation in northeastern Arizona. She immediately told me I needed to be "really careful" around "those people," and that it was not safe to cross the reservation.

I asked her if she had an unfortunate experience on the reservation. She said, "No, I've never been on the reservation." Nevertheless, she was quite adamant about the risk and her fears. I thought about mentioning that I, too, am "one of those people," since I'm an enrolled member of the Cowlitz Tribe of Indians, but I doubt it would have changed her stereotype.

My experience crossing the reservation was completely without incident. The ride was leisurely with miles and miles of open space, sparse traffic, and warm and temperate weather. I pulled into a small trading post, filled my gas tank, and chatted with several of the locals. Everyone was pleasant and helpful and there was nothing to fear.

I dismissed her stereotyping of others as foolish.

* * *

Sometimes, life decides to kick me in the butt.

About the time I get all arrogant and cocky, along comes the Goddess of Smugness to slap me down and put me in my place. This happens to me in Farmington, New Mexico, and I'm really embarrassed to admit this.

As I ride through New Mexico, I realize I'm not without stereotypes myself.

I had heard stories of some Hispanic people being uneducated or unsophisticated, perhaps even drug dealers, and I equated these stories with *unsafe*. Since Farmington has a sizeable Hispanic community, I'm fearful and anxious to get back into Colorado where I will feel safer. Surely the people there are better educated, more refined, and not dangerous.

As I'm leaving Farmington, however, I pass a cemetery. What catches my eye is that the entire cemetery is covered with fresh flowers, potted plants, mementos, and Hispanic decorations. I have never seen a cemetery with so many expressions of love. In my mind, I run through the holidays, and I recall that yesterday was Father's Day.

That is when it occurs to me that the Hispanic people must be caring and considerate if they honor their deceased fathers and family members in this way. I imagine these are the type of people who would help one another and probably help me. My fear vanishes; I relax and enjoy my ride through New Mexico.

If this is a different stereotype, that is okay with me. I like this one better.

* * *

I ache like I have the flu, and everything hurts even if I'm lying still.

A couple days ago, I was in Durango, Colorado, and enjoyed listening to a wonderful thunderstorm while the wind and rain buffeted the tent. However, after I fell asleep, water leaked in and soaked my clothes and foam pad, and I ended up spending the night on the wet ground. The next morning, I was sick and only managed to ride the bike 150 miles before deciding that it was safer to get off the road and rest.

Besides tent space, the KOA has small wooden cabins called Kamping Kabins, and I opt to spend the night in one. This cabin reminds me of something that might have been found out West in the early pioneer days; it is a rustic structure without a bathroom, running water, or bedding. However, it does have electricity, a floorboard heater, a table and chairs, bunk beds, and a mattress for my sleeping bag.

The inside of this cabin is decorated with a western motif. There are pine boards on the walls and ceiling and striped orange-and-turquoise curtains cover small windows. Three coyotes are cut out of plywood and attached to the wall; each wears a small bandana made from the curtain material stapled to its neck. They sit near a corner, and someone has painted a yellow moon on the opposite wall so the animals can howl at it.

The cabin is a huge improvement over my tent. Most of my clothes are still wet from the thunderstorm and it is best to spend the extra money and sleep on a bed that is off the ground for a couple of days. Hopefully I will heal quickly while everything dries out.

I find it aggravating that despite today's modern scientific discoveries, someone has not yet come up with a cure for the common cold. The pharmaceutical companies would not be happy about that, though; I'm sure they are making billions off sad-looking creatures like myself. Nevertheless, I'm doing my part to support their booming business and have stocked up on Alka-Seltzer, cold pills, aspirin, and allergy medicine, just in case it is something other than a cold.

Last night I was feeling sorry for myself and called Robert, thinking that might cheer me up, but it did not help. The conversation, instead, left me feeling depressed and I'm not sure why. While we have our problems, yesterday's discussion was no different than any other talks we have had recently.

When I'm completely honest with myself, I'm happier when I'm *not* talking to Robert at all. If that is not a big red flag flapping in my face, I'm not sure what is. Still, I'm not prepared to call it quits with him. Why does my fear of living alone overpower my otherwise relatively sound judgment?

If a friend were in a similar situation, I would tell her, "Wake up, dump the guy, and get on with your life." Why do I not take my own advice? What is it that makes me act like this? Why do I throw common sense out the window, even though I'm troubled that this may not be a long-term match for either of us?

If this fear of loneliness is the true culprit, then maybe other fears are contributing to it as well. I do not consider myself a fearful person, and I have always been willing to take a calculated risk. However, perhaps there are other clues that are more significant than I realize. I will pay more attention and if I discover an unacceptable fear, I will figure out a way to conquer it. Maybe addressing and attacking different fears will help me address my fear of loneliness.

My first chance comes as I'm sitting on my bunk bed, staring at the cabin door. It has a lock on it! Of course it does. Since this cabin reminds me of a small house, I locked the door out of habit, an old instinct to protect my things and myself.

My first night in my tent was unsettling because I could not lock the tent; I was afraid, and my nerves were shot. Now I'm comfortable in the tent and do not concern myself with my safety. If I'm taking a shower, eating, or away from the tent for any amount of time, the tent is vulnerable to thieves.

The truth is, my things are as safe in this cabin as they are in the tent. If someone wants to take something, they will find a way to break in and take it. So I'm going to attack this fear by replacing it with trust. While camping, I will have confidence in my neighbors and not lock my cabin door.

It is important to say that trusting my neighbors does not mean that I intend to be reckless or careless. As an attorney, I have dealt with a lot of criminal clients and people with mental health issues. It is important to be wary and pay attention to my surroundings and how people act. I like to think that I'm *street smart*, which is to say I have a personal alertness to situations that have the potential to become dangerous.

This is also a good time to mention that I'm not a willing victim, either. I carry two small, loaded handguns with me and one is beside my bed at night. I was raised in the country, learned to shoot at an early age, am completely comfortable with guns, and have had a concealed weapons permit for a number of years. This certainly helps with my feelings of personal security.

I create fear in my mind, though, and often it is not justified. Like many of the folks I have talked with, mine is a fear of the unknown. Negative stereotypes and preconceived notions about people or places continue to creep around in the dark crevices of my mind.

This is illogical, and it drives me crazy. I decide to commit to attacking my fears with a vengeance and to not letting them control me.

I leave my cabin door unlocked, take some cold meds, and collapse into bed.

* * *

I'm loading the last few bags onto my bike the next morning and watch a thin, young woman, maybe thirty, with short brown hair stagger toward me. She is smiling, but her steps are slow, even deliberate, and she balances herself on a wooden cane with a worn handle.

"Hi, I'm Nay. I saw you pull into camp the other day, but since you're rarely out of your cabin, I thought I'd check to see if you're okay." She glances at my loaded Harley.

"Thank you, that's really thoughtful of you. I'm fine, although, I have a nasty cold or maybe the flu, so I thought it best to stay off the bike for a few days. You don't want to stand too close to me. I'm Carolyn, by the way." My physical condition does not seem to concern her, and she continues to stand near me, looking at the bike. I see a wisp of sadness cross her face.

"I saw your Oregon license plate and wanted to talk to you. I'm impressed that you're traveling alone and that you're so far from home." I mention my birthday, and we chat further. I can tell from her questions that she has ridden a motorcycle and we have an enjoyable conversation. She talks about owning a Honda motorcycle and her love of riding.

"Are you still riding?" I gesture toward her cane.

"No, I have MS. Multiple sclerosis. It affects my balance, so I'm really unsteady. I can't even ride on the back of a motorcycle anymore because the motion makes me dizzy, and then the dizziness turns into a negative physical reaction. It's no fun."

"I'm so sorry to hear that, Nay." I reach over and gently touch her arm. "I have a friend in New Jersey with MS, so I'm familiar with it." She shifts her cane to the other hand.

"You're awfully young to have to struggle with this. How are you doing?" I know that MS is a serious, progressive neuro-logical disease that is painful and debilitating.

But Nay does not answer me; she only smiles a sad half smile.

"I'm sure you miss riding." I know the answer, and as tears well up in her eyes, I wish I had not said that. She moves closer to me, reaches over, takes my hand, and looks directly at me.

"Take me with you." She squeezes my hand tighter.

"In this small way, I can be a part of your trip and I'll be able to ride again." We both understand that she means "in spirit."

"Of course I will, Nay. I would love to have you come with me."

"Thank you, Carolyn. You have no idea how much this means to me." She immediately begins to cry. I step into her, take her in my arms, and gently hold Nay, a complete stranger, but a kindred soul. Both of us are crying and I'm overwhelmed that my motorcycle trip impacts her life in such a powerful way. We stand there for a few minutes and then she reaches up and gently touches my face. "Thank you."

I ache for Nay as she stumbles away. Why does life have to be so difficult for this sweet young woman? This seems so unfair to me.

Later that morning, I ride out of the KOA with my first *passenger* tucked securely behind me.

Chapter 7

MOTHER'S WORST NIGHTMARE—THE BIKER

I have been on the road for over a week and have yet to see another woman rider traveling alone.

There are women riding, but they are always sitting behind the security of a man. So imagine my delight when I pull into a parking lot and spy a single woman standing by her packed bike. We spot one another, rush over, and give each other a tight warm hug like we are long-lost friends.

She smiles broadly and then rattles off some statement, a guttural spray of words that means nothing to me. She is a big woman, six foot or more, large boned, with short brown hair. Her heavy motorcycle jacket encases her like a shield, and with her solid, broad shoulders, she presents an imposing figure. Happily pumping my hand, she says, "Bertha. Germany." *Big Bertha*, I think. From Germany. And, I'm *little tiny Carolyn*. From Oregon.

Since I cannot speak German and Bertha understands little English, we begin a comical conversation. Both of us are anxious to explain who we are, what we do, and why we are traveling alone on motorcycles. Unfortunately, the language barrier prevents accurate communication, but through a series of hand gestures and attempts at understanding, I finally decide that Bertha is a masseuse.

It is my turn, and I try to communicate *Attorney*, but she does not get it. I offer words like *lawyer, judge, jury, black robes*, and *courthouses*, but she still does not understand. Finally, patting my chest, I say, "I keep people out of jail." A horrified and upset Bertha stares at me and then quickly turns and heads back to her bike, loads up, and leaves me standing in the parking lot.

I think she understood "I" and "jail" and must have thought I was an escaped felon—a bank robber or an unsavory criminal on the lam. This strikes me as funny, because that was the same appalled reaction that my parents had when their professional daughter brought home *the biker* to meet the family.

It did not go well.

* * *

In 1967, I ventured out for my first solo ride on a motorcycle. It was distressing and daunting.

Newlywed and twenty-three years old, Joe and I owned one car and one motorcycle, a 1966 Honda 305. Joe's job as a salesman required that he use the car daily. As a young housewife, I discovered I did not care to be stuck at home without any transportation. One day I found myself in the garage staring at the Honda. To me, at five foot, three inches and 115 pounds, the bike looked huge. I climbed up on it, straddled the seat, and noticed that my legs dangled almost a foot above the ground.

Since no one had ever mentioned the importance of a bike fitting the rider's body, I never suspected that an improper fit could cause a problem. When a bike fits, a person can comfortably sit on the seat, with both feet firmly planted on the ground. Also, your hands can easily reach the handlebars so you are able to control the gears.

Back in those days, mobility reigned supreme in my mind; nothing else mattered. I had seen Joe start the Honda, knew generally about the clutch and brake, and wondered, *how complicated can this be?*

That was back in my invincible days—no motorcycle lessons, no helmet, no leathers, no sense. Just get on the bike and ride.

I left the garage and headed to the open road. When I reached the first stop sign, the uneven road tilted to the left, so it seemed reasonable that I should lean the bike to the left. Since my feet did not touch the ground, I leaned too much, and the bike began to pitch over. Knowing I was physically unlikely to prevent the fall, I abandoned ship. Off I jumped and the bike crashed to the ground. Unable to lift the bike, I stood there, a disgraceful sight, until some nice man stopped, picked up the bike, and away I charged again.

I spent the next two years aggravated and frustrated in my riding. In a vain attempt to teach myself to ride, I placed myself in dangerous situations. Disgusted by the entire experience, I was ecstatic when we bought a second car.

When we sold that ghastly motorcycle, I decided right then that the day would never come when I would straddle another motorcycle

* * *

The first hint that I might change my mind about motorcycles came in the summer of 1988 with the entrance of, as they like to say in the movies, a "tall, dark, handsome stranger."

I had been divorced for four years, and seven of my female friends and I had just graduated from Northwestern School of Law in Portland, Oregon. Before we tackled the task of preparing for the Oregon State Bar exam, we decided to go away for the weekend to a small resort town in Eastern Oregon. On Saturday, we attended the area's annual rodeo. So there we sat, kicking back in the bleachers, eyeing the local cowboys, when *the biker* swaggered in and captured our full attention.

He had obviously ridden there on a motorcycle. Dust covered his black leather coat, chaps, and sturdy boots. A large Bowie knife hung from his hip, housed in its studded leather sheath. His wallet was attached to a long chrome-linked chain secured to a belt loop. A worn bandana draped in front of his neck, ever ready—I supposed—if he needed to pull off a robbery.

A dashingly good-looking man with a neatly trimmed black beard, he strode confidently up the bleachers and flashed us a disarming smile, his teeth perfectly straight and white. He headed straight toward us, then stopped about five rows down and sat beside a couple with a small girl. The little girl let out a squeal, jumped up, and rushed to him. She gave him a big hug, promptly shifted her dad over with her butt, planted herself next to this man, and then slipped her arm through his.

I watched the biker remove the rubber band from his long ponytail. His black hair fell casually over his weathered jacket. I was confident that the women who sat beside me also could not help but notice the width of his shoulders and the way his lower back narrowed and then wedged into his hips.

That evening I saw him at a dance. We made eye contact. He simply walked up, introduced himself as Steve, and suggested we go for a cup of coffee. This man had a soft-spoken sweetness about him, and our conversation flowed easily. Still, his easy-going demeanor did little to conceal a physical presence that intimidated those who filled the café. People took this man seriously. He spoke candidly about his current involvement with a woman he had known a short while. We talked late into the night, hugged, said goodbye, and went our separate ways.

Several months passed before I heard from Steve. His relationship had ended, and he wanted to see me again. But life takes some strange turns and now I was the one involved in a relationship. Over the next two years, Steve called, sent flowers, and stopped by occasionally on his way through Portland. He would just appear at my downtown law office, his question always the same: "Hey, Red, you still going out with that guy?" I was, but he always charmed me with that smile, and we would head out for a cup of coffee, Steve with his leathers, heavy boots, and clanking chains, me with my three-inch heels, business suit, and red hair twisted into a smart bun. The office staff assumed he was one of my criminal clients.

Before he would leave, he would wink, lean down and deliberately brush his soft beard across my cheek while whispering in my ear, "I don't suppose they have any motels in this city?"

"Not a one," I always replied, but as soon as he left I regretted my answer. Our attraction was highly sexual and we both knew it, and I know he intentionally did that beard thing to set me off. I was committed to my current boyfriend; however, Steve's allure kept me on edge. He was hard to forget.

One day Steve called again and my relationship with the other guy had ended. Steve offered to take me to the Pendleton Round-Up, a professional rodeo located about two hundred miles east of Portland.

"Carolyn, I want you to come with me," he urged, his voice deep and coaxing. "Be ready next Thursday, and I'll pick you up on my Harley."

Now that sounds like quite the adventure, doesn't it? Just jump on the back of a Harley with some badass biker you hardly know and off you go for the weekend.

In a moment of bravado, I agreed. *No problem. Sure. This will be fun.*

* * *

We heard the roar of his Harley's engine long before we saw his imposing figure. I smiled weakly at my two teenage sons.

"I know you'll like him, guys. Really. He looks a little rough, but he's a very nice man." Neither of them spoke or moved from their watch at the window. I panicked; I was beginning to think I had made a big error in judgment.

"Now give your mother a break and don't stare when he comes in the house." I tried to sound stern, but the tension in my throat made the words come out stiff and high-pitched.

It was the fall of 1990, and for days I had tried to prepare Brian, seventeen, and Travis, sixteen, for this moment. Although I had been divorced for six years, neither son felt comfortable with the idea that Mom planned to go away with a biker for the weekend. In fact, I could not believe it myself. A respectable Portland attorney who, up to this point, had only dated respectable Portland gentlemen, intended to leave town with a *biker*, on a *Harley*.

We watched, transfixed, from our upstairs apartment window as Steve pulled into the parking lot, settled his bike with its painting of the Grim Reaper under a brightly lit streetlight, and shut off the engine. He slid his leg easily over the radically lowered Harley, removed his Nazi-styled helmet, slipped the rubber band out of his hair, and headed our way. His dark hair flowed with each long, confident stride. He wore a heavy ankle-length black oiled duster that blended into the dark night, and it was easy to imagine he had an Uzi tucked inside his coat.

Both boys whirled simultaneously and stared at me.

"Is *that* him?" Brian stammered, as if there was some possibility this guy meant to stop by some other apartment in our ritzy complex.

"Mommmm?" This was the long, drawn-out sound Travis made when he was convinced I had finally lost touch with reality and all hope was lost. Then, "You gotta be kidding me," he whispered. The three of us stood frozen as we listened to the sound of Steve's heavy boots on the stairs as he came closer and closer to our front door.

Bang, bang, bang. Overcome with curiosity, Travis bolted for the door, threw it open, and gawked, wide-eyed and open-mouthed, at the large, bearded man who framed our doorway. Brian stepped forward, ready to protect his dazed mother if this suddenly turned ugly. But Steve smiled broadly, stepped into the room, extended his hand, and introduced himself. He walked over and gave my arm a warm squeeze. Then he asked the boys if they could help him unload his bags from the bike. In a flash they were gone.

I watched the three of them from the window. It became obvious that the motorcycle and this mystery man fascinated my sons. They laughed, talked, and hung around the bike. Brian and Travis each took a turn and sat on the motorcycle. When they returned, he asked them about school, sports, and the things they liked to do. He showed them his Bowie knife and said he carried a gun in his jacket, and if they wanted to see it, to ask him first because he kept it loaded. When asked why he carried a gun, he simply stated, "I hope for the best and plan for the worst."

Then, I noticed he kept sniffing. Sniffing? Why does he keep sniffing like that? Then I knew. Drugs! It had to be drugs.

Oh my God, I had committed to spend the weekend with a man who snorts cocaine.

"Steve, you must have a cold." He stared at me. "With all that sniffing," I mumbled.

"No, Carolyn, I don't have a cold. I've been riding a motorcycle for the last five hours. The wind goes up your nose. You'll see."

* * *

In the spirit of the weekend, I had borrowed a leather coat and bought a pair of motorcycle boots. Travis offered his studded leather belt. Steve brought a Harley-Davidson tank top with a single red rose boldly printed across the front of the knit material. When I held it up to me, I thought he had made a mistake. Or this had to be a joke. This minuscule piece of cloth would not fit a three-year-old. No way could I wear this. But the fabric stretched, and the rose became bigger than life. The cut of the tank top ruled out the option of a bra and, as I am rather busty, the entire outfit made quite the statement.

Early the next morning as I packed, both boys came into my room, shut the door, and said, "Mom, you don't have to do this. It's okay if you want to stay home."

"I'll be fine, guys, really. I want to go. If we don't take a chance on life now and then, it slips away from us. We must be brave and create our own adventures. I don't want fear to hold me back." I hugged my handsome sons. "I really do want to go.

Think of the experiences I'll have. Everything will be fine. Now don't worry."

"Well, you can always call us and we'll come and get you."

The boys repeated the pact I had with them for years, and I never wavered on my commitment. I always said to them, "No matter what happens or what you do, good or bad, if you need help, call me and I'll come and get you. It doesn't matter where you are, I'll be there. No questions asked. If necessary, we can discuss things later." How strange it sounded to hear these familiar heartfelt words spoken back to me by the young adults who stood at my side.

As we prepared to leave, I twisted my long hair, formed a bun, and pinned it on the top of my head. Steve quietly suggested, "You might want to braid your hair and let it hang down your back. That way the helmet fits closer to your head and is more comfortable."

"Nonsense," I answered with a feigned cockiness in my voice, "The bun works fine." Then he wanted to know if I had any other sunglasses, the kind that would lay tightly against my cheeks and properly protect my eyes.

"Yes, I do, but I liked the look of these better." When I started to put on one more layer of lipstick, he said in that soft-spoken way, "I don't believe I'd do that."

"Why not?"

"Because bugs will stick to your lips!"

Men are so weird. What was the matter with him, anyway? Did he actually believe I would be out there, stylin' on the back of a Harley, extended rose thrust toward the east, without my lipstick? I added an extra coat. Without another word, Steve handed the boys a piece of paper. He had arranged for us to stay with his grandmother; the paper contained her name, number, and address. Then he looked at my sons. "Don't worry. I plan to take very good care of your mother."

The moment of truth had arrived. I hugged the boys again, mounted up, and we were off.

* * *

I sat behind Steve, perched precariously high on a flimsy four-inch seat, and clutched his black leather coat in a death grip. The passenger foot pegs attached high on the sides of the motorcycle, and I swear my knees came up almost level with my shoulders. His large bowie knife hung out from his hip, and because I felt too embarrassed to move it, I could not get my legs closer to him. They jutted out spectacularly from both sides of his body, and I looked like I was all set for my gynecology exam.

As we headed out of town, the wind swirled around my face and shot right up my nose. *I can't breathe.* I gasped for air and commanded myself to calm down. *Of course you can breathe.* People ride on the back of motorcycles all the time, and they do not flop off for lack of oxygen. Since this was my first experience on the back of a Harley-Davidson, I figured I felt breathless due to Steve's excessive speed. How fast was this maniac going, anyway? I clung to his leather jacket and cautiously peered over his shoulder.

The speedometer needle set steadily on thirty-five miles per hour.

By the time we hit the freeway, the increased speed caused the wind to catch the front edge of my helmet and wrenched it upward. This tightened the chinstrap under my neck and practically choked the life out of me. I quickly tried to push the helmet closer to my head, but it was hopeless. My tidy bun held firm.

The wind swept around the inside of my helmet, and my head began to bobble about uncontrollably, much like a bobblehead toy. The sunglasses did not hug my cheeks, so the wind burned and stung my eyes. This in turn caused them to water like mad, and black mascara streamed down my face. And yes. You guessed it. Small bugs, caught in the extra layers of lipstick, started to pile up on my lips. Since I was afraid to let go of Steve's jacket, I sputtered and spit in an effort to get rid of them.

I caught a glimpse of Steve as he watched me in the rearview mirror. I noticed that even though he had clenched his jaw, the corners of his mouth was turned up in a controlled smile. I'm sure he wanted to burst out in wild laughter, but instead he reached back and patted my leg to reassure me, much as you would a child.

How had I ever let myself get talked into a motorcycle trip to Pendleton? Suddenly the two hundred miles of road seemed endless. What kind of an idiot would think this is fun? Tense and uncomfortable, I wanted off this hideous contraption. I wiggled, squirmed, and counted down the hours until we arrived. Four more hours. Three more hours. Mercifully, Steve took pity on me, and we stopped often. By then I was sniffing with the best of them. I sniffed and snorted, massaged my throat, wiped mascara, picked off smashed bugs, and attempted to force my knees together.

I wanted to be a good sport and not complain, but I was not happy. Somewhere along the way, we stopped at another rest area. I dashed cold water in my face, glanced at the pathetic sight in the mirror, and limped back to the torture rack.

Steve had the bike unloaded.

What on earth did he mean to do? Why did he have my things off to one side? Maybe he intended to leave me there. Why not?

Who could blame him? Then I saw foamy stuff oozing from my bag. The vibration from the motorcycle had shaken the canister of hair foam I had brought until it had erupted and emptied its contents all over my clothes and everything else packed inside my bag. Perfect.

The mental countdown continued. Two more hours. One more hour. At last we arrived at the Pendleton rodeo. I gratefully dismounted the disgusting contraption and planted both feet on solid ground.

Looks like I will be giving the boys a call.

Later, as we headed toward the arena, people looked at us and stepped aside. Their body language changed from a relaxed mode to a tense, wary posture. Why did they do that? We did not act aggressive. These people had taken one look at us, saw *bikers*, associated that with *bad bikers*, and instinctively guarded themselves. When we headed up the stairs to our seats in the bleachers, happy faces turned serious. No one wanted to sit beside us.

I did not blame them for the way they felt about Steve. He did look bad. But why did they look at *me* like that? Did they not understand he was the real biker and I, a proper attorney, just happened to have on a leather jacket? I realized they had no way to distinguish the difference between us. With a few articles of clothing, I had been transformed into a biker, or, more precisely, a biker's ol' lady.

Only the day before, I had represented clients in state court, a respected professional woman who argued her cases before judge and jury. And now, less than twenty-four hours later, respect had been replaced with suspicion and fear.

The way people label and stereotype one another has always fascinated me. But I had never had the labels applied quite so dramatically to me. And that was not the end of it. Later that weekend, I met some of Steve's cousins. They acted polite enough but otherwise had no particular interest in me. After we had been in their home for well over an hour, someone finally asked me if I worked in a bar. When they discovered I practiced law, they moved their chairs closer and solicited my opinion on a variety of legal issues. The biker vanished, and the attorney appeared. I was *somebody*.

When I thought about the way people judge and label one another, it dawned on me how unfair I had been to Steve. Because of my own preconceived notions of how a badass biker must act, I too had fallen into the stereotype trap, believing Steve snorted cocaine or could be a knife-wielding fanatic. I had assumed the worst and hoped for the best.

Steve's behavior with my sons, and knowing his relatives, friends, and strangers confirmed my initial impression of him being a kind, sweet person. He always smiled—he was an open, friendly man who tried to put people at ease. His clothes did not change his basic personality any more than a leather coat changed mine. He was a sweetheart. This man, I expected to see again.

When we reached Steve's grandmother's house later that day, we had a chance to visit with her, a sweet, kind woman who reminded me of Steve. She had our separate rooms ready in the basement. Earlier, I had a chance to wash my foam-covered clothes and had hung them up on the clothesline downstairs near the bedrooms. As we were getting ready to go to bed, Steve walked past my short black negligee that swayed on the clothesline, touching it lightly.

"This is nice," he said softly while rubbing the lace between his fingers, "but you won't have it on long."

"I hope I don't."

With that, he took two long strides across the floor, swooped me up in his arms, and carried me into his bedroom, pushing the door shut with his foot. His wet lips melded to mine, his tongue pressing deep into my mouth. Our clothes were off before we reached the bed, and landed intermingled across the floor. Neither of us slept much that night, and the sheets on his twin bed were a tangled, sweaty heap the next morning. I hoped his Grandma could sleep, but with all the commotion going on downstairs, I rather doubt it.

I would not be giving the boys a call after all.

Over the next few days, we made many short motorcycle trips around the area. It surprised me to discover that the Harley itself drew a crowd. After they overcame their initial reservations, people wanted to know more about the motorcycle and, as a natural progression, more about the riders. We became the center of attention.

I have to fess up here. I loved all activity the Harley generated and believe I'm a frustrated movie star wannabe at heart, and that my rightful place is in the limelight. The motorcycle and the commotion it created fired enthusiasm and excitement in me.

Little did I know, those exhilarating feelings would transform the direction of my life.

Soon we had the motorcycle packed and were headed back to Portland.

We cruised through the beautiful Columbia River Gorge. My braided hair hung down my back, and I sported a new pair of sunglasses that fit snugly to my cheeks. I adjusted Steve's knife and pressed my breasts tight into his back, my legs tucked firmly against his sides. The lipstick, I would save for later.

The sun warmed my body, the balmy wind massaged my face, and I relaxed and settled into the bike. The sun dipped low in the west, and our two shadows danced on the pavement. As Steve moved the motorcycle smoothly in and out of traffic, our shadows followed, the graceful dance of two ballerinas blended as one.

Our shadow dance held me spellbound. Mesmerized, I watched the dark silhouette sweep along the broken white centerline that divides the lanes. The shadow flowed, and I sensed a smooth cadence as the lines passed. *Whoosh, whoosh, whoosh.* The wind blew across the river, and I felt occasional hints of dampness on my face. Small hawks hovered on the air currents above the iridescent water.

Caught by the rhythmic, sensual rumble of the Harley's engine, I realized I did not want the ride to end. Would it really be over in three more hours? Two more hours?

You have time to reflect when you are on the back of a motorcycle. The strong, steady rumble of the engine has an almost hypnotic effect, and I recalled the carefree days of my childhood. From the time I was five years old, I had a horse and eventually rode unrestricted on my parents' 650-acre ranch. The Harley reminded me of riding my horse and the wild, unbridled innocence of youth.

Sheltered from the outside world by loving parents, I did not concern myself with burdensome complexities such as old age or the loneliness it might bring. Those fears would find me easily enough later in life. Oh, to feel safe and secure again. What freedom that would bring!

I wished Steve did not live so far away, and at any moment I could pick up the phone and say, "Let's go riding today!" Tucked securely behind Steve on the Harley, that idyllic feeling of childhood freedom and safety could be mine again.

I'm not sure when it happened. Days before, I had been a miserable passenger, but now the strong, steady rumble of the engine captivated me, its power a reminder of a time when all things were possible. I wanted to ride again, and I did not want to wait until Steve came back to town. Ignorant of the full impact and the changes the future might bring, I made an astonishing decision. As soon as I returned home I would place an ad in the local paper.

Wait until I tell Brian and Travis the news: their mother is going to buy a motorcycle!

And it had to be a Harley.

Chapter 8

THE WOMAN IN THE MIST

I'm near the last high pass in the Colorado Rockies, and then I must carefully trek down the mountains.

It is stunning up here with the vast vistas of green forests, deep valleys with clear rivers, and the occasional dancing waterfall. The air is crisp but nippy. I should put on my rain gear since I'm moving in and out of light showers, but after being sick for several days, I'm too tired to stop and unpack my saddlebags. This should be my last major mountain range for a while, and I'm looking forward to returning to the heat of the desert.

As I head downhill, my thoughts drift to my dissatisfaction with law. Would I want to return home, inspired by this freedom, only to be back in the throes of the law? I had decided to leave my practice even before this trip. This frustration surprised me because I was excited to be accepted into law school at forty-one years old, a single mother with custody of two active little boys.

* * *

Joe and I had been married for eighteen years, and his demand for a divorce stunned me. Although our life was physically active and we had lots of friends, it was not particularly emotionally or sexually fulfilling for either of us. However, I thought we had adapted and would continue to raise our children together. I assumed we would muddle through for another forty years or so, and then at the end of our lives we would wonder what it had all been about.

Prior to our divorce, we attempted marriage counseling. When that did not work, the psychologist suggested I attend law school. He said, "You will be in and out in three years," as if there was nothing to it. His suggestion astounded me because the law was not an option I ever considered, but I valued his opinion, applied, and was accepted.

I found learning about the law challenging and satisfying. Once I began practicing, I enjoyed meeting new clients and liked the interaction, the diversity of their issues, and my ability to help them solve their problems. What I discovered, however, was our time together was only a small portion of the practice of law.

The bulk of the practice was sitting in my office, door closed, with mounds of paperwork stacked high on my desk. Family law, the majority of my private practice, is extremely paper intensive and relates to all issues dealing with families: divorces, custody, child and spousal support, visitation rights, adoptions, division of assets (both physical and monetary), retirement funds, wills and trusts, etc. The issues and problems were infinite. As if that were not enough, this body of law is constantly changing, so researching the latest updates was endless. It was tedious work: exacting, precise, and mundane. It was time for a change.

While still practicing law, I signed up for a Lawyer in Transition class offered through the Oregon State Bar / Professional Liability Fund, which focused on helping lawyers transition from the law to other professional areas that are better suited to them. I discovered that I'm happiest when around large groups of people. I like spontaneity, a free flow of activity that is not mired down in fact-specific information.

My perfect job would be fast-paced, allow me to be flamboyant and dramatic, and require me to think on my feet. I might consider television, radio, or an area of sales or marketing. This insight explains why I enjoy the KOA interviews—my law practice was the polar opposite.

As glamorous and fun as the possibility of another career sounded, I still had Brian and Travis to consider. It is important for me to make a living and contribute to the support of the boys. And, at nearly fifty, I had no job experience in these other areas.

It is a big decision to make a career change. I sat down with the boys and explained my dissatisfaction with the practice of law, and discussed my dilemma. I could stay in the legal field or choose a different profession. I told them that it would affect them financially, and I might not be able to help them as much with college as I had planned.

For many years, I have said to the boys, "Do what makes you happy." I guess they were paying attention, and much to their credit, both of them repeated these words back to me. But it was not that simple. Where do I draw the line when deciding what is best for them and what is best for me? Should I change careers now or continue to practice law until they are out of college?

Which way should the scales of justice be tipped?

Another big question for me is, do I want to give up being in business for myself and become an employee who works for someone else? I like making my own decisions and being responsible for myself. I'm temperamental and headstrong, so it is hard for me to imagine working for someone else.

There is a status that comes with being a lawyer. Do I want to give that up? Besides the money, I feel an enhanced sense of worth that is different than when, as some professionals liked to put it, I was "only a housewife." People do respond differently when I tell them I'm an attorney, even though I'm the same person with or without the title.

As I continue to traverse the high mountain range, I realize there is a lot to consider, and I need to give this decision more time.

* * *

I leave the Rockies without incident and enter the Midwestern plains.

The terrain is flat, the sky clear, and I'm heading due east toward Kansas. The desert temperature increases and the arid wind dries my wet clothes and warms my body. I relax and settle into the bike, and hour after hour, I reflect on my past and think about my impressions of life.

When I was a child growing up in the rural town of Winston, Oregon, my mom would take us kids to the Christian church on Sundays. Mom did not have any particular church preference, but this church was only blocks from our house, and she wanted us to learn the Bible stories. Our exposure was very generic and a particular church affiliation was not pushed.

Today, I do not consider myself religious; rather I think of myself as spiritual. After learning about various religions over the years, I could not accept any religion or belief in which people were killing and torturing others in the name of their gods. It did not make sense to me.

I believe many people use the name of a god as a vehicle to control people, maintain power, and increase their personal wealth and status. It is more about them and what they have or want, rather than sincerely trying to help the unfortunate, poor, or sick.

This dishonesty bothered me for years. What I now believe is that we are all on the same journey toward perfection and each must find our own way. Who am I to say what is best for someone else? Or what they should believe? In the same vein, I do not want someone else telling me what is best for me. I will decide that for myself.

I did not push religion on Brian or Travis, as I felt confident that they, too, would figure out what was best for them. We did talk about ideas, and the boys and I have had some interesting conversations.

One day Brian and I were sitting at home when he asked me to describe my belief about tapping into the greater consciousness, something I called *the source*. Travis, who always amazed me with his insightful perspectives on life, had just headed out the door to throw Frisbees in the local park with some of his buddies.

"Well, I believe the source is an energy force where positive thoughts attract positive energy, and negative thoughts create negative energy. I think of it like holding a magnet near a piece of metal; the object is attracted to the magnet—that is the positive energy. But if you try to hold two magnets against each other, they repel one another and neither of them work. That is the negative energy."

"Where do you think this source comes from, Mom?" I watched Brian settle into his chair.

"Well, I believe that positive universal wealth and knowledge is all around us and accessible to everyone. We can receive guidance and direction, but we have to ask for help. I think it is like going to an ever-flowing stream and scooping up a cup of water. It is my responsibility to go to the stream myself. But, I have found that if I do ask for help or guidance, many times it comes to me."

"So, I'm supposed to go to the river and scoop up a cup of universal wealth?"

"Yes, or something like that." I smile at my son.

"And, seriously, Mom, that works for you."

"Yeah, honestly Brian, I know it sounds weird, but many times it really does. Over the course of my life, there have certainly been dark periods, but now I have you and Travis. There was a time after your sister died that I did not think that was possible."

"So, give me an example of when it worked." He runs his hand through his thick blond hair.

"Well, when your dad told me he wanted a divorce, I was devastated and scared. I did not know how I was going to be able to raise you and Travis by myself. So I asked the universe for help and for me to find a *teacher*, or a *guide*, or something like that. I felt pretty desperate at the time."

"I know that wasn't a fun time." He turns toward the window and nods in agreement.

"Well, nothing happened at first—in fact months passed. Then one night when I was really stressed and could not fall asleep, I saw a vision of a woman standing back in a thick white fog or mist. She wore a black, full-length cape with a large hood that covered her hair. She stood a good distance from me and, with the heavy fog, I couldn't see her face."

Brian was quiet, so I continued.

"She never said anything to me or moved. She just quietly stood there, and I felt like she was watching me. What was so strange about it was when I looked at her, I was filled with this overwhelming sense of peace, and I knew I would be all right. I came to think of her as the *Woman in the Mist.*"

"No kidding? How often did you see her?" He leans forward, resting his chin in one hand while fiddling with a tear in his jeans with the other.

"Maybe four or five times, and only when I was especially upset and stressed out. But, I always felt so peaceful when she came that I relaxed. But even if I didn't see her, if I recalled the image of her in the mist, it gave me a feeling of calm."

"Do you see her anymore?"

"No, I don't. The last time I saw her was several years ago. It was after I had graduated from law school, started the practice, was happy, and settled into my new life as a single parent. But, the last time I saw her was a shock."

"How come?" He looks up and sits back in his chair.

"Because I wasn't stressed. I was happy and content, so it surprised me that she came at all. This time, though, as I looked at her, the mist started to clear, gently drifting away from her. For the first time, I could see her face." I paused.

"The Woman in the Mist, Brian—she was me."

"Wow, that gives me goose bumps!" He quickly rubs his hands over his muscular forearms.

"Me, too, and it makes me cry to think about it." We both sit there quietly for a few minutes, and, since he seems interested, I continue.

"While I believe the source is all around us, and available, often I forget to ask for help. Or I don't feel comfortable asking for something that is not a necessity. It doesn't seem right to request things that fuel my ego, like money or fame. It makes me feel uncomfortable to ask for those things."

"Really? Why do you feel that way?"

"Because, I'm concerned that if these things come too easily to me, I will have missed out on some important life lessons that I need to learn."

"I wouldn't mind getting all the things I wanted." He is smiling.

"Yes, I know. But my personal search is to find an inner peace of mind, a deeper understanding of who I am."

"Well, I can understand that, but I don't know if I believe all that stuff about the source. What if it doesn't work?" He straightens up and studies me.

"But what if it does? It can't hurt to give it a try."

He gets to his feet. "Fine, I'm going to go to the river now and scoop up a cup of knowledge. Or, maybe I'll go meet Travis and the guys and throw the Frisbee instead." As he heads out the door, he pauses and calls over his shoulder to me, "I'll think about it."

"That's the important part, honey. Have fun."

As I continue on toward Kansas, the memory of an old church on the east coast resurfaces in my mind and stubbornly coerces me to return. I must go back—or the excruciating ache in my heart will never end. But, if I do go there, I will have no choice but to confront my painful past, my demons, and that is unbearable. My will wavers; I cannot commit to returning.

I do not know which is greater: the pull of the old church . . . or my resistance.

Chapter 9

A GUN OR AN ATTITUDE

I cross into Kansas and this road with its unusual rolling hills is intimidating, and my heart is racing.

As I ride up the front side of each hill, my vision is obstructed and I have no idea what is on the backside. There may be a stalled car in my lane, an animal on the road, a wreck. Or, as I discovered at Bryce Canyon, there may be some reckless kids out for a joyride. Maybe the local kids think it is exciting to go over these hills side-by-side, which would put their car in my lane.

The state of Kansas is relatively flat where I am riding, with few mountains but a lot of rising and falling hills. Long, tubular, rounded mounds stretch out across the landscape on both sides of the road. As I reach each crest, it seems like I can see the rim of the earth far into the distance. I imagine reaching the top, rocketing off into space, and then dropping into a vast void. I wonder if this is how Columbus felt when crossing the ocean for the first time, seeing nothing beyond the curvature of the earth.

These rises are frightening, and I instinctively reduce my speed as I near the crest of each mound. This is not good, because it forces the cars behind me to brake unexpectedly.

I need to get my mind right. These rises require a leap of faith. On the next rise, I force myself to hold the throttle steady as I approach and ride over it. Repeating the same thing with the next rise, and then the next. My confidence returns and the ride begins to remind me of being on a roller coaster, it is actually fun. That is the way it goes for me—with some trust and a steady course, I go through life more smoothly.

While on the road, I have had a chance to talk to a number of people, and many are quick to offer warnings that I be vigilant. My favorite caution so far concerns Kansas. I'm supposed to keep my eye on "those Kansas people." Seriously? Kansas? If I were going to pick the states that I was *least* concerned about, Kansas would be at the top of my list.

Any time I stop for food or gas, I like to ask the friendly local folks about the area. Once I passed miles and miles of wheat, corn, and produce fields, but I did not see any rivers or lakes and was curious to know how these fields were watered. One rancher told me there is a huge underground river, almost the size of a lake, which most farmers can access. He said they use an irrigation system that floods the land so the crops thrive.

There are hundreds and hundreds of miles of land that could produce an abundance of wheat to feed people who are starving, yet the government pays farmers not to grow wheat. Our politicians want to keep the supply of wheat low so the price remains high. This financially benefits the few, while many people go hungry. I do not think that this is right.

I'm spending another night in a KOA cabin. I still do not feel well, and I rest better on a bed than the one-inch piece of foam out in my tent. There are a lot of people, mainly men, in this camp tonight, far more than normal. When I ask about them, I learn they are *harvesters*.

These folks, many of them from Canada, come into town with large pieces of machinery—thrashers, cultivators, and other equipment—to process the wheat. One neighbor tells me some pieces of equipment cost around $150,000. A cook and crew travel with them and they spend the summer moving around the state, harvesting the local crops.

I like Kansas. There is a laid-back peacefulness here. I wonder if it is because there is more space so people have a chance to spread out. The people I have met are kind and helpful and I cannot help but think that this would be a wonderful place to raise children.

Not once did I worry about "those people in Kansas."

* * *

What I do worry about is that the woman who returns from this trip might not be the same woman who left.

I like myself now. While I recognize there are problems I must address, overall I'm happy with my life and who I am. What if, after months on the road, I change somehow and it is not for the better? What if I become more insensitive and begin to look at life from a negative, rather than a positive, perspective? What if I become discouraged or hurt and have to stop my trip early, and this disappointment permanently complicates my life?

As I'm riding this morning, though, I realize I'm calmer and more confident. I feel an unexplained peace of mind that I did not expect, a settled sense of well-being. This has taken place in only a couple of weeks and I'm optimistic about the future. I hope the woman who returns will be stronger, grounded, and more self-assured, and that my life will take a different direction, one that will be for the best.

Then, while I'm blissfully motoring along to these esoteric thoughts, a swarm of large black bugs smacks into me. Bugs are flying across the road in a dark mass right in front of me and there is no way to avoid them. As I ride through them, they splatter across my windshield, half helmet, leather jacket, pants, and face. It hurts. I duck under the windshield as much as possible, yet they still smash into me. This huge cloud of bugs has a death wish. They are like kamikaze pilots, each determined to be the one to take me out.

It is nasty—blood and guts everywhere—and now I'm going to be forced to stop.

* * *

As I scrub squished, sticky bugs off my windshield in a Dairy Queen parking lot, a man riding a Kawasaki motorcycle pulls up and parks next to me.

Without so much as a hello, he starts talking. Traveling alone as a woman is a unique experience, because people seem comfortable walking up to me and will start a conversation without feeling threatened. I can just stand there, and they happily chat away.

"Are you from Oregon? Boy, that's a long way to come on a motorcycle. You're really loaded down. Where are you headed?" Without going into a lot of detail, I mention that this is the year I turn fifty, and to celebrate, I'm riding through all fifty states.

I always give those I quickly interact with this short, non-personal version of what I'm doing, rather than honestly explaining my true purpose. Most people are quite candid and straightforward about their feelings, but I have not reached that point, even with myself.

"That's fabulous. I'm fifty-three, and I've been married for thirty-two years, and I think I'm having a midlife crisis." He rattles off this information without taking a breath. I find it fascinating that people will tell me, a total stranger, the most personal things.

"I'm thinking about getting a divorce, and what bothers me the most is that if I did get divorced, I think I'd be all right." He seems to think he has an obligation to suffer if he makes this decision.

I do not mention that I am a divorce attorney, agree with him that he would be all right, and add that it might take more time than he thinks. But I can tell he is not interested in my opinion; he only wants to talk, to give his feelings a voice. So instead of talking, I listen.

"I think your trip is a wonderful idea." Then, "I'm going to go with you for a while." At first I think he means in spirit, like Nay, but I can tell by the look on his face he is serious. He climbs on his Kawasaki and roars out of the parking lot. I'm concerned that he is going home to pack, so I hurriedly start my bike and head out of town, smeared bugs and all.

I check the rearview mirror and hope he does not catch up with me.

* * *

Looks like I was able to outrun the guy on the Kawasaki, but I'll add him to my passenger list anyway.

As I cross into Oklahoma, the thought of encountering enormous dust storms has me worried. I have never been to this state, but I carry mental images of dry, scorched land with huge dust storms blowing constantly, similar to the descriptions in

John Steinbeck's book, *The Grapes of Wrath,* published in 1939 and set during the Great Depression.

America's Great Depression, often described as the longest, most widespread, and deepest depression of the twentieth century, affected countless people, many of whom never recovered emotionally or financially. Both Joe's and my parents were children or teenagers during this era.

My parents told me stories about how the Depression affected their families. My mom's parents lived in Oregon, owned a farm, and raised cattle, so for a number of years, they were able to get by. Eventually, though, they were forced to sell the remaining farm animals, the property went into foreclosure, and her parents and their seven children had to move in with a neighbor. Still my mother said they were luckier than most.

My dad's family was destitute, and his father deserted his wife and seven young children. My father quit school in the sixth grade and said he stole chickens so the family could eat. My father mentioned this casually a time or two, but he never dwelled on the past.

Looking back, I admire my parents for choosing to look forward, not backward. They made the decision to instill a sense of wealth in their children and I grew up believing we always had plenty of money. I was an adult with children before I understood how tight money really was for our family, especially during the years after my father returned from World War II, and later when he started the construction business.

I never knew if the Depression negatively affected Joe's parents, or if their past history impacted their children's lives. When I met them, Joe's parents were successful and their adult children had a good standard of living. But somehow, Joe developed a fear of not having enough money. While we were married, we never did without, but Joe had what I called a poverty mentality. He could not bear the thought of spending money on anyone other than himself; to do so was almost physically painful to him.

We would often stay at my parents' home for the weekend. Joe would go out with my dad or brothers, and they would share pitchers of beer, but Joe rarely put any money on the table. If we went out with my family or friends to eat, Joe figured our portion of our bill (down to the exact penny) and would pay only that amount. It was as if each dime he spent on someone else had a thousand dollar value to him.

Joe's behavior seemed irrational to me since we had money and Joe never skimped on things we needed. We had nice cars, beautiful homes, clothes, and all the recreational toys Joe wanted, from rafts to scuba to skydiving equipment. This idiosyncrasy never made any sense to my family or me. However, this baffling money anxiety was always there, the effect cumulative. In time, his fears intensified until they became an obsession bordering on a neurosis.

The magnitude of Joe's underlying fearfulness—and his continual dread over money spent on someone else—would eventually crush our lives.

* * *

As I continue on through Oklahoma, the land is flat, spacious, and dips into small, lush valleys where people congregate. Quaint little communities with green trees and red brick houses have sprung up in most valleys; the houses are neat and clean, the yards well landscaped. Each town has a church and most are identified as the First Baptist Church; all are older buildings with tall spires and a bell. I presume I'm in the Bible Belt, where Christianity is deeply embedded in daily life.

While traveling I usually eat at small cafés, because I want to visit with the local people as much as possible. After stopping at a rural diner, I head into the bathroom to wash up, and a small, gray-haired, elderly woman comes in at the same time. The bathroom is an open room, and both the toilet and sink are in plain sight of each other. I tell her I'm only here to wash my hands and then she can have some privacy. She is sweet and gracious and says it is fine for me to stay.

Before I can leave, she walks over to the toilet, pulls her dress up and her panties down, sits, and starts peeing. She repeatedly reaches back and flushes the toilet, I guess so I'm not offended by any disrespectful sounds. She is quite the lady throughout the entire process. She asks me what I'm doing, where I'm going, and what kind of car I'm driving. When I say I'm traveling on a motorcycle, she says, "Oh dear, you be careful, and may the Lord bless you." That is so sweet. It is comforting to think someone beside Ada might be watching out for me, guiding me on my trip.

This blessing is one of many well wishes and kind thoughts I continually receive from the American people during my journey.

* * *

This guy is going to be trouble.

He zooms past me in his car while driving in the left-hand lane, then suddenly brakes, slows his speed until I catch up, and then sits next to me on the highway, staring at me.

Normally I ride in the right-hand lane if I'm on a four-lane highway; the pace is slower, and I can check out the people when they pass. A quick glance tells me a lot. Usually, they smile or wave and I nod back.

I nod chin up, not chin down. This may seem like a small thing, but it is not. A downward nod appears submissive, while a chin up nod is assertive. It is all about body language and having a don't-mess-with-me attitude. I do not nod at this guy at all; there is nothing friendly about his behavior.

Shortly after starting my trip, I decided to leave the main freeways and take America's back roads. Someone has dubbed these back roads *blue highways* because they are colored blue on some road maps. These roads are rural and often quite isolated.

This decision came with an added risk: I'm more vulnerable to danger. Although there is less traffic and thus more time to reflect, if I have mechanical problems or any unforeseen concerns with people, I am virtually alone out here. I was willing to take this chance, though, so I could concentrate on my feelings and simply enjoy riding the bike.

I have had two uncomfortable incidents on the bike so far. The first was a wary feeling rather than any overt behavior. I stopped for gas at a remote spot in the desert; the attendant was a man of about fifty, and we were the only ones at this small, rural gas station. He did not say anything that I found alarming, but he had an odd demeanor and kept watching me, as if I might steal a piece of gum or something. He did not ask me any questions about where I was going or what I was doing, which was unusual. Our total lack of interaction felt weird and uncomfortable.

The only toilet was an isolated outhouse behind the service station. But there was something about the chance of being locked in that secluded outhouse that did not feel right. To make matters worse, it was hot so I had left my leather jacket on my bike. My gun was in my jacket. Great, huh? When I came out, I noticed another car had pulled into the station, so I quickly paid for my gas and left. But this man's abnormal behavior stuck in my mind, and from then on I vowed to always keep my gun with me.

The next incident was when I was at another out-of-the-way store in a rural, mountainous area. While filling my bike's gas tank, a beat-up, rusted brown pickup rolled in behind me. There were four guys in it, two in the front seat and two sitting in the bed of the pickup. They quickly jumped out of the pickup and all four of them moved close to me, too close.

They were a dirty, ratty-looking bunch, some with a couple of teeth missing, and, even though it was early in the morning, their breath reeked of alcohol. They started asking me general questions about my trip, but then they wanted to know specifics; which road would I be taking, when was I leaving, was I always traveling alone?

Across the road from us a large semi-truck was idling, and a beefy trucker was walking toward it with a cup of coffee in his hand. Gesturing his way, I said, "I run with the truckers. They have CBs and can call for help if I need it. They keep an eye out for me." We watched the trucker climb into his cab and I said, "Well, it looks like we're off." As the trucker merged back onto the road, I pulled in behind him and kept an eye on the guys in my rearview mirror. I was relieved when they stayed at the gas station.

I do not know if the truckers are looking out for me or not. However, since there are a lot of trucks on the road, I like to think one of the truckers would stop if I needed help.

Now, alone on the road, I have to deal with this jerk. I increase my speed and pull ahead of him, then watch him speed up beside me a second time. He begins to mirror my actions. If I speed up, so does he. If I slow down, so does he. He continues to sit directly beside me. I wave him on, but he does not change his speed; he continues to stare at me and moves his car closer to my lane. We are the only ones on this back road.

I'm right-handed and carry my gun in the right front pocket of my leather jacket. I control my speed by adjusting the throttle with my right hand. I could set the cruise control to keep the speed steady, reach into my pocket, get my gun out and let him see it, but the process is awkward, and I will have to control the bike with my left hand. This is not my best option. Nor is it a good idea to stop and get off my bike; it is safer to stay on it.

It is also a bad idea to point a gun at someone; I would not do that unless I was serious about following through and believed my life was in danger. So far, this guy is only being intimidating. If he moves his car into my lane, though, or tries to run me off the road, then we have moved to a different level.

I hold my speed steady, look over, and scowl at him. Slowly I unzip my left jacket pocket, put my hand inside and make an adjustment like I have a gun. He gets it, hits the gas, and drives out of sight. I'm relieved for the moment, but that kind of contact has my nerves on edge.

I'm carrying two loaded guns, but the other one is packed at the bottom of a large bag that is strapped onto the bike near the rear fender. I could not get to it unless the bike was completely unloaded. When repacking tomorrow, I'll tuck this gun into a fold of a bag that is right behind me. It will be out of sight, but easy to reach.

This guy is gone for now, but this may not be my last interaction with him.

Chapter 10

THE BURNED MAN

The fool that had been staring at me never reappeared, but such interaction makes me wary.

Jerks aside, though, I think the American people are getting a bad rap. It seems like all I hear on the news anymore are negative things: people killing one another, rapes, fights, and so on. What I'm discovering is that most folks I meet are nothing like those in the sensational stories in the news. They are warm, kind, and generous.

As I ride through small rural towns, I see children playing Little League games, cars in front of churches, and grange halls with young and old people chatting outside. Each small town looks and feels much like the others to me. When I stop to eat at a local diner, people are open, friendly, and sociable, and they appear content. Everything has a similar, comfortable feel about it, only the location is different.

I'm endlessly overwhelmed by the kindness of strangers. When in camp, people come up to me and want to know about my motorcycle trip. They are anxious to tell me where they have been and where they are going. Since I'm not cooking, it is not uncommon for them to invite me over for dinner, breakfast, or a cup of coffee.

I think what I find the most appealing, however, is how open everyone is about sharing his or her hopes, dreams, and intimate thoughts and feelings. I would like to know if this is the norm for travelers. Do most people talk so freely with strangers? My guess is no, but rather that it is because I'm a woman traveling alone, and strangers do not find that threatening.

When I traveled with grumpy Robert, people were not as open or willing to come up and start a conversation. It was different with Steve. Even though he looked like what he was—a tough biker—he had a warm and open personality, so people were comfortable approaching us. Although both men rode motorcycles, there was a vast difference between them. Steve had a zest for life and for his motorcycle; Robert did not. I need to pay attention to this difference in men.

Several years ago, I had a chance to meet a number of other bikers when they started coming to my law office for assistance. They talked passionately about their love of riding motorcycles, and many spoke of their preference to ride alone.

Before I started riding, I did not understand why they felt that way, but now I do.

* * *

Motorcycles offer a completely different experience than when traveling in the protection of a car. Riding a motorcycle incites the senses, inflames my complacency, and demands that I participate in life.

Sight, smell, hearing, taste, and touch bombard me; they barrage my body and mind, each sensation specific, yet cumulative. I'm far more aware and attuned to my surroundings on a motorcycle. It is like waking from a dream state.

Think of how excited a child becomes when feeling wet grass for the first time, tasting ice cream, or discovering the prickly hairs on a caterpillar. When I ride a motorcycle, my enhanced impressions excite me, imprinting a new mental image or refreshing a recollection, or provoking thoughts on a vast array of subjects.

Unrestricted by the confinement of a car, an expansive range of vision becomes possible. The landscape opens and a panoramic view of the surrounding countryside erupts before my eyes, each scene a snapshot of color, texture, and depth—reminiscent of a master painter's canvas. I watch the top of the trees bend in the breeze as I witness the bright sunlight shimmer through the leaves. I look down and greet the highway as it scurries to meet me, only to blur as I sweep by.

As I cross a grated bridge, I lean out from the side of my bike and steal quick glimpses at the water below. The rough grids of metal create a vibration in the tires that cause the front wheel of the bike to wobble erratically, a frightening sensation that leads me to think that the bike might fall over.

Cars cruise by, the occupants mere inches away. I look fellow travelers in the eye, see the expressions on their faces—either smiling or rigid with stress. This personal invasion of privacy does not appear to offend most travelers.

Odors physically adrift on the shifting winds penetrate the nose. Most are pleasurable. Newly cut hay smells sweet, a reminder of home and hot summer harvests. Trees, fruits, and flowers are distinguishable: crisp pines, strawberries, mint fields, gardenias, and roses. The heavy smell of yeast from freshly baked bread hovers in the air, so thick my mouth begins to water.

Then, as quickly as I savor one smell, another casts it aside. The pungent tang of a paper mill stings the inside of my nose, its grasp strong and biting. Stagnant water reeks with the stench of decay, as do animal carcasses. Some stink with such vigor that it becomes necessary to hold my breath until I pass. I can smell rain a few minutes before I encounter the precipitation. The temperature drops ten to fifteen degrees, and the air smells clean, crisp, colder.

Sounds are amplified. An ambulance or police car's siren wails loud and piercing. City traffic's heavy hum reverberates from honking horns, construction site machinery, and shouting pedestrians, all a source of enhanced clamor. The country, desert, and mountains offer renewed silence with only the familiar rhythm of the Harley's engine for company. Sometimes, however, even the Harley's noise wears on the ears, so earplugs are necessary to diffuse and mute the sound.

I can taste more than I first suspected when riding on the open road. Some flavors are obnoxious, such as the acid, crunchy bug that invariably flies into my mouth or the dry, gritty dirt blown from a farmer's plowed field that clings to my tongue longer than I would like. I can now distinguish between the taste of smoke, hot tar, and car exhaust. There are wonderful tastes, too. I like the zesty taste of charcoal from burning fields because it reminds me of licking the head of a burned match as a child.

My favorite day to ride is when the temperature is about eighty-five degrees. The sun heats my body, and warm winds bathe my face with gentle fingers that knead and relax my muscles. Too much time in the sun and my face blisters, especially my nose and lips. Sunglasses protect the eyes, but they create a raccoon effect with a light area around the eyes contrasted with darkened skin.

Half helmets are light and comfortable but do not protect the face from the elements. Rain stings—sharp needle pricks jab into my flesh until it becomes necessary to cloak my face with my hand or a bandana. Temperatures vary radically. In the same day, or even within a few hours, I'm too hot or too cold. The desert may be a hundred and ten degrees, while mountaintops plunge to twenty degrees or less. At these temperatures, my stiff, frozen fingers struggle to bend in order to undo the helmet's strap.

Occasionally, a flying insect slaps into me—a smart, unexpected whack or sting, or sometimes a disgusting splat. Excessive speed increases the thrust of the wind against my chest, causing an unnerving sensation that feels as if I will be sucked backward off my bike.

The vibration of the bike wears on my body. There are times when my arms and hands ache, my butt gets sore, and every physical part screams for mercy so that I wish I had never seen a motorcycle, much less owned one. Then, when I almost reach the point that I'm sick of the whole enhanced-stimuli experience, a vision awakens and quietly slips into the recesses of my weary mind. A faint impression becomes clear as the soreness fades away.

I ride on a long, straight back road in the desert, a sparsely populated area with virtually no traffic. I settle into the bike, lock the cruise control to maintain a constant speed, grip the gas tank with my knees so I will not fall off, and take a deep breath. My head tips back; I feel the bike steady, and then trust envelops me. My hands release their grip, my arms spread fully to embrace the warm desert wind, and I *fly*.

The wind grasps my arms, which gently rise and fall on the currents of air. I close my eyes for a second, and suddenly my spirit is set free. I float, drift, become one with the bike, the wind, the universe. All worries vanish, whisked away by the wind, and I'm immersed in absolute serenity.

For that fleeting moment in time, I unquestionably accept what I know in my heart to be true: *I am not alone.* I'm an indispensable piece of a mysterious multidimensional puzzle. The piece has only been misplaced, but it can be found.

I try to hold tight to that confidence, but when I open my eyes again, it is gone.

* * *

I'm covering my bike for the night when I hear a man approach from behind me.

"How do you like your bike?" I turn and am startled by the way he looks, but then I quickly regain my composure and smile.

"This bike is new to me, but I'm very happy with the way it handles. How about you, do you ride?" I watch him look reflectively at my motorcycle.

"I used to love to ride, but I was riding my BMW motorcycle when I was hit from the rear. There was a defect in the motorcycle's gas tank, it exploded, and I was severely burned and almost died. I can't ride anymore, because my fingers are too stiff to control the gears."

"Yes, I can see you were burned. How are you now? Are you okay?"

"I'm trying to adjust, but it's difficult. I'm Johnny, by the way." I look at him and see that his ears are gone and most of his face is distorted, scarred, and twisted. He has on shorts and a short-sleeved shirt. His arms, hands, and legs are as badly scarred as his face. I figure he is in his twenties or thirties, but it is hard to tell.

"I'm Carolyn. I have a couple of Cokes in my saddlebags. They're warm, but come and sit with me. Tell me where you've been and where you're headed." I walk over, partially undo the cover from the saddlebag, take the Cokes out, and we walk over to a picnic table and sit across from each other.

He tells me he received a large settlement from his accident and is traveling across the country with a new RV. I glance at the RV and notice he is pulling it with an expensive-looking red pickup. Johnny says most people do not talk to him because he is so disfigured, or they simply do not know what to say, and that makes him feel bad. He says he is the same person on the inside; only the outside has changed. We spend several hours talking about his ability to cope with the changes in his life.

For the first time, I causally mention my concern about spending the rest of my life alone, but it seems so inconsequential compared to the magnitude of his problem.

He sits up and looks at me. "I think you're right to worry about loneliness." There is exasperation in his tone, and the scars between his eyes deepen.

"People really don't understand how devastating it can be, or, if they do, they don't talk about it. I never felt lonely before my accident; I was friendly and outgoing and I think most people liked me." He slumps forward a little and looks down at the table.

"Now I feel isolated, like I'm not a part of anything anymore. It's terrible. Getting burned and recovering was horrible, but honest to God, sometimes I think the loneliness is just as bad." His breathing is heavier and I'm shocked to hear him say that.

"Do you really feel that way? That the loneliness is almost as bad as being burned? That's hard to imagine." He raises his head and I see tears glisten in his eyes.

"Yes, it's different of course, but really I do. I think we belong with other people, and we shouldn't have to feel like we're outcasts, just because we're different. It's wrong. It's really hard for me to relate to people now." He twists his Coke can between his stiff fingers. "I know it's uncomfortable for people to look at me, but I wish they would just *say* something to me." He is quiet for a few minutes and changes the subject.

"Why are you traveling by yourself, if you don't like to be alone?"

"Yeah, I know it seems strange, but I read this interesting quote many years ago by Ralph Waldo Emerson. He said, *Do the thing you fear and the death of fear is certain.* What he meant was, if we confront our fears, we'll overpower them and they won't scare us anymore."

"I like that, but tell me that quote again."

I repeat the quote and continue. "And that's why I decided to travel and camp alone. My idea was, if I spent a lot of time by myself, the nagging fear of living alone would vanish. I'll probably be on the road about three months."

"Is it working?"

"I don't know yet. I've only been on the road for a couple of weeks and I haven't given it a lot of thought. I'm not used to riding so many miles every day, so I'm exhausted most of the time and at night I just fall asleep. You know, you're the first person I've told this to."

He smiles at me. Before he gets up to leave he says, "I can't begin to tell you how much it means to me that you talked to me. I felt like a normal person for a while. I know this may sound forward, but I was wondering if I could follow along behind you with my RV?"

I sigh. "You know, Johnny, what I'm doing is nothing compared to what you've been through, but I think we have a similar goal.

We're both searching for peace of mind. I do get lonely traveling alone, and it would be nice to have a companion, but for me to get over this feeling, I've committed to traveling by myself." I take a deep breath, "I'm so sorry, but you can't come with me."

He hangs his head and looks sad. "That's probably for the best. I need to force myself to interact with more people. It's hard, but I have to stop being afraid of the way I look."

I reach across the table and take his hand in both of mine. "You're going to be all right. I want you to know that I think you have great courage. You're an inspiration to me, and you'll be an inspiration to other people, too. You can do this, so don't give up."

As he leaves, I call out to him, "Hey, Johnny, do what you did with me. Be the *first* to say hello. You're a great guy, and when people get to know you, they won't even see the scars." He waves at me and walks back toward his RV.

When I wake up the next morning, Johnny is gone.

He does not know it, but when I ride away—I take the burned man with me after all.

Chapter 11

REALITY CHECK

Good Lord! There is a tarantula sitting on the floor near my boot in the Oklahoma KOA bathroom.

It is early in the morning; I'm the only one in here, and I missed seeing him when I came in to brush my teeth. But I can sure see him now. I zip out to my tent that is pitched behind the restroom, get my camera, approach him slowly, thrust one foot forward, and carefully lean over to take his picture as he sits near my boot. I want my friends to see how big he is. I'm nervous about taking his picture, though, because if the flash startles him and he jumps, he may land in my hair. I tuck my hair inside the back of my shirt.

In general, tarantulas do not scare me. Brian had one for several years and Travis had a large iguana that hissed or bit if you tried to touch him. How come my kids did not want goldfish?

Brian's tarantula's name was Cleopatra, CP for short, and she was a fascinating pet. Tarantulas by nature are timid creatures, but if the kids were careful, they could pick her up and carry her around. While it did not bother them to pick her up with their bare hands, that was not my thing, so if I had to handle her,

I wore gloves. I did the same thing if I had to handle Travis's iguana.

All of us had to be careful not to let CP jump from high distances, because tarantulas' legs are fragile and can easily break. I'm not sure why, but tarantulas seem to have a fear of dogs. Since we had a dog, Kelly, we made sure to put Kelly in the garage if CP was out of her cage.

One day Brian charged into the kitchen all excited and said, "Mom, I'm so lucky. I was holding CP in my hand when Kelly ran into my room. I quickly put my hand behind my back, and CP jumped out of my hand, but she didn't fall on the floor. Instead, she landed and clung to my rear end. That was so lucky."

"Brian, if CP jumps out of your hand and lands on your mother's rear end, that tarantula is going to get a ride she can't believe."

Fortunately for me, the tarantula in the KOA stays put, but the photo will probably be blurry because my hand is shaking. I talk to the manager about the spider, and he says he will take care of it. I go with him to make sure he does not hurt it, but he assures me that this is a common occurrence in Oklahoma.

He picks up a broom and dustpan, and we walk back to the restroom. He sweeps the spider into the dustpan, walks behind the restroom, and calmly deposits it right next to my tent.

I considered staying another night at this KOA but decide to move on.

* * *

I'm riding along a river on a winding road, trying to locate a large white two-story house shaded by enormous, sprawling oak trees.

I crossed through Texas and then Arkansas, and now I plan to spend the night in Louisiana to get a sense of the Old South: the plantations, the fields of tobacco, cotton, and mint, and the slave quarters. I want to try and imagine how people lived during that era.

The house by the river is a magnificent structure reminiscent of another time; it is quiet and serene. I walk toward the house and then climb the stairs to a wide porch with white wood railing. A number of rockers are interspersed along the porch and I can visualize people sitting on the veranda, fanning themselves, and sipping mint juleps. The house and surrounding grounds are restored, immaculately maintained, and open to the public. I decide to skip the guided house tour and instead walk around to the back of the house.

Away from the house, and certainly not within sight of those fanning themselves on the veranda, are rows and rows of small wooden shacks where the black slaves once lived; these are drafty weather-beaten hovels, most with dirt floors. I suspect large groups of people were crammed together into these tiny spaces. There is no room for any beds, so people must have slept on the grimy floors. The plantation house is impressive; the living accommodations for the black slaves are appalling.

I leave and ride for miles and miles. On both sides of the road and as far as I can see are flat open fields. For the people who once worked these fields, there would be no escape from the glaring sun or the oppressive, burning heat and humidity. It is beyond imagination that many had to work their entire lives as captive slaves in fields like these. I imagine young and old people, pregnant women, those with babies and small children, the sick and weak.

Then, after hours in the blazing sun, they had to come home to shacks with no water or electricity, and someone had to cook and care for hungry children and adults. If it had been my children or me out there, I would have been constantly enraged at the inequality of life and man's inhumanity to man. No wonder, generations later, many are still furious at the way their ancestors were treated, and the way many black people are treated today.

As I ride past the vast open fields, I continue to see images of the hopelessness of the slaves working endlessly in the scalding, oppressive sun.

These images remain imprisoned in my mind.

* * *

Manhandling the bike in this heat is physically wearing, and my riding is getting dangerous and sloppy.

I constantly need to be aware of my surroundings, which means I need to get off the bike to look at maps, figure out where I am, and decide where to spend the night. Even on the back roads, the ride itself is fatiguing in this sweltering heat. It is hot, and wearing my leathers and heavy helmet does not help. I could change into my jeans and a light shirt, but wearing my leathers is safer, and the risk of injury is less if I were to have an accident.

One of the attorneys in my law office gave me a great piece of advice before I left Portland. He said if I got tired to stop and rest for a few days. Nevertheless, I feel an underlying pressure to continue riding. I must be on the west side of the Rockies by the middle of September, before the snow starts to fall. If the pass is covered with snow, I will risk being trapped on the eastern side of the mountain range and unable to cross back into the West.

Right now, though, my schedule does not matter. I need to get off the bike, reorganize my stuff, and relax for a day or two. The heat is wearing me down, I'm exhausted, and my riding is becoming compromised.

The humidity in the South is unreal.

Last night I woke up several times to find my sleeping bag soaked with sweat. At first I thought I was getting sick, but it was the persistent heat that is continually trapped inside my enclosed tent, even if the flaps and windows are tied open. You cannot escape it day or night, so I have to find another way to cool down. Pulling into camp, I notice a couple of huge rocking chairs on the KOA porch. I unpack, set up the tent, change out of my heavy leathers, put on a lightweight sleeveless dress, and head over to sit and rock.

The chairs are massive and made of heavy, sturdy pieces of wood. There is a small table between the rocking chairs, with a couple of folded fans lying on it. This is perfect. I can sit, rock, and fan myself.

I join a heavy-set woman sitting in the other rocker with her eyes closed. I do not want to disturb her, so I sit down and say nothing, my toes barely touching the wooden floor. She sits and is slowly rocking in her chair, loosely holding a fan in one hand. She takes up most of the chair and sits with her legs spread far apart, each arm draped casually over an arm of the rocker as she moves the chair in slow, slow, rhythmic rocks.

The rocker creaks. The sound is low and aching, like the hinge of an old door that was never oiled. She gently pushes with her feet, and the rocker tilts backward with a long, drawn out *creeeeaaak*. There is a lingering pause at the end of the tilt, a holding pattern with no sound, and then with a slight shift of her body, the rocker moves forward with another prolonged *creeeeaaak.*

An almost undetectable movement with her foot pushes, and the rocker tilts backward again. *Creeeeaaak,* hold, hold, hold; small shift forward, *creeeeaaak;* hold, hold, hold; gentle push back *creeeeaaak.* The sound is mesmerizing.

I give my chair a hardy shove and start to rock, *creak, creak, creak, creak, creak.* Back and forth I go, moving with the speed of sound. *Creak, creak, creak, creak, creak.* Honest to God, my movements look like a jackrabbit in heat.

My rocking partner stops, gradually turns her head in my direction, slowly opens her eyes and stares at the absurd creature sitting beside her, the one who is whipping back and forth like a maniac. I stop rocking, and she smiles at me. It is obvious that I'm a hyped-up westerner, not a relaxed, refined, southern lady.

She continues to rock, and I try to match her speed. I lean back, spread my legs, and hang my hands over the rocker's arms. It is hard, but eventually the methodical rhythm gets the best of me and I manage to slightly slow down. She tells me she lives in the South and is here visiting her sister.

Her speech is as slow as her rocking, each word considered so as not to expend unnecessary energy in this heat. I ask a question, and it appears to be socially acceptable to rock and think before eventually answering with one drawn out word after another. I try to relax and slow down even more, but it is not as easy as it looks.

On the second day, I'm sitting in the KOA rocker alone, thinking about all the small towns I have passed through. I have come to the conclusion that if everything is about the same wherever I go, then it is impossible to run away from my problems. I can only take them with me, lugging them along like a gigantic bag of misery. What good would it do for me to move to New Mexico with Robert? If we do not make it as a couple, my issue of loneliness would be the same there as it would be in Oregon.

It is not like I can somehow escape from myself. I can choose to be happy; allow myself to be sad, angry, and annoyed; or find peace and serenity within myself. It is up to me. I must find a way to leave my worthless bag of woes behind and instead pursue peace of mind.

Rocking clears the mind. As I sit here, I come to another shocking realization, and I do not like this one.

I thought I was handling my loneliness issue remarkably well. What is really happening is that I'm so busy, tired, or surrounded by people, that I have not had time to think seriously about being alone. It has been fun and enjoyable meeting and visiting with all sorts of personalities, blabbing away during my KOA interviews.

Now I'm sitting by myself, not chatting with anyone, with time to kill while regaining my strength. Loneliness takes on a different perspective when it is just me and I'm not on the run. Suddenly, this is not fun.

I think about Johnny, the burned man, and the idea of living alone looks bleak. What I need to do is spend more time away from others, but that is a depressing thought. Now I want to be back on the road and wish I had not taken the day off.

Maybe if I just keep riding, loneliness cannot catch me.

* * *

As I'm leaving Louisiana, a large pack of Harley riders almost all dressed in black leather passes me. They hoot and holler, honk their horns, give me the thumbs-up, and yell encouragements.

The women sitting behind the men wave and smile, and I smile and wave back at them. I do not see any women riding by themselves. They are traveling fast and the group of about forty passes effortlessly, moving out of sight within a few minutes.

I have ridden in packs like that, at times with several hundred motorcycles or more. It seems strange to think that it was less than four years ago, after my return to Portland with Steve, that I placed an ad in the local *AutoTrader* with the catchy phrase: "Lady Lawyer will exchange legal services for Harley."

The ad certainly raised some eyebrows in the legal community, but the phone began to ring. Male voices usually opened with a cautious, "Are you the lady lawyer who helps the bikers?" Soon they arrived, a parade of men dressed in black. I did not know what the other tenants on the eleventh floor of our downtown Portland, Oregon, office building thought of this group as a whole, but they seemed to agree on one thing: no one wanted to be trapped in the elevator with one of these guys.

The standard biker attire included worn leather pants, chaps or jeans, a leather coat, a T-shirt, sunglasses, a bandana, a hat, gloves, and formidable boots. I eventually learned this look was more than just a menacing fashion statement. Leathers crafted out of sheepskin—or cowhide—had a fourfold purpose: to protect the rider against the elements, to protect the body in case of an accident, to make upkeep easy, and, of course, to look tough.

One might imagine these men to have continual run-ins with the law. However, their legal problems covered a range as broad and diverse as anybody dressed in a business suit. That is not to say criminal issues never arose. But their issues typically revolved around custody or visitation rights with children, or a will, trust, or contract matter.

Obviously, these bikers had a passion for motorcycles. This zeal dictated a way of life they prized, revered, and protected. These men displayed a fierce independence; they struck me as a proud, loyal group with a strong sense of who they were and what they wanted. When they spoke, their conversation was candid, straightforward, patriotic, respectful, and fascinating.

I liked them immediately.

What intrigued me most about the bikers tramping into my office was that they loved to ride alone. They would take to the open road and be gone for hours, days, even weeks at a time. Not only did these bikers not fear riding by themselves—they actively sought out and became protective of their time alone. They talked about being "one with the bike," the wind, earth, and sky their only companions. Riding alone fulfilled and revitalized them.

These men claimed they were not lonely and, as strange as this seemed to me, I believed them. As I talked with the bikers sitting across from me in my law offices, an excitement rose up within me. If motorcycles made these men feel this way, then perhaps a motorcycle could bring me freedom from insecurities and force me to become even more independent. If I could master a large piece of machinery, there was no telling what else I might be able to do. I longed to feel the passion and independence these bikers felt, before it was too late. I wanted to ride, wild and free, without personal limitations or fears.

I had ridden behind Steve on a few trips, but my confusion and ignorance about motorcycles was soon clear. The bikers offered support and advice. They patiently explained about motorcycles, told me what to look for and what not to buy, and said to call them if I had questions or concerns. New riding friends offered to accompany me when I went to purchase a motorcycle, their mere presence defying anyone to take advantage of me. I wanted a Harley and, by God, they would shepherd me through the maze.

Through the conversations with my biker clientele, a pattern of advice began to emerge. At first I had no idea what they were talking about. When the bikers described their used motorcycles or motorcycle parts, terms like *basket case, modified* or *raked frames, Knucklehead, Panhead,* and *Shovelhead* made no sense to me. Often they talked in letters. "It's an FXDL," or an "FLSTS," they might say. A Harley might be called a Low Rider, a Wide Glide, a Fat Boy, or a Softtail. Wasn't a Harley a Harley? Why did the same motorcycle have so many names? The language they spoke sounded bizarre and foreign.

Eventually, it became apparent that a smaller Harley, a Sportster 883, would work best for me. Physically lighter, and with less horsepower, it would be a manageable bike when taking into account my height, weight, and inexperience.

I was wholly unaware of how much this world would impact my life, but my interest grew, as did my desire to do something dramatic with my life. The year I turned fifty was the year this came to a head.

I watched the ads in the newspaper and came across a 1988 Sportster 883 with low miles. The owner took me for a spin around the block, and I plunked down my $3,600. He brought the bike to our condo and parked it in the carport. I had become the proud owner of a Harley-Davidson motorcycle!

A shiny black beauty that I could not ride.

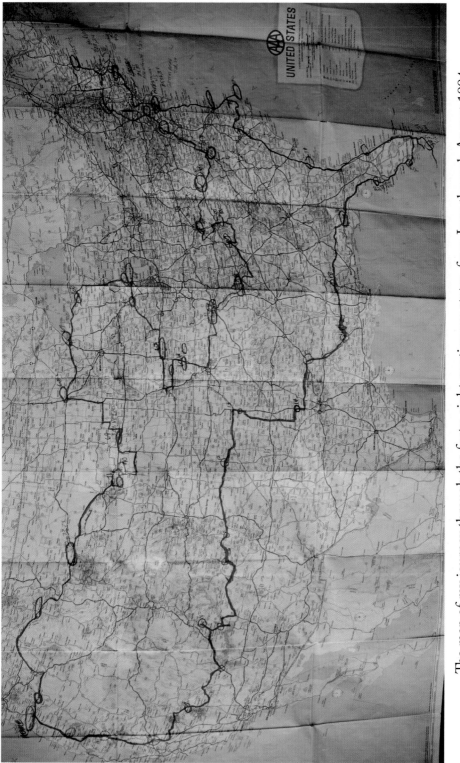

The map of my journey through the forty-eight contiguous states, from June through August 1994. (Later that year, I completed my trek in Alaska and Hawaii.)

A photo from the marketing packet I sent to Kampgrounds of America (KOA). KOA sponsored me and provided free camping when I stayed at their campgrounds. They also arranged for numerous interviews, as I shared my experiences as a single woman traveling across America on a motorcycle, alone.

Packed and ready to roll on my newly purchased 1989 Harley-Davidson Springer. I carried a tent, sleeping bag, warm/cold weather clothes and gear, shoes, maps, tools—entirely too much stuff!

Death Valley. The air was so hot, each breath burned my throat and lungs, thus the bandanna. It was less than a week into the trip, and I was convinced I had lost my mind for making this trip alone.

Utah: I had never seen rocks like these before, turning an intense red when the sun hit them. Being in this area gave me some hope that this trip might be fun after all. Time, a lack of stamina, injuries, and stupidity would dampen my enthusiasm.

I stayed in this KOA "Kamping Kabin" in Colorado for three days while recovering from the flu. No water, toilets, or bedding inside. However, there was a table, chairs, and two twin beds with mattresses. Much more comfortable than sleeping on the hard, cold ground.

The inside of my Kamping Kabin where I dried my soaked clothes and recovered from illness.

Louisiana: The heat in the south is unbearably hot and humid in the summer. After several weeks on the road, I spent two days here trying to regain my strength and reflect on things. Maybe if I just kept riding, loneliness couldn't catch me.

I spent five days with people I had never met who lived on the Weeki Wachee River. It was like spending time with family. "Gus," a great egret, lands on the deck every morning, then marches into the house and pecks on the refrigerator door until someone gives him a treat.

My biggest thrill was this rare opportunity to swim with the manatees in Florida. I didn't want to disturb these endangered creatures, so I bobbed around in the water until they cruised past like silent submarines.

Riding along the Atlantic Ocean, I took my boots off and cooled my feet in the sea.

These are the steps that drew me to the Old Narragansett Church in Rhode Island, built in 1707, and seen in the distance. It was here that I confronted the guilt and fears of my past.

Pennsylvania: One of many Harley-Davidson factories and dealerships that I visited on my journey.

My only mechanical breakdown on the trip (in West Virginia) was caused by a defective voltage regulator. Luckily, I had purchased an extended warranty before I left. While the lost time was a concern, I stayed in a motel for three days and slept in a real bed. The reprieve ended when I encountered a dangerous male predator.

One of the numerous TV interviews arranged by KOA; sometimes there were several in a day. This one was in Kentucky. The interviews were always exciting and enjoyable. Getting there on time was an undertaking.

The Badlands of South Dakota: This area is surreal. On one side of the highway are endless grasslands as far as the eye can see. On the other side of the road, about twenty-five feet away, is this wasteland.

It was here at Mt. Rushmore that I met a man who had recently had his heart replaced. He was traveling alone on his Harley.

The appearance of this cloud in Montana warned me of a dangerous storm system approaching, but I chose to ignore it. I was convinced I could outrun it, but I was wrong. I was almost killed.

The Dalles, Oregon: I liked the dichotomy of an old shaker village contrasted against a modern dam. It reminded me that in time, all things change. Seventy-seven days on the road in the contiguous United States, and 14,200 miles.

I flew to Alaska and borrowed a friend's Sportster and her hat. Thick, large, odd-shaped pieces of jagged rock covered most of the roads in this area. It was unnerving to ride on the gravel.

Hawaii was my fiftieth state. I flew to Hawaii and rented this 1994 H-D Lowrider. I spent the day listening to the cadence of the ocean, as I have always found it peaceful and healing. This was a bittersweet time for me. There was the joy of completing my personal journey and finding forgiveness, mixed with the tragedy of losing a family member in September.

A recent shot of me. Over the years I have personally owned six Harley-Davidson motorcycles; my latest is a 2005 Harley-Davidson Fatboy. All told, I've ridden over 100,000 miles. Not bad for a seventy-one-year-old woman.

Chapter 12

TAMING THE HEINOUS BEAST

The good thing about aging is that with it comes sense. Good sense.

Right?

My *AutoTrader* ad was a success, and I was now the owner of a beautiful Harley. After my earlier disaster with the Honda, I decided I needed motorcycle lessons. No more invincibility for me. With lessons, learning to ride a motorcycle would be a piece of cake. How hard could this be?

It was hard. Really hard.

Travis and I signed up for a motorcycle skills course. We successfully passed the required basic skills portion and I prepared to complete my final test: I was to ride to the instructor and then come to a controlled stop in the shortest distance possible. To this day, I cannot explain what occurred next. Blame it on the rain, the cold, perhaps on my fatigue, or that I longed for a Snickers bar. I do not know. Honest to God, I can only say I had my first out-of-body experience.

All I remember is when the instructor yelled "Go!" the transformation took place. Carolyn Fox stepped out and Evel Knievel stepped in.

The engine revved and the tires squealed as Evel and the bike exploded forward and rocketed down the course. First. Second. Third gear. Faster and faster he went. No one could stop him now! All eyes beheld his splendor as the divine moment of glory drew closer. He would show that Travis kid what a real biker could do.

Evel observed the instructor's chin and clipboard drop simultaneously as the instructor watched the bike streak out of the controlled riding area and straight toward a six-foot drop-off. Perhaps the horrified look on the instructor's face caught Evel's attention, or maybe memories of the Snake River Canyon mishap came to mind. Who knows? But at that precise moment, Evel decided to skip the glory. He exited stage left, and I returned to the bike.

I panicked and grabbed the front brake lever *hard and tight*. Motorcyclists consider this the big "Oops" or the "Oh shit!" or the "I wish I hadn't done that" moment.

We learned in class that the brake on the right handlebar controls the front wheel and the right foot brake controls the rear wheel. We are taught to *squeeze* the front brake *gently* while we simultaneously apply the right foot brake. This makes for a smooth, controlled stop. If you grab the front brake lever hard and tight like I did, it locks the front wheel.

Simply put, the back wheel continues to turn and the front wheel does not. The resulting momentum hurls the weight of the motorcycle, rider included, toward the front of the bike. When I locked the front brake, the front wheel, being mechanically sound, stopped. I did not.

I sailed through the air like a gazelle.

Out of the corner of my eye, I watched the bike topple over and crash to the ground. Sparks shot everywhere as it slid on its side and continued to follow my pattern of flight.

Midair, I curled up into a ball like a sow bug.

I reached maximum velocity and then slammed onto the pavement with a thud that resonated throughout my body and reverberated across the parking lot. I bounced several times, rolled, slid, and then skidded some thirty feet before I came to a stop.

When Travis determined I would live (and when he could stop laughing), he described the spectacle in true teenage skateboarder language: "Wow! Mom! You really *caught air!* I think you had about a three-point-five second *hang time!*" Then he collapsed in hysterical laughter again.

I will admit—it was the soar of a lifetime. I obtained undreamed-of height and distance, the envy of all who ever rode a skateboard. The Russian judge would have given me a 9.8.

Needless to say, I flunked the class. Travis passed.

Except for aches and pains, I thought I had survived the crash in remarkably good form. However, within a week I sat in the doctor's office as he probed for internal injuries and discovered badly bruised body parts, though nothing had been broken. As his professional duty demanded, he lectured me to stop riding, saying I was too old. Too old? I was only forty-six.

The accident had taken the snap out of my enthusiasm for riding, though, and my bike sat in the driveway, untouched, for over a month. That shiny beauty appeared as a hideous, leering beast that defied conquest. I tentatively paced around it, and then finally I decided to buck up and ride the damn thing. I was back on the bike, determined but wary. I took a few short nerve-racking rides on back streets, but for the most part it was not fun.

However, on quiet morning rides, I occasionally spotted a glimmer of fresh dew reflected on tall shimmering cattails, or a cloud formation configured in fanciful shapes. A farmer's newly plowed field carried the sweet, damp smell of freshly turned earth; a pig farm bore a strong, pungent odor. I would have missed these sights and smells if confined to a car. This sprinkle of unusual experiences began to make the rides bearable, even pleasurable.

Slowly, with each mile, I began to develop a cushion of comfort for riding alone. That is not to say I liked riding alone, because I did not. But I realized my focus had to be on improving my poor riding skills for the time being. First things first: I would learn to ride and then look internally at my fears.

I decided to commit to riding the bike one thousand miles. I felt this task would be a fair test. Other people learned to ride. Who knows, maybe some riders even lived in my area. After the one thousand miles, if riding continued to be a wretched experience, at least I had done my best. If I had to sell the bike, so be it. I would search for another medium to confront my fear of living alone.

Steve came to Oregon as often as possible, but his work as a construction foreman in Seattle limited his flexibility. When he was in town, though, we rode together and he offered instruction, suggesting he lead and I follow. My goal would be to try and duplicate his riding style, which ultimately increased my confidence and skill. Steve handled his bike smoothly and proficiently and, through observation and practice, I became more comfortable in corners and on the open road.

Riding with Steve was far more fun than riding alone, and I felt safe when we rode together. If there was a problem, Steve could handle it. We liked each other and soon became an item. Although I felt more relaxed when I was riding with Steve, my feelings of frustration and tension returned whenever he left town. I needed to be able to handle my motorcycle alone and become more independent, more self-reliant.

One weekend, Steve and I drove down to Roseburg, Oregon, so he could meet my parents and brothers. That was a big mistake. Both dad and my sweet mother, Daisy, who graciously invited everyone into their home, had an absolute fit. My dad cornered me in the bathroom when I was putting on my makeup. He shut the door and was livid.

"Carolyn, what are you thinking? This is a very dangerous man. I've been around his type all my life and I know what I'm talking about. Your mother and I can't believe you would bring this man to the house. My God, you're a professional woman, have you lost your mind?" I tried to defend Steve, but my dad was not having any part of it.

"Dad, he's really a nice guy, and he's not dangerous to me." Without another word my dad shook his head and stormed out of the bathroom.

I had already sworn my sons and brothers to secrecy; they were not to mention that I had bought a Harley. That was lucky, because it was undeniably clear this was not the best time to tell my parents.

We spent one night at the house but decided to leave early the next morning. I loved my parents and had no idea they would be so upset. My father had been a logger and owned a heavy-equipment construction company, and he was a force to be reckoned with in the community. Rough assortments of men were often at our house. I never thought anything of it, because these men were always exceptionally polite to me. I guess my father made it clear to them that they were not to mess with his daughter, and no one dared cross him.

Dad was right, though; when I was with Steve there was an element of danger. But the truth was, I found the experience stimulating and exciting.

* * *

Steve moved comfortably among the hard-core bikers, and I had an opportunity to glimpse the darker side of the mystical biker lore. One night we ended up at the clubhouse of one of Portland's biker gangs.

As we approached the weathered, dark building, I saw dirty, unkempt motorcycles parked inside an enclosed, fenced area. We rode into the enclosure, but no one was outside so Steve opened the clubhouse door and marched in. Low, subdued lights reflected off the dark walls and ceiling. Painted entirely black and covered with dark banners and motorcycle paraphernalia, the room had an eerie, almost surreal quality. There was a bar tucked against one wall. Above the bar, someone had attached ten to fifteen black balloons filled with water. Some person who ordered a drink might be surprised with an unwanted bath.

A pool table sat in the middle of the room; booths, tables, and chairs lined the walls. In one booth, two women helped several young children with their homework. The few men who stood in the room stopped talking when we walked in.

The grizzly bear of a man behind the bar immediately approached us and, in a loud voice, demanded to know why we were there. Clubhouse etiquette required an invitation. You do not walk into a biker's clubhouse unless you are prepared to fight. The men standing nearby tensed. Steve quietly guided me behind him. Since Steve knew one of the club members and asked for him by name, the bartender warily accepted our intrusion. We stayed put while someone located the man.

I did not like this. The confrontation had explosive potential, and I felt the hairs on the back of my neck tingle. I definitely felt out of my element. Steve's friend joined us, nodded at the men in the room, and everyone relaxed.

We walked over to a booth and sat down. The friend wanted to know why a *woman* had accompanied Steve to their clubhouse. I wanted to hear the answer to that one myself. Women in biker gangs do not hold a high status. Most take a backseat to the men and tend to act reserved or intimidated, especially when the men are around. Steve mentioned I practiced law, and the implied clout set me apart from the rest of the women.

My social and professional status promptly elevated me in their eyes. I think these men saw me as a potential resource, an ace in the hole held for some unknown game. I had the distinct impression they believed that the key to the jailhouse door lay securely tucked in my bosom. Whatever it took to gain their esteem suited me fine. Thank God for *stereotypes*! At least no one gave me any trouble.

As much as I enjoyed Steve's company, it became obvious that while I might move in his world, he was limited in mine. As passionate as I might become about my motorcycle, it would always remain a hobby with me and never rise to the level of a lifestyle. Steve and I were not a long-term romantic match, a fact we both understood and accepted. We spent an exhilarating year together and parted friends.

I will always be grateful to him for introducing me to the sport of motorcycling.

* * *

It was an offer I could not refuse—an invitation to the local Harley Owners Group (HOG) in Beaverton, Oregon.

I was trying to locate other riders in the area and the local Harley dealer mentioned the Sunset HOG chapter and suggested I attend one of their meetings.

Harley-Davidson (H-D) Motor Company was the only major American-based motorcycle manufacturer and a leading global supplier of premium quality heavyweight (651cc+) motorcycles. H-D sponsored the HOG chapters. With five hundred thousand worldwide members and over a thousand local chapters, HOG held the record for being the world's largest company-sponsored motorcycle enthusiast group.

In 1992, women who bought Harleys comprised five percent of the market. In the Sunset chapter, a group with approximately 120 members, less than half a dozen women owned their own motorcycles. These women belonged to the Sunset Ladies of Harley, a subset of the Beaverton chapter.

The practice of law can have its tense moments, but nothing prepared me for my first encounter with the Beaverton Sunset HOG Chapter. Eighty men and women filled this room, a sea of black leathers, boots, chains, pins, long hair, beards, and commotion. Add one intimidated attorney.

The hearty, joyful laugh of a woman who enjoyed life, liked people, and was liked in return, soon caught my attention. And I do not mean a chuckle or giggle. Her laugh was hardy and instantly became infectious. As she laughed, I smiled and started to relax.

As the meeting progressed, she stepped forward and began to speak; she was the safety officer. A tall woman, blonde, confident, and well respected, she spoke with the air of a seasoned rider. They introduced her as Joy, which was the perfect name for the woman with the joyful laugh.

After the meeting, Joy came over and introduced herself. I have to admit to being in awe. After all, before me stood the first female biker I had ever met. This virtual stranger seemed to recognize my tension and warmly welcomed me to the group. But the biggest shock came when she *offered to ride with me*.

I explained my inexperience and poor skills, my difficulty negotiating a corner, and my inability to turn the bike around in a small area. I also made clear my drive to learn to ride and my determination to give this a fair try. Joy looked at me and said, "You can do it! If you want to ride, you'll ride. Don't let anyone tell you otherwise." She spoke with firmness and conviction. If she rode, I could too. I had found a riding group, a teacher, and a friend. Thus it began; the mentor had committed to teach the apprentice.

Joy, who was also an excellent mechanic, insisted I buy a service manual. She believed women have the capacity to be self-sufficient. She taught me how to change the oil, filter, and spark plugs; how to install a new battery, tighten bolts, and identify problems; and how to speak intelligently with various Harley mechanics. Through Joy's guidance, I learned to ride and take responsibility for my motorcycle. But most importantly, I found Joy to be an ideal riding partner, and we became fast friends.

Joy and I had numerous things in common. Both single mothers of teenage boys, we often commiserated over the difficulty of raising children by ourselves. We both believed in true love, and the hunt for the perfect love match entertained us on a regular basis. Our outings were fun, adventurous, and always good for a laugh, and hers was as hearty as ever. Surrounded by my new friends and accompanied by my riding buddy, any concerns I had about riding alone or being alone felt far away.

Through Joy, I learned to distinguish the various types of riders in the motorcycle community. Unfortunately, when many people see a motorcycle rider, they think of motorcycle gangs, biker clubs, or the Hells Angels. However, these kinds of groups are the smallest segment of the motorcycle community.

These riders are often referred to as *One Percenters*, since their numbers only include 1 percent of all motorcycle riders. Motorcyclists and the clubs they belong to are a way of life with these men and they value and protect this lifestyle. Thanks to Hollywood and the media's push for sensationalism, any activity by this group usually receives front-page coverage. Thus, the average person may well believe all motorcycle riders are included in this tiny subset of the motorcycle community.

Another small group of riders are called *Independents*. These men do not belong to clubs or gangs, although motorcycling is also a lifestyle with them and not a hobby. Their life revolves around motorcycles. It is what they do and who they are. Steve fell into this group; he was a biker through and through, although not a member of a gang or club.

The rest of the motorcyclists, the ninety-eight percent or so, are called motorcycle *Enthusiasts*. They do not belong to gangs or biker clubs. Motorcycles are their hobby. They may well be extremely passionate about their hobby, but it does not consume their day-to-day living. Joy, myself, the HOG members, and, with rare exception, the motorcycle riders I knew personally, fell into this latter group.

With Joy's encouragement, and often with her company or the HOG members, I rode my Sportster twelve hundred miles. My enthusiasm and passion for the sport increased, and I wanted a bigger bike. I sold the Sportster and purchased a 1977 Shovelhead FXE in immaculate condition. The word *Shovelhead* describes the distinctive shape of the Harley's engine (as do *Panhead* and *Knucklehead* for those bikes). The letters identify the style of motorcycle.

This new motorcycle was *hot.*

It screamed "sex appeal." Painted a bright red, it had the words *Harley-Davidson* emblazoned in a bold blue across the gas tank. The man who previously owned it polished and chromed this baby until the fire-engine-red paint radiated like a firestorm in the sun. Although it was an older bike, it had been reconditioned to showroom quality. And it had stuff on it. Guy stuff. Like two-inch straight drag pipes, an eighty-three-cubic-inch 1984 E motor, wheels and rods, a Sifton Python camshaft 485 lift with solid lifter and Sifton pushrods, and an H-D 40 mm carburetor. It even had Manley value seats, Rowe cast iron guides with thin stem valves, and cut-and-balanced rocker arms.

What did this all mean? At the time, I did not have a clue. What was important was that this motorcycle had mysterious powers, its pull stronger than a cosmic magnet. It accomplished the impossible like nothing I had seen since my divorce. This racy beauty attracted *men!* "Does it have this, or does it have that?" they would ask. I whipped out my handy sheet of typed specs (prepared by the previous owner) and, with a shrewd grin, passed the cheat notes to them. They gushed over this mechanical wonder and the astonishing woman who could ride it. I felt like a black widow and prepared myself for the kill. Which tasty morsel to choose? Natural selection—step aside. Bring on the Harley.

Now, ladies, you have to trust me on this. Forget the Wonderbras! Skip the facelifts! Forego the butt tucks! Bolt to your nearest Harley-Davidson dealership and buy yourself a killer Harley. It was the best eight thousand dollars I ever spent.

With a renewed hue and cry, I charged forth. With all of these men to pick from, surely true love lingered just around the corner, and I would not have to suffer the golden years alone.

When Robert cruised into town astride his Harley two years later, it was one lucky day.

Chapter 13

DEATH'S PREMONITION

Dark, ominous storm clouds loom on the horizon, and even though it is early afternoon, the light in the sky is disappearing.

A television interview is scheduled at the KOA in Laurel, Mississippi, later today. My agreement with the KOA is that they will reimburse me for camping space and arrange for the television, newspaper, or radio interviews, and I will show up on time. So far this has worked fine. As I ride toward the menacing thunderstorm, however, the wind's force increases with a vengeance. Riding in a downpour is one thing, but manhandling the bike in a windstorm is quite another. Still, I feel the pressure to continue on.

The abrupt increase in the wind velocity and the torrential rainfall is fearsome, and I take deep breaths to control myself. The sky turns black, lightning flashes, and thunder explodes overhead. Tall groves of trees line each side of the road; as the trees bend and are forced over, branches break off, fly across the road, and then crash into the bike, and me. Each time a limb hits me, my hands jerk and the front wheel wobbles sporadically and startles me. I catch my breath and strain to focus, to remain calm.

Although I'm watching for them, the branches fly across the road so quickly that they cannot be avoided. The rain increases, heavy and forceful, and it obstructs my visibility. The wind becomes ferocious and shoves the bike into the oncoming lane as I try to maintain control. Fortunately, it is rare to see another car. I search for a safe place to pull over, but there is nowhere to stop or protect myself from the trees.

After an exhausting couple of hours, the wind and rain lessen, and the sky begins to clear. I do not need gas but stop at a service station to get a cup of coffee and rest. The man behind the counter looks up and is shocked to see me.

"Did you just ride through that storm on a motorcycle? That's not a good idea. Ya' know there are storm warnings all over the television and radio? It's a bad storm, and it's knocking trees over. Everyone's supposed to be off the road." I missed that bit of news. After resting for several minutes to settle my nerves, I continue on and arrive for my interview haggard and exhausted, but I am right on time.

The interview is canceled.

Supposedly, the TV folks got a call from a woman who claims to have a talking rooster, and, God knows, they do not want to miss that. I nearly kill myself to get here, and a chicken has upstaged me.

In retrospect, it was dangerous and reckless to continue when I knew the sky had all the signs of a terrible storm. In order to meet the media's deadline, I was rash and deliberately put myself in a situation entirely beyond my control.

The next morning, I'm still enraged with myself for my irre-sponsible decision and want to transfer the blame to someone else. I contact the KOA corporate office and rant that I'm no longer willing to put myself in physical danger in order to meet a media deadline, as if my stupidity was somehow their fault. Then I tell them they either adjust the interview format to accommodate *my* schedule or we are done. They are apologetic and upset that I could have been hurt and agreed to modify the schedule. From now on, I will give them as much notice as possible, and they will give the media a tentative, flexible agenda.

It has finally come to me that when I ask about the weather, the local people often have a completely different assessment of it than from what I experience. I think this is because storms are normal occurrences where I'm traveling. People are used to heavy rains and high winds, and, when warned, they have the good sense to stay off the roads. Nor do most people (other than that gas station attendant) have any concept of a rider's vulnerability, since their usual mode of transportation is in the safety of a car, not out in the open on a motorcycle. Much as I hate to admit it, this is my fault for not understanding weather concerns sooner.

My judgment must be better next time. From now on, I will confirm the weather trends for the area where I expect to travel. This will not always hold true because I'm never sure where I'll end up for the night, but at least I will have a general idea of the weather and can better prepare for it. If I do not stop taking stupid and unreasonable risks, I'm going to be seriously injured or killed. Setting my jaw, I resolve not to deliberately ride into another terrible storm.

I was lucky this time—but fate can only be tempted so many times before luck runs out.

* * *

One minute I'm standing in the shower, enjoying the hot water, and then in an instant, I'm crumpled on the cement floor, stunned, and gasping for breath.

I'm in a Mississippi KOA shower, shaving my legs, with one foot propped up against the opposite wall, when my other foot slips and I fall. It happens so quickly! As a reflex, I raise my arm to protect myself, but my head and body strike the wooden bench in the shower stall, leaving me dazed. I'm on the gritty floor scrunched up in a ball, afraid to move in case something is broken, while the hot water pours in my face and soaks my hair. After a few minutes I'm able to carefully lift my hand and feel a large raised lump on the side of my head. Bruises start to appear on my arms and legs while the rough cement scrapes my skin as I shift positions. Nothing seems to be broken, and I'm finally able to stand up by holding onto the bench and lugging myself up. After dressing, I manage to stagger over to my tent and rest for a couple of hours.

Any injury is serious. This is the one thing that can end my trip permanently. A fall or an accident is more apt to happen if I'm tired, hungry, unfocused, or careless. This time I'm fortunate the injury was not worse, but I have to pay more attention and pace myself. It is important to stop, rest more often, carry healthier food, more water, and eat at regular intervals.

Each morning I must take the tent down, pack everything back on the bike, figure out where to eat, and get on the road. It is time consuming. Often, when riding in remote areas, there is no place to have lunch, so I end up buying junk food when paying for gas.

In the evening, I regularly skip dinner altogether because I'm too tired to find a restaurant; I usually eat a candy bar or chips purchased at the KOA office. But eat or not, there is still the process of unpacking everything, setting up the tent, conducting media interviews, and getting organized for the next day. The ride is grueling and my body aches. Each night, I slather myself with BenGay to ease my aching arm and leg muscles. I reek, but I do not have the energy to care.

About a week ago, I was still sound asleep late in the morning when some guy outside my tent commanded me in an authoritative voice to *please step outside*; he wanted to talk to me. It was a policeman. Turns out one of the RV campers at the KOA caught on fire the night before and there was a lot of noise and confusion: fire trucks, police cars, sirens, people yelling and moving their vehicles. The policeman wanted to know what I saw or heard—which was nothing. I slept through the entire incident.

Many people think sitting on a motorcycle all day is relaxing. It can be, but usually it is a physical workout, and mental concentration is mandatory.

On the handlebar's right side, my right hand controls the speed, and the hand break slows or stops the bike. I must exert constant pressure on the throttle to maintain a steady speed, or I can roll on or off the throttle to change speeds. To brake, my fingers extend to grasp, pull in the lever while I slow the bike, or hold the hand brake tight when stopped. My right foot controls the rear wheel brake.

On the left side, if I need to shift, I hold in the clutch with my left hand and shift the gears with my foot. My body is constantly adjusting to the movement of the bike, and this time of year, many roads are being repaired. When required to stop, I must balance the bike upright with my feet until it is time to move again.

In time, all of this comes naturally, but it is still a lot of physical exertion. After eighteen days on the road, my endurance has improved and I am stronger. However, it is time to rearrange my schedule—I'll leave earlier in the morning when I have the most stamina—then settle into camp around four or five in the afternoon. This should give me adequate time to find a place to eat.

The fall in the shower gives me a headache, and I'm beat up, but this is a good wake-up call.

One more freak accident like this one, though, and the trip could be over.

* * *

I'm enchanted to see fireflies; they remind me of an earlier time when our family lived in New Jersey.

Fireflies are not flies or bugs—they are beetles. Their rears light up now and then, tiny specks of flashing light to brighten the night sky. We do not have them in Oregon, so the first time I saw a firefly was when Joe was promoted. AT&T had transferred him back east to begin an upper-management training program.

The family flew to the East Coast and we arrived several days ahead of our furniture. It was dark when we took the boys to see the new house, and we spotted a lone firefly in the yard. We searched the basement, came up with a fruit jar, and chased the poor thing around the yard until we caught him. All of us were thrilled, as none of us had ever seen a firefly. We looked him over and then turned him loose. Those were happier days for our family; I had hoped the move would rejuvenate our marriage.

Several nights ago, while staying in one of the KOA cabins, I turned off the light and spotted a firefly flashing on the ceiling. Since my tape recorder has a light on it, I grabbed it, flipped the light switch on and off, and waited to see if he would respond. He did, with one quick flash! I flashed the recorder again, and he signaled back. I suspected he wanted to mate with my tape recorder, but he never moved from his spot on the ceiling. As we continued to signal, a pattern to his flashing emerged—it was consistent. Too consistent.

I got up, turned on the cabin light, and discovered I was trying to communicate with the smoke detector.

* * *

This sounds eerie, but as I move closer to the east coast, I'm developing a preoccupation with cemeteries.

In Oregon, when riding on the major highways, it is fairly rare to see a cemetery. Usually they are located away from the main roads, tucked back among the trees, or placed somewhere pleasant. Oregon cemeteries do not have a lot of massive headstones, either; there are some, but many headstones or markers are small or lay flat on the ground. As it is easier to mow over or around them, the grounds upkeep is less onerous, and many cemeteries look like well-groomed parks.

It is also unusual for people to be buried directly on church grounds. You see this sometimes in older, rural areas of the state, but it is not the norm. As I'm riding through other states, though, it is common to see the graveyards placed right next to the highway or beside a church. Their headstones are dreadfully visible: large, numerous, dramatic, and packed tight against one another. Maybe this is because of the larger populations in these states, and grave space is limited.

There are winged angels, arms outstretched toward the heavens, and rectangular concrete boxes that sit above the ground on a slab—perhaps to keep the body from getting wet, although I'm not sure why that would matter when you are dead. Sometimes, the smaller headstones of an entire family surround an enclosed mausoleum in the shape of a church. Crosses are popular, as are American flags. Usually, rusting retainer fences enclose and protect the cemetery.

When seeing grave markers in close proximity to churches, it makes me wonder: did people who wanted to be buried near churches believe they would be closer to God, or that they could get into heaven sooner? Maybe the location is merely a matter of convenience, so the bodies would not have to be moved so far. In freezing weather, this makes sense; the same reasoning would apply to hot, humid weather.

Sometimes when riding, my mind wanders. However, I'm not comfortable with my new fascination with graveyards and hope this curiosity in cemeteries is normal, since these monuments are so unusual looking. I worry, though, that this may be a premonition of a death in the family, or my own death. This fixation bothers me, yet I slow my speed and stare at the headstones as I pass.

An unexpected wave of panic rushes through me; I cannot shake the persistent feeling that something bad is going to happen.

I recall the last time I saw my family as we gathered at Jim's restaurant in rural Winston, Oregon, for a farewell breakfast. My mom, dad, Travis, and my brothers—Gary and Jim—were there.

Jim, forty-five, and his wife, Lorraine, owned and operated the Treasure House Restaurant, a popular hangout for the locals. They were renowned for their generous portions of food and the positive, good cheer. Jim, six-foot-two and overweight, never wanted anyone to leave hungry, and they certainly did not. The restaurant overflowed with families, farmers, local workers, cowboys, and lonely people who wanted the company of others. Lorraine had Mom's sweet, kind nature, and folks flocked naturally to her. Jim and Lorraine both worked hard and raised two great sons.

Gary joined us that morning. At fifty-one, he had the rugged good looks of a movie star. A tall, handsome man, his charm won the hearts of men, women, and children alike. Gary had three daughters by three different women, and, as incredible as it may seem, his exes, their new husbands, and his present paramour all loved and saw one another often.

Travis had seen Brian off to Europe, and he drove down for one last goodbye. Bless his heart. Whatever trait Gary possessed that made others love him had passed on to Travis.

Robert stayed in Portland. He had pulled some muscles in his back and did not feel up to the drive to Roseburg for a *bon voyage*, although I heard he managed to attend a party. His absence hurt my feelings, but I understood if he could not manage the trip.

We gathered outside the restaurant for several photographs before I left.

The last one snapped showed the five Foxes lined up against the side of the restaurant. Dad, eighty-four, his health deteriorating, stood on the far right and steadied himself with a cane, while resting his right hand on Mom's shoulder. Mom, seventy-nine, and with heart problems, looked rather serious and had her right arm tight around my waist. I stood between Mom and Gary, my right hand grasping his forearm. Gary held a cup of coffee in his left hand, and with his right hand he held a large, American flag back away from Jim's face. Jim, arms crossed, smiled happily into the camera. I remember the flash and how normal everything felt. I was safe and secure, surrounded by the family I loved.

Over the years we have taken many photographs of our family. This picture of the five of us, snapped so innocently, did not seem that different from so many others. But in time, this picture would come to have special import. I would look at this photograph often, study it, cry over it, put it away, and bring it out again.

I did not know it then, but that instantaneous bright flash of light had created the last Fox family photo.

Goodbyes are emotional for me, and I hurried to be on my way. When I steered slowly out of the parking lot and began the first leg of my trip, I felt happy and relieved that the journey, at long last, had begun. Destiny had whispered my name, and I responded to her gentle, constant murmur. I had willingly chosen this path, and now I needed to continue forward.

My family stood in the parking lot and watched me ride away. No one spoke. Later I was told that my mother said, "I can't believe it is Carolyn doing this. It should've been one of you boys."

Jim put his arm around her. "Don't worry, Mom. You know Carolyn doesn't like to be alone. After one night in her tent, she'll be ready to come home."

Gary chimed in, "That's right, Mom. She'll spend the night and then give us a call in the morning. Tomorrow Jim and I will take the pickup and drive down to Mount Shasta, load her up, and be back home before dark." That settled the matter, and everyone felt much better.

They marched back inside for one more cup of coffee.

When I left that morning, I did not consider our family's future or even think about what it would be like if one of us died. My concern was with the present and my immediate need to begin this journey; my focus was on myself, not on what might happen to my family. I hugged everyone goodbye and told each one that I loved them. In retrospect, it was not enough, not nearly enough.

If I had only known, I would have held on to everyone tighter—and stayed home.

* * *

I'm following behind a logging truck with overhanging logs that bounce up and down and look like they could slip off the back of the truck bed and crush me.

I reduce my speed and widen the distance between us. The long logs, stacked high on the bed of the truck, hang off the end about fifteen feet or so. A small red cloth is secured on the end of the longest log, the only caution to stay back.

Logging trucks are not loaded this way in Oregon; the trees are cut to fit on the bed of the logging trucks, and it is rare to see any logs hang over the end. I'm worried that if another logging truck that is loaded like this one passes me, and the driver inadvertently switches lanes in front of me too soon, the overhanging logs could swing out and knock me off the road. I widen the distance between us.

My father was a logger when he was younger, and logging is a major source of revenue in Oregon. The Alabama trees are slender and fragile looking, unlike Oregon's large, solid firs. Although the smell of the logs remind me of my childhood, it is a relief to ride out of this area and onto a less congested road.

Alabama is a beautiful state with its flourishing forests of tall, thin trees. Today is perfect for riding, not too hot or humid, and I have a chance to think about my upcoming visit with a family in Florida. These are folks I have never met, but they have graciously invited me to stay with them for a few days.

The opportunity to visit came from a mutual friend, Katie. We were talking about my upcoming trip, and she mentioned she had friends who lived right on the Weeki Wachee River in Florida. She went on to say that if I stopped by, maybe I would have a chance to swim with the manatees.

Manatees, or sea cows, are water mammals that are mainly herbivores. They are ten to fifteen feet long, have a round tubular body with a flat, semicircular tail and small front flippers, and can weigh eight hundred to a thousand pounds. They have a small head with a rounded nose and a lot of wrinkles on their face. I think they look adorable.

The idea that I might swim near these large endangered mammals, with their soft, endearing faces and gentle demeanor, captures my imagination. I want to swim with the manatees—and if it works out—it will be one of the highlights of my trip.

Katie arranges for me to stay with the Wilson family: Max, a laid-back bachelor, his brother, Bill, and their mother, Louise. Another brother, Tommy, and his wife, Shelly, live nearby, and everyone happily cares for their elderly mother. It sounds like they are a close-knit, loving family much like mine.

Yesterday I talked to Max, and he said it does not matter when I arrive, that his family is excited to meet me. I have been on the road for three weeks now and am sick of spending time by myself. I want to spend some quality time with a family. I'm curious to meet Max, who seems like a nice guy; he was relaxed and low-key on the phone.

I sense there is an undercurrent of something happening, but I have not figured out what it is.

* * *

Yesterday, I had another television interview, and now that I'm several thousand miles from home, the questions have changed. Originally, reporters wanted to know my motivation for the trip, my experiences on the road, what my interactions with the American people are like, the hardships I have encountered, and always, *Are you afraid?*

I tell them I am willing to take a calculated risk, one I have thought through, and that I think the odds are in my favor, but that dangerous, unpredictable storms have caught me off-guard a number of times. But no, I'm not afraid to ride across America alone, and I believe the American people are kind, helpful, generous, and wonderful.

Now the reporters include a new question, and it appears more and more frequently: *Are you lonely?* This question surprises me. How did they know? Before I left home I never suspected loneliness could be a widespread concern, or one that the media interviewers thought would be of interest to their viewers or readers. They also want to know if being alone *bothers* me, and if not, why not—as if I have some secret immunity against it.

I tell them the truth.

I am honest about loneliness. I explain my anxiety about living alone and say that this trip was to overcome and conquer this fear. I share Emerson's quote with them and encourage people to be bold, to confront their fears, to take a chance on life, and to reach out to others.

But I'm not completely honest. I won't reveal my deep-rooted fear, or my concealed and unspoken guilt over a horrifying decision that I carelessly agreed to go along with many years ago. I'm certainly not going to discuss that unconscionable, hidden part of my past with strangers. Nor will I even concede to myself that I was a willing participant in the decision. It is easier to believe that somehow my input did not count, that I only acquiesced to the suggestion. It is more tolerable to bury my shame and deny my involvement in the decision. Even better, to not think of it at all. But this ride is doing something to me, to my psyche, rattling long buried truths out of the ground.

The closer I come to facing my past and admitting the truth, the more prevalent my anxiety becomes. I do not know if I can confess my sins, even to myself.

The interviews are different, exciting, and add a little glamour to my life, but my moment of stardom only lasts a few minutes before the media folks scurry off to their next appointment and I'm left standing there by my motorcycle. These interviews are not as much about me as they are about meeting deadlines and filling a news spot. It is a stimulating experience, though, and I enjoy the interaction and commotion while it lasts.

Those experiences are similar with the people I meet in camp or on the road. Usually we have quick snippets of conversation or brief discussions about my trip, and then they head back to their families or move on with their lives. I long for a conversation with substance, and I hope to find it with the Wilson family. This is the Fourth of July weekend, so it is a perfect time to get off the road for a few days and act like a normal person again.

Katie, unbeknownst to me, has prearranged this visit with the Wilsons hoping that Max and I will be a romantic match.

Chapter 14

A CONVERSATION OF
SUBSTANCE

As I cross into Florida there are more swamps, unusual assortments of birds, and odd-looking trees.

The trees grow in the water, which seems abnormal because if trees in Oregon stood in water for any length of time, they would rot and die. But these trees look perfectly healthy; they have tall, thin, white trunks without side branches, and tufted shoots of green leaves sprout on top. They remind me of skinny, curved telephone poles, devoid of wires and with a gigantic topknot.

The land is flatter, the view unrestricted for miles. It is picturesque here; the sky is an intense blue with few clouds, the grass and treetops a deep green that reflects in clear, motionless ponds and estuaries.

As I'm riding, the noise from my motorcycle engine startles small white cranes. They fly off in pairs, usually in twos or fours, and then glide across the horizon as one. I ask a local merchant about them, and she says these small cranes mate for life.

I envy those cranes. How ideal it would be to meet the right person at the right time and live happily ever after. No divorces, no conflicts, no trying to find another "perfect" mate. I long to be part of a unified, committed, spiritual, and permanent partnership, but I worry that, while Robert and I may live with one another, I cannot envision us growing old together. What happens if we split up and I'm sixty or seventy? How do you start over at that age? I should stop being so stubborn, so bull-headed, and try harder with Robert.

I'm on my way to meet the Wilson family and ride for another couple of hours. Without warning, the sky abruptly turns black, and blinding, heavy sheets of rain begin to surge from a torrential cloudburst. My visor is closed, my breathing fogs up the inside, and it is impossible to see; I crack the visor up several inches until the face shield clears.

This helps, but now this downpour gushes into my helmet, runs down my chin and neck, soaks my shirt, and then streams into my pants. The rain is warm, but my jeans under my leathers are getting waterlogged, and I'm sloshing around on the seat. When I arrive at a restaurant, the parking lot is covered with two inches of water and I'm sopping wet. My hair is soaked and stuck to my head, and my makeup is running. I had hoped to make a good first impression, but that is not going to happen now.

After calling Max, he says he will come and meet me and then I can follow him back to the house. When he arrives, I'm standing in an instant lake, dripping and steaming like an over-cooked sausage plucked from the microwave. Bless him, he graciously gives me a hug, seems genuinely happy to meet me, and manages to control any horrified looks.

When we arrive at the house, Max helps me unload the bike and shows me where I'm going to stay—a quaint, small bungalow next to the main house. I change into something dry, make an attempt to put myself back together, and join everyone next door.

Louise, Max's mother, rushes over and gives me a tight squeeze. She is so sweet and reminds me of my own kind, loving mother. She introduces her son, Bill, the brother that shares a place with Max; and Tommy and Shelly, the other son and his wife. Everyone is warm and inviting. We hug and chat, all of us as comfortable as if we had known each other for years. Max, the more reserved one of the bunch, stands back and watches the fuss. For the first time in weeks, I feel like I'm home.

The next morning I'm up early and go outside to sit on the deck and dangle my feet in the crystal clear water of Weeki Wachee River. The water is transparent; it is like looking into a pristine aquarium. Schools of fish swim and move together as one, in coordinated, causal shifts as they drift with the current. Single fish, looking quite self-reliant, wander by with their long, skinny bodies that remind me of pencils. Fifteen feet below the surface, small blue crabs scurry around on the sandy bottom, snatching bits of waving grass.

Across the river is a luxurious, thick jungle with swamps, marshlands, and a vast assortment of foliage in intense shades of green. Numerous birds fly in and out of the undergrowth, their squawks shrill and insistent as they crowd for legroom in this tropical paradise. It is phenomenally beautiful, peaceful, and relaxing; I could be happy living in a place like this.

Bill tells me the Weeki Wachee River is about seven miles long and flows westward toward the Gulf of Mexico. He says what is unusual about this river is that it begins from a spring that is a surfacing point of an underground river and is the deepest naturally occurring spring in the United States. The water temperature remains a consistent 74.2 degrees year round and is perfect for swimming and supporting the tropical forest undergrowth and wildlife.

He goes on to mention that this river is where they filmed an old American classic *The African Queen* with Humphrey Bogart and Katharine Hepburn. The setting reminds me of pictures of the Amazon River, with its evocative jungles and humid, sweating rainforests.

Quietly walking outside, I meet and feed Gus, a great egret. He stands about three feet tall when he stretches out his elongated, skinny neck to peer around. He comes onto the porch every morning for breakfast, and Louise feeds him a treat. Gus has been known to march into the house and peck on the refrigerator door if Louise dawdles.

The Wilsons are a kind, considerate family with a live-and-let-live philosophy. Max mentions that Bob, a palmetto bug, lives in the shower in my bungalow; Max asks if I could be careful not to step on Bob.

Bob turns out to be a speedy insect about an inch and a half long, with a hard brown shell. This morning when I head into the shower, he scurries under the shower curtain and stays put, so he does not bother me. Later, when I ask Max what type of bug Bob is, he offhandedly says, "Oh, he's a giant cockroach." I will remember that intriguing detail the next time Bob and I share the shower.

The Wilsons welcome me like a member of the family and give me the grand tour of the area, including a dazzling Fourth of July fireworks show over the Gulf of Mexico. Earlier, Max and I putted out into the Gulf in their small fishing boat to watch for manatees, but we do not spot any.

The next morning, Bill, Tommy, and Shelly take me up the Weeki Wachee River in the family boat to look for wild alligators. Tommy says the wild ones still have spikes on their back, while zoo alligators' spikes have been rubbed down from groups of alligators climbing over one another.

We see wild pelicans, buzzards, cranes, herons, wood owls, turtles, countless fish, and a rickety shack tucked deep into the woods. I want to check it out, but a large sign warns, DANGER! KEEP OUT! EXPLOSIVES. Tommy says the backwoods people who live on this side of the river are serious about protecting their property and privacy. I decide that taking a picture of the sign and shack is a more reasonable option.

We spend the day snorkeling in the river and see one six-foot alligator slip from his post high on the riverbank into the water, his peaked spikes clearly visible. Shelly points out long, muddy stripes from the top of the riverbank into the water, saying these are the alligator's *slides*. She mentions that if we do not see any alligators, it probably means they have already slid into the water when they heard us coming. I can feel the hairs on the back of my neck tingle. Alligators aside, though, I'm becoming more and more relaxed.

It is going to be very difficult to leave this paradise and the Wilson family.

* * *

Max and I are outside in lawn chairs, looking at the stars and listening to the birds chitchat across the river.

This is the first time we have had a chance to sit and talk, and he starts right in. "Carolyn, I think you're drop-dead gorgeous. You have beautiful teeth, a perfect shape, a fabulous smile, and you're a wonderful person." After the aggravation I have been through with Robert, these comments astonish me, and I'm about to gush with gratitude and graciously thank him when he adds,

"*And, you're simple.*"

"Simple? You think I'm simple?" My nostrils flare; I instantly suck in air and inflate like a puffer fish.

"Jesus, Max, are you out of your mind? I don't know you very well, but whatever made you think you could open up a conversation with a woman with a statement like that? You'll never have another date in your life if you start out by telling women they're simple. Frankly, that offends the shit out of me. I'm surprised a smart man like you doesn't understand that." I watch a flock of birds bolt from the trees.

Max continues talking, as relaxed and casual as ever, with no reaction whatsoever to my eruption.

"What I mean is, you have a simplicity of *values* and candor and a more simplistic appreciation for life, a live-and-let-live attitude. You have integrity, you're honest, and you have character. There's a depth to you, and I can tell you have a genuine love of people and things. There's purity with simplicity. You're straightforward, and those qualities are extremely rare and should be treasured."

This sounds a little better, and I exhale.

I never thought of it like that, but Max could be describing himself. His live-and-let-live philosophy includes everything that surrounds him: bugs, plants, and animals. Max tells me, "You will have fully arrived when you wake up in the night, lift a crawling bug off your chest, drop it on the floor, and immediately go back to sleep." The bugs down here are large, and I cannot imagine being that casual with sizeable bugs creeping over me, especially since I sleep in the buff.

Max is a handsome man, fiftyish, tall, slim, with dark hair, a black mustache and beard, and glasses. He is a solid, grounded guy who values his family, and I'm drawn to his intellect, character, and kindness. I admire that he is outspoken and truthful. I have not run across many men like Max, and so I change the subject.

"This place is beautiful, Max. How long have you lived here?"

"I've lived here about seven or eight years, since after I stopped working."

"Oh, you're retired?"

"No, I just stopped working. I'm content here on the river. I'm an elitist, so I don't work . . . I think."

My eyes widen and my eyebrows shoot up. "You mean you're content to sit here all day and do nothing? What do people think? Don't they consider you lazy?"

"The working people do, but they don't understand."

"Well, I'm sure they don't. It's hard for me to imagine how someone who has as much going for him as you do could choose not to work." I shake my head and take a deep breath. "I think work is important."

"Yes, I know you do." His words are level and unruffled. I can visualize him sitting in that big rocking chair, slowly creaking with the best of them.

Max goes on to explain that I'm tied up in the work-ethic philosophy. I have a working-class mentality, he tells me, in that I develop my sense of worth by working, and I think people who are not working are lazy or worthless. I do not think much of his opinion, but he continues with his analysis.

"An elitist belongs to a group of people who don't work and consider themselves to be the thinkers. The working class doesn't see the big picture. It takes the ones who aren't working to be able to sit back and think about things and make decisions for the masses."

The muscles in my jaw tighten. "Doesn't that strike you as a bit uppity? What makes you think your opinion should have more weight than someone who's working his or her ass off? I think physical labor is important; it builds character and contributes to the betterment of mankind. Just because you have money and are in a position to sit around, why do you think that entitles you to have a judgmental opinion about other people?"

"I don't think of it as judgmental at all; it's a statement of fact. Those that aren't working have the time, energy, and luxury to think. They're the ones who can move the masses forward because they're able to observe and reflect." His voice is steady and smooth.

"Frankly, I think that is a lazy man's cop out. People like the Kennedys and Rockefellers worked. They didn't sit around all day and ponder the mysteries of their navels. They contributed to society. I think it's a way to justify the fact that basically you don't want to do anything."

Max just smiles.

We stay up until two in the morning having our lively, opinionated discussion. Max is the first person I have met who considers himself to be an elitist and is willing to admit it. It is hard for me to relate to Max's point of view, but different opinions are the spice of life and I like his feisty spirit and conviction.

Max is an impressive guy, snooty opinions and all.

* * *

On Monday, with the Fourth of July weekend over, I tell the family it is time for me to move on.

They immediately ask me to stay, even if only for a few more days. By now, we feel like family, and it is difficult to leave.

Max says, "Stay awhile, Carolyn. I think we should talk more." I had been looking for a conversation of substance and, like it or not, I got it, and so I agree to stay a couple more days.

I'm glad I stayed, because the next morning, while out on the deck in my swimming suit, Max yells that several manatees are headed downstream. I jump in the water, swim out a ways, and hold as still as possible so as not to disturb them while they cruise by like silent submarines. Max snaps a few pictures, and I get the thrill of a lifetime.

That night as we sit outside, we talk about flirting.

"How come you don't flirt with men? You owe it to your public to be flirting with them. It gives men a sense of excitement and allows them to hope they could have a woman like you."

"Well, actually, Max, I do flirt, but only when I'm in a committed relationship. I flirt because I feel safe and there's no way I'm going to cheat on my partner." Max watches me, but does not say anything, so I continue.

"If my flirting makes someone feel good about themselves for a brief time and they understand nothing is going to come of it, I think it's fine."

Max sits up and shifts slightly in his lawn chair.

"I don't want anyone to misinterpret it, though, as a come-on. There's a fine line, and I only flirt with people I know well."

The conversation shifts.

"I can tell you're looking for a man." It is getting late, and we are once again looking at the stars. What I like about my conversations with Max is that no subject is off limits.

"No, I'm not. I'm involved with Robert."

"Robert is not the man for you, and you know it. You deserve a Cadillac of a man and shouldn't be settling for a Ford. You're entitled to have the same quality in a partner that you bring to the relationship."

"Are you a Cadillac?"

"Yes, I am, but then you know that, too."

I have to admit that Max is the kind of man I admire, someone who can see and appreciate my qualities in the same way I can see and appreciate his.

"You know, Carolyn, when someone is so attractive, so innately appealing to men, you have to be more candid and direct with them. You literally have to say, 'I wish that this weren't true, and I wish it could be another way, but I simply am not sexually attracted to you. That feeling is not there for me.' Otherwise, if the person has feelings for you, they still have hope that in time you'll change your mind. If you're honest with them and close that door, it will set them free."

He continues, "If they don't get this, then you have to say, as gently as possible, 'Look, there's absolutely no possibility, whatsoever, that I'd find myself intimately involved with you. The idea that I'd be buck-ass naked with you is a total turnoff.'"

"Well, that doesn't sound very gentle to me. How am I supposed to say something like that? It's heartless and cruel. Besides, sometimes feelings can change. It would be awful to close that door permanently. How do I balance keeping the door open versus setting someone free?" Our talks continue well into the night.

Katie was right—she had picked a good match for Max. All of them would be happy if I stayed, but I belong in Oregon with my family. I could no more abandon my children or my parents in their old age than they could desert Louise. That is one of the things that I admire about Max and his family, and I consider them good friends.

After five days, it is time to leave, and all the Wilsons are there. Louise keeps crying and saying how much she will miss me. Tommy and Shelly say if I will just come back, I can stay the summer at their house. We are all in tears.

I give Max a quick peck on the cheek. He grabs me and holds me tight against him. "I'm so glad that I met you. I will remember you all of my life," he whispers. I know he genuinely means it and it feels good to know I enhanced his life, as he enhanced mine.

Then he says, "Carolyn, I want you to kiss me goodbye." I give him a brief kiss. "No, I want you to kiss me like you mean it."

And so I kiss my good friend, Max, goodbye.

Chapter 15

"DO THE THING YOU FEAR"

---

aution—Panther Crossing Next 5 Miles.
The sign is in the middle of the Florida Everglades. Since I'm destined to attract attention with my long red hair, fringed gloves, and flashy motorcycle, I constantly scan the trees and underbrush, expecting a large black cat to lunge at me at any moment. I want to stop and take a picture of the sign, but then I visualize the morning paper headlines: *Stupid woman killed by panther while taking picture of sign about panther.*

The Everglades is a national park; sometimes it is called the River of Grass because the area is largely a river—not a marsh or swamp as many people think. It covers approximately 1.5 million acres. I pass by small marshes, mangroves, cypress domes, and sloughs, then stop at a boardwalk and walk over to an observation tower to look for alligators, wading birds, and other wildlife.

Immediately, mosquitoes bombard me; swarming in from all directions in huge, thick clouds, they plunge their sharp needle mouths into my skin.

The park ranger at the entrance of the park warned me that this is the hatching season and the mosquitoes are brutal, but I did not expect this onslaught. I rush back to my bike waving my arms and covering my face, but it is not enough to ward them off, and welts rise on my face and hands. The mosquitoes swarm near me until my speed increases and I outrun them.

Nevertheless, the park is beautiful and enjoyable as long as I keep moving. Near the end of the park, a controlled burn is underway to minimize the potential of wildfires. While I'm waiting for my turn to proceed, a ranger tells me this kind of burning reduces the old vegetation that can easily ignite, and the fires are only carried out when certain weather temperatures permit. Although the sky is clear, the smoke is thick. I tie a bandana across my nose and mouth, but my eyes continue to water and breathing is a struggle. At least there are not any mosquitoes around.

Leaving the park, I ride toward the Florida Keys, where I intend to celebrate my fiftieth birthday. Looking back on my life, it is amazing how quickly the time passed; how did fifty arrive so soon?

Now that I have been on the road almost a month, I have had time to seriously consider my relationship with Robert. We have our issues, but that is the nature of people living together and making continual adjustments to each other's needs, which adds complexity and interest to the relationship.

I have been single for ten years. It is time for me to grow up, to be more accommodating, and to try harder to adapt my life to fit another's. I will be fifty in a couple of days and I'm sure Robert will give me a call on my birthday to tell me how much he misses me, and for me to hurry home. I have finally decided to tell him that things will be better when I'm home, and we can move to New Mexico shortly after I return.

I cannot wait to hear how excited and relieved Robert will be to know that we can spend the rest of our lives together. If I start moving quicker through the states, I should be able to be back home within another month.

I have heard that turning fifty is hard for a lot of people, but my fiftieth birthday will be a celebration, a gala event! *I am one lucky woman.* Fifty is the perfect age to start over.

What could possibly go wrong at fifty years old?

* * *

Fifty! The number that strikes fear into the hearts of many and can make a grown man cry.

Fifty screams for recognition. As a young kid, I never thought about being old or lonely. Each day flew by, a lifetime of adventures between one Christmas and the next. Old age and its implications did not apply to me. I looked at others and decided people fell into two defined classes: young and old. Anyone over twenty counted as old—a sad, unfortunate fate that befell them.

In the United States, approximately 76 million people were born between 1946 and 1964. This eighteen-year span became the most fertile period in US history. Folks born in those years were dubbed the *baby boomers.*

After World War II ended in 1945, a large number of the men and women overseas bolted home, hormones ablaze. They were anxious to reunite with loved ones and get on with life; many wanted to have children. If that did not appeal to them, at least they aspired to practice the fine art of procreation. Birth control choices were limited back in those days, so whatever their intent, they produced babies. Babies boomed, an explosion of humankind never witnessed in the United States before or since.

Now, some fifty years later, many of those babies, myself included, had grown up. The fifty-year watermark of life approached. Like it or not, we were forced to warily look down the barrel of middle age. The worth of our life's accomplishments and the reality of our own mortality confronted us.

In and of itself, old age is not so bad, especially if you are well and happy, and have someone to share life with you. But what if you do not have anyone? How do you reconcile the insult of a deteriorating body and years spent alone?

Married at twenty-two, my life's important landmarks then centered on our marriage, homes, cars, Joe's job, and my looks. Materialistic and consumed with presentation, what we owned and what others thought loomed high on the value scale. The cleanliness of the house became a compulsion. Toilets sparkled and furniture gleamed in the event the Fuller Brush man should arrive unannounced at the door.

We entertained our friends on a weekly basis, the state of the house and my morning weight of monumental concern. Extra ounces and dust mites dared not invade the serenity of a young yuppie couple that demanded perfection. We gathered a lot of possessions in that acquisitive decade. Middle age and what it meant did not concern me. After all, that was light-years away.

By the time I reached my thirties, Brian and Travis rounded out our family. Joe's successive promotions kept him away from home often, which meant I became more involved with the boys. More money brought bigger houses, nicer cars, and a comfortable lifestyle. On the surface our life looked charmed, and in many ways those years were our best. Life changed with two babies, though, and without warning the years slipped away at a quicker pace. I turned thirty-five before I realized the first half of that decade had vanished in a frenzy of dirty diapers, sick children, toddlers, and constant fatigue.

Overall, I thoroughly enjoyed my thirties and gained a new appreciation for who I was. My boundaries expanded, and I tentatively began the search for the substance of life. I remember the day I turned thirty-five and reflected on the year 2000. In the new millennium, I would be fifty-five. Twenty years away. To live twenty years is such a long time, an almost unattainable feat, when you are only thirty-five.

In retrospect, I smoked through the ten years from thirty to forty at an alarming clip. Everyday life consumed my thoughts and energy, potential loneliness a distant star. I woke up one day and, lo and behold, I turned forty.

I loved my forties. The best years ever. Single and independent, self-reliance welled up from within. I chose my paths, for better or worse—the decisions and results my responsibility alone. Each year, I grew stronger emotionally and attacked life with a vengeance. I became a better person, clearer in purpose, wiser. Brian, Travis, law school, the practice, and friends filled my life.

But my forties also awoke a new reality: what would happen to me when the boys left home and I was alone? That once-distant reality suddenly had the configuration of an asteroid hurtling straight toward me as I neared fifty.

Fifty is a coming of age. I certainly deserved this insignia of recognition after the years spent in the trenches. The time neared for me to step forward and accept it with grace. I envisioned my strut toward the podium, head held high, the half-century honor within my grasp. Trumpets would sound, white doves would soar toward the heavens, and the stage would glimmer with angelic light. *Wait a minute! Stop!* What is that part again, that bit about a *half century?* That could not be right. *Yesterday, I was a kid!* I could not be fifty. Fifty? That is *old!*

Looming old age had reared its ugly head.

So fifty patiently waited for me while I got my attitude right. It lingered, ever present, secure in the knowledge that I, too, must join the ranks of those who had gone before. It was like being nine months pregnant—there was no graceful way out of what was to come. I decided to buck up and make the best of it. Why make myself miserable over the inevitable? Fear, stress, and depression would not erase the future.

Consequently, I chose to view fifty as a highlight in my life, to see it as a celebration and not a midlife crisis. Life slips away on an ever-receding tide if we are not bold, or if we do not take a chance to live our dreams and follow our passions. I wanted to celebrate this day in a special way, to challenge myself and take a risk.

When my birthday was six months away, I considered marking the day by taking a long motorcycle ride, alone. I thought a trip to the Oregon coast and back might be a good length. Always accompanied by friends or a group, I had never spent a full day alone on my motorcycle. And I loved the ocean; its magnificence and power reminded me that, while our place in the universe may be small, within us lays great personal strength. As my fiftieth birthday approached, I needed to step outside myself.

The idea frightened me, but I would be fearless and ride to the coast alone.

* * *

One day Joy and I discussed solo travel, and she relayed the story of a young man who had ridden the perimeter of South America alone, something no woman had ever done. My interest was piqued, and I actually spent a good amount of time considering the possibility of being that first woman—but then I realized I did not know Spanish or want to travel through jungles and dangerous, isolated mountain chains. However, the story put the notion in my head to pack the motorcycle and try an extended trip.

After Robert's and my three-week motorcycle trip last year, I felt marginally comfortable riding to an adjoining state and back. A few days on the road alone would be challenging. It would test my abilities, increase my confidence, and address this fear that lurked beneath the surface.

After Joe and I divorced, I spent the first blocks of time by myself. When you have been half of a couple for so many years, it takes some doing to adapt to single life. But time passed, and I forced myself to attend activities alone. I pretended to have a good time, but I never felt completely comfortable.

These occasional single outings did not change the fact that I still had custody and responsibility for the boys. The house bustled with an endless assortment of kids. Joe's work kept him out of state often, so my weekends alone were rare.

Even if Joe had the boys, though, I knew they would return Sunday night. However, these smidgens of isolation signaled a factual certainty. In a few short years, the boys would become adults and move away. An unchangeable fact remained; I would have to face old age alone and perhaps be lonely. This brutal truth paralyzed me with fear.

For many years I have followed Ralph Waldo Emerson's advice, "Do the thing you fear and the death of fear is certain." He believed the things that frighten us are manageable if attacked head-on, ruthlessly, and without hesitation. Once we confront fear, it retreats, driven away through self-confidence. Over the years, I had done stressful things: attended college, married, divorced, raised children, completed law school, opened a private law practice, and ridden a motorcycle.

But, for a reason I could not clearly identify, the underlying fear of loneliness unnerved me. I had considered remarriage but decided that to remarry was dishonest and unfair. Remarriage would provide companionship, but it would not address my fears. Where do I start to eradicate this feeling? Maybe a few days on my motorcycle by myself might bring the answer.

One morning while brushing my teeth, an extraordinary idea came to me. This year I would turn fifty. *Why not pack my motorcycle with a tent and sleeping bag and ride alone through each of the fifty states?* If I rode alone and camped alone, perhaps I could conquer this persistent apprehension once and for all. A trip across America had possibilities.

How do you prepare to ride through all fifty states? To travel through each of the states takes time, money, and effort. I needed to consider Brian and Travis, my relationship with Robert, the law practice, and give this more thought. Think it through. Perhaps if I actually made it, my success would encourage others to face their fears as well.

Panic gripped me. How could I possibly survive alone; what if I needed help?

A month passed, and one morning a woman with intense blue eyes stared at me. Her hair fell softy over her shoulders. She had long hair—too long, I thought—for a woman her age. Her eyes caught and held my attention, her gaze steady.

"You can do this!" I encouraged. She smiled ever so slightly at me. That odd little smile I had seen so many times. In an attempt to convince and bolster her, I continued. "Really. You can do this. You must try. You'll never forgive yourself if you don't try." She quietly stared at me, so I persisted, my voice firmer. "Do you want to be an old lady who sits in a rocking chair and regrets the fear that held you back? That you never took a chance on life?"

She continued to stare at me, and then I saw it. The way her jaw began to set, the upward tilt of her chin. She straightened her shoulders and held herself a little taller. Determination took hold. She had listened to the inner voice that emboldens forward movement and decided to take a risk. I saw it in her eyes.

That is when we made our pact—the woman in my mirror—and me.

I would ride the fifty states. Alone.

Chapter 16

FIFTY AND ALONE

Robert has dumped me!

I'm in the Florida Keys at a phone booth, relaxed and enjoying the flickers of light that sparkle on the ocean waves, when Joy tells me she ran into Robert earlier in the day. Robert told her that, as far as he is concerned, the relationship is over. Over? This is news to me.

Joy lowers her voice and I can tell she is not comfortable continuing. "Carolyn, Robert is carrying an extra helmet on his bike."

I'm stunned and brace myself against the glass wall of the phone booth. Carrying an extra helmet means only one thing— Robert is looking for another woman to go riding with him. This instantly infuriates me. Joy and I hang up and I call Robert.

"Robert, I just talked with Joy, and she tells me you're carrying an extra helmet on your bike." My breathing is ragged and I sound desperate.

There is only silence on his end of the phone.

"I still want to be in a relationship. However, I have the distinct impression that you don't." It is all I can do to get the words out.

There is a long pause before he answers, his voice low and composed. "No, I don't. I don't want to be in a relationship with anyone."

"Oh please. Give me a break." I'm fuming now—furious and hurt. "You're carrying an extra helmet on your bike. You want to be in a relationship with someone, just not me. Thanks for having the balls to tell me first. I think this is really chicken shit of you. I didn't realize you were such a coward." My voice is shaking, and my words come out shrill and harsh. I'm mad and can't control myself as the volume of my voice increases.

Then he has the nerve to say, "I was hoping we could still be friends."

"Friends? You must be joking! What do you think we're going to do, double date? No thank you! I'll find someone whom I consider a real friend, not someone sneaking around behind my back. Frankly, Robert, I think you're a total asshole." I have lost all composure and am screaming into the phone; I notice people looking at me, but I do not care.

"Okay then, I guess this is goodbye." I hear him sigh and we hang up.

The relationship is over.

To say that I'm upset and pissed is the understatement of the year, especially since I had decided to make this work. There was no time to tell him the fabulous news, and I'm certainly grateful for that. At least I did not make a complete fool of myself, although what possible difference does it make at this point?

A couple of hours pass before I calm down and have some time to think. Why should I be so angry, since the relationship has been in trouble for the last six months? I suppose it is because I like to be the one who ends a relationship. That way,

I'm the one in control and it is easier to save face. The truth is, I'm as big a coward as he is for not ending it earlier. Still, I am totally pissed off. *God damn him!*

It makes no sense to me why I fixate on one person when there are other opportunities. I unrealistically hang on and think, *if I just stick with it long enough, love will rekindle.* But this time, that is not going to happen.

If I'm honest, Robert does have some good qualities, but our interpersonal relationship has been almost nonexistent, and we have been in a nonsexual relationship for months. Nevertheless, I feel deceived and abandoned. When we first met, he told me he was absolutely, madly in love with me, and I was the woman he had waited forty years for. I remember how he was pumped up about how lucky we were to have met one another. However, when I made a commitment to him, he immediately put on the skids, and for all practical purposes, the relationship was over after three months.

What am I supposed to do now? Erase *New Mexico* off my packed boxes? Where am I supposed to live when I get home, or find work, since I have closed the law office? Robert was my backup plan, my ace in the hole, the one who was going to save me from myself.

My hands are trembling and I feel weak. I take a couple of deep breaths and continue to stare at the phone. For the first time on this trip, I clearly understand the brutal reality that I'm four thousand miles from home and utterly alone.

Tomorrow, I will be fifty years old.

* * *

Yesterday I was depressed and despondent over my breakup with Robert.

Today it is harder to feel as sorry for myself, because it is so incredibly beautiful here. I know I'll feel better if I get on my bike and ride. It clears my mind.

To celebrate my fiftieth birthday, I decide to ride the length of the Florida Keys. First, I will head north to the beginning of the Keys, and then I will turn around and head back to the Fiesta Key KOA where I'm staying. This KOA is near Key West, the last island accessible by highway. I ride on US 1, also called the Overseas Highway, which has small green mile markers starting with MM 0 in Key West and ending with MM 126 just south of Florida City.

As I head north, the Gulf of Mexico is on my left and the Atlantic Ocean is on my right. Only this small strip of islands and highway separates the two bodies of water. There are a total of forty-two bridges connecting the islands, but the Seven Mile Bridge is the longest. The highest point on one of the bridges is about sixty-five feet above sea level. As I glance down, the water below is multicolored with different shades of greens, blues, and mauves, the most prominent color being turquoise. Everywhere I look reminds me of a painting created by one of the masters, as each panorama is perfect.

The Florida Keys are tropical. The warm air massages my face, and I settle into the bike and attempt to relax, focusing on how fortunate I am to have the opportunity to spend my fiftieth birthday in this magnificent place. I reach MM 126, find a place to turn around, and head south.

I'm on the road about an hour, enjoying the view while simultaneously assessing my relationship with Robert, when a huge black cloud sneaks up behind me. A loud crack of thunder makes me jump, and then sheets of heavy rain pound me. In an instant, I look like I have jumped into a swimming pool and then slogged back out. It is hot outside, so my leathers begin to steam, my visor fogs up, and with the driving rain, it is impossible to see the car in front of me.

Fortunately, I'm on some island and see a road to my left where I can pull off, park, and wait out the rainstorm. It is raining so hard, though, that I can barely make out the building in front of the parking lot. I run inside and stand there, saturating their floor with large pools of water. After removing my helmet, I see a group of policemen staring at me. It looks like I have found my way into a sheriff's office. It looks like even the fortunate can get an unexpected bath.

Cloudbursts are normal down here, and as quickly as it starts, it dissipates. The weather is hot and balmy, and my leathers are dry by the time I arrive back at my KOA.

I decide to spend several days down here, sit by the pool, clear my head, and see if I can make some sense out of what the hell I'm doing.

One lucky woman, my ass.

* * *

"Carolyn, where are you?"

Joy has left a message on my cell phone, a big, bulky thing with limited service, which has to be plugged in and charged every night if it is to work. Three days have passed since my breakup with Robert, and I'm still at the KOA, hanging out by the pool, feeling depressed and miserable. I give her a call.

"I'm still in Florida. It is warm and beautiful down here and I think I'm going to stay another week." I know my voice sounds whiney.

"No! You can't stay there. If you don't start moving, you'll never make it over the Rockies before it starts to snow." Her voice is firm and bossy. "If that happens, you're screwed. Now get on that damn bike and head north!" Sometimes Joy has such a sweet way with words.

"Fine, fine. Calm down. I'll leave in the morning. You're really no fun, you know?"

Since I have had a lot of time on my hands the last couple of days, I reorganized my things, kept what I needed, and will ship the rest back to Travis. It has been so hot; I find I'm only wearing a few items of light clothing. Most of the heavy, bulky, warm things take up a lot of room in my bag and I do not need them. Besides, it feels good to unload the extra baggage.

One of the guys, Fred, who I met in camp, is going to take my overflowing box to the UPS store in his pickup and then show me around the island. After checking out some of the fresh fish markets, we head back to the KOA. Fred tells me that he is an alcoholic and is impressed with the idea of a trip like mine, which requires a person to face her or himself.

Then he says, "If you'd consider letting me go with you, I'll stop drinking and buy a motorcycle today. I've got plenty of money, and I'm retired. I'll be ready to go by tomorrow and won't hold you up. I can travel with you as long as you'll let me. I think this would be an excellent way to turn my life around and start over."

This is a tough one. I can hear the stress in Fred's voice, and I know he is looking for a lifeline. I have to tell him the same thing as others about traveling alone, and then add, "Fred, if you think this type of experience would help you, maybe you'd consider a smaller trip, perhaps around the perimeter of Florida. There's no reason you couldn't take your truck, if you don't want to buy a motorcycle." I reach over and touch his shoulder. "There's a lot to be said for spending time alone. I don't think it's fun a lot of the time, but I do think it's a seasoning experience."

"I'm not sure how to start." I watch him tighten his grip on the steering wheel.

"You'll start the same way you would if you went with me tomorrow. Pick a destination, pack some things, and leave. Make a commitment to be gone for a week or so and see what you think. If you don't like being by yourself, you can always come back here. I found it hard at first to be by myself, but it does get easier. You can do this if you make up your mind. Why don't you give it some thought?"

"All right." I thank him for the ride and wish him the best of luck. Fred sounds defeated and I doubt he will try a solo adventure, but I hope he proves me wrong. One way or the other, though, I'll add Fred to my passenger list and take him with me.

When I head out the next morning, both the bike and I feel lighter. It feels liberating to leave Robert and the majority of my warm, heavy clothes behind.

Little do I know, I will come to deeply regret this cathartic spur-of-the-moment decision.

* * *

After leaving Florida I head up the eastern coastline through Georgia and South Carolina. I am heading to New Jersey to visit with some friends.

Last night when checking the map, I spied an island with sandy beaches off the coast of North Carolina, a spot called Cape Hatteras, which is the easternmost point of the United States. I decide to stop, and it turns out to be a nice break, a real island retreat that is relaxed with a slower pace.

It is hot and sunny, and my walk on the beach is healing. I walk toward the KOA store to buy a Coke and notice a man lying on his stomach on a cot that was placed outside on one of the cabin porches. By the way he is propped up with pillows, it looks like his movements are limited, so I stop and call out to him.

"Hi, I'm headed up to the store. Can I get you anything?

"No, I'm fine, but thanks for asking." On my way back, he waves me over.

"I wanted to tell you that my family and I have come here the last couple of summers; they play on the beach, and I lie here during the day. Do you know you're the first person who has ever asked me if I wanted anything? That's really nice. Why don't you sit with me for a while?"

"Well, thanks, I'd love to." I sit down on the porch step so that I'm lower than he is and ask him what happened.

"It was a freak hunting accident, the kind you're always warned about in hunting classes. In class, we were told that if you ever need to leave your gun unattended, check the chamber of the gun first." He shifts his hips a little and moans. "If there's a bullet in the chamber, you always need to remove it, because there's a chance the gun could fire accidently." I notice he has deep frown lines in his forehead.

"I was out hunting and getting ready to climb over a wooden fence. I leaned my rifle against a fencepost, but I was in a hurry and didn't check the chamber." I see his eyes squint as he moves again and then looks back at me. "As I was climbing over the fence, the gun fell and discharged, and the bullet struck me in the back. I'm not paralyzed, but if I stand up or sit, I get these terrible, debilitating shooting pains through my back and legs, so it's best for me to lie flat."

"I'm really sorry to hear that. When did it happen?"

"Several years ago. I've seen a lot of specialists, but no one has figured out how to stop the pain."

"It must be difficult for you not to be out on the beach with your family." He squints again, looks toward the ocean, and shifts his hips.

"I'd like to be out there with them. I have young kids, but this was my fault, and I'm fortunate to be able to enjoy them." He glances back toward the beach and his eyes look sad. "At least I wasn't killed. I'm grateful for that. The truth is, I feel really blessed. My family is very devoted to me, and I'm lucky I'll be able to see my children grow up." His voice softens, and his words drift off. "I feel confident that someday someone will figure out how to help me."

"I have to tell you, I'm impressed with your courage and positive outlook on life. Your family is lucky to have you, too."

"Thank you. It was really nice of you to stop and spend some time with me. It means a lot." As I start walking back to my tent, he yells out, "Good luck with your trip."

After leaving, I think about his attempt to be optimistic, even with his unbearable pain. My problems are nothing compared to his, or the burned man; I add this courageous man to my passenger list.

I need to quit whining, buck up, and stop feeling sorry for myself.

* * *

The next morning, I slip on my bathing suit and walk down to the beach, spread out a small towel, and sit with my toes dug into the warm sand.

I watch children playing near the ocean and wonder if some of the kids belong to the man on the porch. As her mother stands nearby, a little girl, maybe five years old, with long black hair, lets out a happy squeal when the waves roll in and touch her toes. As I watch her, tears well up in my eyes and I'm swept back in time.

Ever since Elizabeth died, I watch little girls with black hair and a fair complexion. I never bother to check the color of their eyes because I did not know the color of Elizabeth's eyes. Maybe they were blue like mine, or brown like Joe's eyes. She was in so much pain that she kept her eyes closed most of the time, and the oxygen mask they placed on her covered most of her tiny face.

Each year, on February sixth, I say to myself, *today Elizabeth would be two, or five, or fifteen, or twenty,* and I look for little girls, teenagers, or young women that resemble that age. The hardest ages were children under five, darling little girls often dressed in pink skirts, pink shoes, and usually a pink bow to match. I would smile at them—more with a look of longing than with the polite smiles one usually gives little girls.

The day she was born is always difficult for me. I choose the day she was born, rather than the day she died, as I feel that somehow this keeps her alive for at least one day, one day out of each year. This year Elizabeth would have been twenty-two. Maybe she would be graduating from college, or married with children of her own; grandchildren I cannot envision even when I try. All vanished, nonexistent, because she was born six weeks too soon.

When a child dies, it changes you. Or at least it changed me. Honestly, I'm not sure if it made that much difference to Joe. I think Elizabeth's life did not count for him because she *only lived one day.* We both said those words because they were true, but his tone was different, more nonchalant, and each time he said it that way, it infuriated me and my resentment grew.

It was as if her name was written on a blackboard, then quickly erased, leaving a slight smudge where her life had been. Something to be forgotten and wiped away, an inconsequential memory.

When does a life count? Would it have counted if she lived one month? Six months? A year?

One day counted for me; her life counted. Maybe it was different for me because I felt her moving and kicking my ribs until they ached, as she stretched to change positions. Maybe it was my helplessly standing outside the nursery window watching her die, listening to her anguished cries. Or maybe it was my unrelenting, unforgivable guilt that followed her death. Whatever it was, one day counted for me. And it nearly destroyed me.

When overwhelmed with grief, it is easier to deny reality, to pretend the decision I contributed to was not my fault, to excuse my participation in the unconscionable. As the years passed, I have tried to close those doors and shut out those last memories, to say it was not my fault, but the damn doors would not stay shut.

I came to believe I did not deserve forgiveness. What I deserved was to suffer.

Elizabeth's death, Brian's premature birth, and Travis's complications created the irreversible drive to be ultra protective of the boys. I became a lioness with injured cubs. No one, including Joe, dared step between my sons and me. I would have ripped their heads off.

I became a lenient mother, too lenient according to Joe and most people I knew, but that did not concern me. The things that were important to other parents did not matter to me: the boy's escapades as teenagers, the length or color of their hair, baggy pants that hung low in their crotch and exposed their underwear. Those things did not matter because I knew they were phases that the boys would outgrow.

The line was drawn at tattoos and piercings; nothing permanent before they were eighteen was my rule. We also talked at length about the importance of reaching adulthood without the trauma of unplanned-for babies, drugs, or police records. They were great, bright kids and our relationship was solid—the three of us were devoted to and protective of one another.

I felt blessed that they were alive. I wanted them to grow up and be happy; I wanted them to live.

Gathering up my things, I head back toward the tent to pack the bike. I'm ready to be on the road. As each eastern state is clicked off one after another, my chest tightens and my breathing becomes shallow. My anxiety mounts as I move closer and closer to an old church in Rhode Island where I intend to confront my past, if my courage holds.

I must force myself northward if I am ever to find any peace.

Chapter 17

PEOPLE ARE LIKE FROGS

I do not believe this—I lost my tent!

When leaving Virginia this morning, I neglected to properly secure the straps that held the tent to my saddle-bags. After several hours on the road, I stop for breakfast and discover my mistake, but it is too late. The tent is gone.

Fortunately for me, I'm on my way to meet a family friend, Dotsy, and her family who live in New Jersey. I plan to spend a couple of days with them and will buy another tent then.

Dotsy's mother, Jan, and my mom were best friends when we were children. Later, Jan and her husband divorced, and Jan and her daughters moved back to the East Coast. I have not seen Dotsy for years, so I'm looking forward to meeting her husband, Kevin, and their three children, Carolyn, Jennifer, and Michael. Five-year-old Carolyn is my namesake. Her mother tells me she reminds her of me with her cowboy boots, jeans, and independent ways.

Little Carolyn sits on a bucket in the driveway all afternoon waiting for me to arrive. She follows me everywhere for three days and even stands patiently outside the bathroom door, until her mom tells her to go sit on the couch. They are a lovely family: kind, thoughtful, and devoted to the Baptist church. They warmly welcome me into their home.

Tomorrow, Kevin is going to drive me to a sporting goods store so I can buy a tent.

* * *

The salesman slowly raises one arm, extends his index finger, and points to the green one.

"That," he says, with a noticeable haughtiness in his voice, "is our best seller."

Looking up at the ceiling, I'm awestruck. Suspended twenty feet above the floor, several tents hang from brackets, each tent a different size, shape, and color. These beauties are assembled and seem to be inflated as they billow and float, moving gently with the cool air from the air conditioner. I have never purchased a new tent before and this quickly becomes obvious to the salesman. Spotting an easy mark, he continues to point at the green one, praising its virtues. Then he leans closer, his shoulder touching mine, and utters a taunt in my ear.

"You can put this tent up in five minutes, *flat*, without reading the directions." There is a challenge in his tone and a smirk on his face that implies: *Anyone, that is, except someone who looks as stupid as you do.*

That is all it takes.

I buy the tent, accept the challenge, and we head back to the house. With an air of defiance, the first words out of my mouth are, "I can put this tent up in five minutes, *flat*, without reading the directions."

Kevin, stopwatch in hand, is in the yard. Dotsy and the three kids are in the yard. The tent is in the yard. I lay out the pieces, and with a *click* of Kevin's stopwatch, I begin.

I have no idea when or why they leave. Perhaps it is from heat exhaustion after standing in the hot sun for so long, or maybe they simply do not want to see me disgrace myself any further. I do not know, because I'm down on my hands and knees with my ass in the air. I pore over the blueprints and schematics contained in the three volumes of instructions necessary to erect this architectural marvel.

Everyone leaves but little Carolyn. She sticks with me, but eventually she does somersaults in the yard, plays with the dog, swims in the pool, and takes her afternoon nap. At some point, she returns with a glass of lemonade sent by her mother. She looks at me with big, sympathetic eyes and says, "Has it been five *hours* yet?"

I guess I really am as stupid as I look, because when the tent is on the verge of collapsing for the twenty-seventh time, Kevin takes mercy on me, and between the two of us, we finally get the disgusting thing to stand.

When the salesman described this beauty, he said it was a "three-man" tent. When I crawl inside, my first thought is: *Which three men?* Not any three men I know—or any two or even one. I can barely fit inside. I can, however, sit upright if I align myself perfectly with the highest point in the center. If I turn my head left or right my nose scrapes, and, in no time, I could pass for Rudolph the Red-Nosed Reindeer. Since I mean to dress inside the tent, I'll have to lie flat on my back and squirm in and out of my tight jeans.

Once standing, the tent is a bright, neon-green atrocity that looks completely different from the magnificent one that blended subtly into the multicolored store ceiling. What is more, my new tent is flimsy, the fabric paper-thin. I doubt the aluminum poles will withstand the first hint of an evening breeze, let alone any type of windstorm. But I'm committed now and feel the pressure to continue on my trek north.

Soon it is time to leave. I fasten my humiliation securely to the bike and hug everyone goodbye. Little Carolyn and I both cry. Spending time with their family has meant so much to me, and it was wonderful to reminisce with Dotsy about our time together as children.

As I head up the East Coast, I'm nervous about returning to an old cemetery that persistently calls to me. When I'm there I mean to detail my past, but I'm apprehensive and scared. What happens if I cannot find the serenity I seek? Will I forever be haunted by my guilt?

It is hard to ask for forgiveness—when you know in your heart—you do not deserve it.

* * *

Twelve years ago, when Joe and I lived in Sparta, New Jersey, my best friend was Leslie.

We would laugh and joke and tell each other our deepest secrets. She still lives in the same area, and one might think that time and distance would change the way we feel about one another, but it has not. We instantly reconnect as though we have never spent a moment apart. We hug and cry, and I decide to spend an extra day so we can catch up on each other's lives.

When I first met Leslie, she had been diagnosed with multiple sclerosis (MS). The disease affected her eyes and legs, and she often had different physical ailments. We lived less than a mile apart and William, her husband at the time, needed their only car for work. Often, we would trudge back and forth and hang out after the boys left for school. She was on a new MS drug regimen then, and she had to have a daily shot. Since she did not like to give the shots to herself, I would give them to her.

Leslie, still a beautiful woman with large brown eyes and long dark hair, has been married to Jack now for ten years. I find out she is frustrated and angry with Jack for his insensitivity to her MS. She tells me he is eight years younger, has never had any health issues, and cannot relate to the leg, vision, balance, and fatigue problems associated with her MS. She is really aggravated and is considering a divorce.

We drive to the Sparta boardwalk, buy ice cream cones, and sit down on a bench overlooking beautiful Lake Mohawk. We have sat on this same bench with ice cream cones many times before while discussing our personal issues. Today is no different.

"Leslie, I know this may sound weird, but let me tell you about my observations of people and frogs. I think they're very much alike."

Leslie snorts. "Well, you've had some unusual thoughts, so I can't wait to hear this one."

Unfazed, I carry on with my inspired analysis. "As you know, tadpoles go through a dramatic transformation during the time they change from a tadpole to a frog. In the beginning, tadpoles can only survive in the water." Leslie pushes her dark hair back from her face and looks out over the lake.

"No matter how much tadpoles want to be frogs and have the freedom to hop around, it's impossible. They'd die if they stayed out of the water. Tadpoles must develop in their own time and in their own way. Eventually, they'll grow arms and legs and develop lungs. They'll become frogs, but none of this can be hurried." She takes a bite of her ice cream.

"Frogs, on the other hand, are also limited because they can't live underwater permanently. They would drown."

My ice cream is melting, so I lick it off the sides of the cone. "I think people are like this. I believe we, too, go through developmental, transitional, and growth stages. Our abilities may be limited by our age, gender, race, education, opportunities, or experiences. Like the tadpole, we mature and develop at our own pace and in our own time, and it can't be rushed." I watch Leslie nod, but she doesn't say anything.

"I do get frustrated sometimes if someone doesn't meet my expectations. However, I think it's unfair of me to damn him or her for not adapting to my timeline or adjusting to my needs."

I lean into my good friend. "Here's the thing: I think you're a frog when it comes to understanding physical limitations, but Jack's still a tadpole. On the other hand, Jack may be a frog in some areas of life and you may be the tadpole. I don't know of anyone I'd consider a frog a hundred percent of the time. Do you?"

Leslie laughed. "No, I can't say that I do."

"You know, there is nothing wrong with having feelings of frustration for Jack's lack of empathy, but from what I can see, he's very devoted to you. He seems like a genuinely nice guy, and it looks like he'd do anything for you." Leslie smiles and looks at me.

"Yeah, you're right. He does spoil me and worry about me."

The next morning Leslie tells me that when she woke up, she felt like she had released the anger and frustration she had felt for years. She would accept Jack's tadpole stage because that is simply where he is today. She won't blame him for failing to be something he cannot be. Relief floods her face, and that makes me happy.

Sometimes I'm like a mini-tornado that blows into town, whirls around, stirs things up, and leaves. My hope is to encourage people to take a chance on life and do what makes them happy. If this whirlwind of activity makes a positive impact on people and my input makes them feel better about themselves, then this trip is a success.

For myself, I'm looking for guidance to tell me what direction *my* life should take, but I cannot think about that now. It is time to move forward and finally confront the demons of my past.

My next stop: the old church in Wickford, Rhode Island.

Chapter 18

ELIZABETH—FORGIVENESS AND REDEMPTION

The first time I visited Jan Chasm, my mother's dearest friend in Wickford, was with my mother about ten years ago.

Wickford, Rhode Island, is a village in the town of Kingston, thought to have been settled around 1637, and is characterized by late Revolutionary and Federal period buildings. Although Jan moved to the East Coast a number of years earlier, she and my mother kept in contact; they wrote, called one another, and both flew coast to coast to visit.

Jan and my mother have studied metaphysics for many years, and both are wise, intelligent women. Jan is crippled with rheumatoid arthritis, a long-term disease that leads to inflammation of the joints and surrounding tissue. Although it was difficult for her to walk, Jan wanted to show Mom and me the area and, in particular, the Old Narragansett Church built in 1707, which she considered to be one of the most interesting and famous buildings in Wickford.

After walking around the small town, we headed over to the church. The walkway leading to the church was a series of large, flat stones, each engraved with writing, and the path was about a block long. At the far end of these block steps, I could see part of the church in the distance, a small building with a brown door. Trees lined both sides of the walkway, but because of the distance between the church and us, the trees appeared to narrow into the church in the shape of an upside-down *V*. As I walked closer, the church seemed to gradually enlarge as the trees stepped back from my view.

As I moved toward the church, I felt a strange sensation in my chest, like I was being physically drawn to this church— something was pulling me forward.

The plain white church was a rectangular two-story building with simple windows. Along three sides of the church was a cemetery with old carved headstones. There were a sizeable number of small weathered rocks stacked up around the base of the church.

That day, as I neared the church, I had the overpowering sense I had been there before.

I stopped and stood frozen, staring at the church, while Mom and Jan continued walking around the building and out of my sight. As I stood there, I found myself saying over and over in my mind, *It's all right. I forgive you. You can go now.*

For some reason, I felt as if someone there needed to be forgiven, but I did not know who, or why. I scanned the headstones, but many of the old words were barely visible. It seemed as though an invisible presence lingered near me. However, I did not feel any fear, only this strong sensation that I had returned to this church for some purpose. *But I've never been here before,* I reminded myself.

Mom and Jan came back into view and started to walk back toward Jan's house. I continued to stand there, the words running over and over in my mind: *I forgive you. You can go now,* when a name came to me: Elizabeth Ann Bartley. The name repeated in my mind.

My mother looked back, saw me standing there, and called to me. "Carolyn! Carolyn, come on."

It was the sound of my mother's voice that finally forced me to move. I caught up with them but did not mention my strange sensations at the church.

Mom and I slept upstairs at Jan's house. Throughout the night, I would wake up and go stand by a window that looked out in the direction of the church. I silently repeated my statement of forgiveness and wondered about the name. I did not know anyone named Bartley.

The next morning when we were having breakfast, I told Mom and Jan about my strange feelings at the church and about the name that came to me. Jan said, "That's so odd that you would mention Bartley, because that's a very old family name here in Wickford." I felt a shudder of apprehension travel up my spine.

A year after that strange experience, I would return to Wickford, when the story would seem to fully develop.

* * *

"Carolyn, tell me a ghost story."

My twenty-five-year old cousin, Debbie, was sitting in the back seat of my car beside her mother, Lucille, my mom's sister. Mom and I were in the front seat and we were headed to Rhode Island to visit Jan. The three of them had flown out from Oregon to visit our family in Sparta, New Jersey, and we had spent the last four days touring Washington, DC. The drive up to Rhode

Island took several hours, and we were all worn out from our Washington excursion. It was dark outside, so I figured a ghost story would be a good distraction from the drive.

"Okay. Several months ago, I was sitting in our living room in Sparta. Joe was at work and the boys were in school. The house was hushed, and it was snowing outside. As I relaxed and watched the snowflakes slowly swirling down, I saw an image of two little girls playing in the snow. One of them was about four or five, the other maybe eight or ten. They had on long white dresses and unusual-shaped bonnets that made me think of the colonial era."

Debbie settled into her seat as she listened, and I related the rest of the story to them.

"The girls were playing a game that reminded me of hide-and-seek, and I noticed that the light in the sky was fading. I watched as the younger child ran far into the woods to hide. After a while, no one came for her, and she started crying. She called for her friend, *Anna, Anna,* but Anna didn't come. She looked for Anna, but because it was getting dark, she became disoriented and went deeper into the woods. She finally sat down at the base of a tree, curled up and fell asleep, softly calling Anna's name." No one in the car spoke, so I continued.

"Next, I saw the older child. She was yelling, calling out the name, *Elizabeth, Elizabeth.* When she couldn't find Elizabeth, Anna ran home. Many men and women went into the forest to search for Elizabeth, and they were carrying some type of lanterns, but they couldn't find her. The next morning, they found Elizabeth near the base of a tree. She had died during the night from the cold.

"Anna never forgave herself for losing little Elizabeth in the woods or for her death. As I watched, transfixed, I had the sense that Anna married, lived to be in her twenties, but died early from her overwhelming guilt." Everyone in the car was quiet.

"Here's the ghost story part. I think the lost little girl's name was Elizabeth Ann Bartley. And I believe I was that child in a former life." That got everyone's attention.

Then I told them about my strange experience at the Wickford church and how I continually repeated the words, "I forgive you. You can go now." We decided that when we arrived at Jan's, we would go to the church and look at the old headstones to see if we could find a marker for Elizabeth or Anna.

The next morning, we were talking with Jan about our plan. She told us that back when the church was first built, it was common for people to honor their dead children with small rocks since so many children died young. Jan said some rocks had the child's initials carved on them, but most did not. When I was there before, I had wondered why the church had so many rocks stacked near its base. The stones now had a more powerful and gripping meaning.

Jan did not feel up to going with us, so the four of us walked to the church and saw the stones piled against the base. None of us wanted to disturb anything, so we did not touch or move them. There was no headstone for Elizabeth Ann Bartley.

I came across an old marker that said, *In Memory of Anna S. Thomas, wife of George B. Thomas and daughter of Lemull S. Elizabeth Burge. She died August 27th, 1845 in her 24th year.* I was not sure if the spelling of *Lemull* was correct because the stone was faded and difficult to read. Nor did I know what type of clothing children wore in this area in the early 1800s. I believed the little girls in my vision wore Colonial-looking dresses.

Nevertheless, Debbie took a picture of me with my hand on Anna's headstone. I did not know if this grave had anything to do with my vision. What I did know was when we all left the church, I felt a tremendous sense of relief. I no longer felt it was necessary to forgive Anna.

I believed Anna was in a better place.

* * *

Since I began my motorcycle trip, I have been trying to prepare myself for this current visit with Jan.

My intent is to return to the old church alone. I want to detail my daughter Elizabeth's life, her death, the horrendous aftermath, and the devastating effect it had on my marriage and on me.

I approach the church the same way as my first encounter, via the long stone walkway, to see if my feelings are different today. The ominous pull toward the church is the same as before, and I'm convinced I once lived in this area, but the need to forgive Anna is no longer there. This time, I go inside the church and listen to a woman talk about the church's history to a small group of people.

The inside of the church is painted a soft gray color. The beams and trim are a very light green, and the pews are white with narrow brown trim around the backrests. A small door on each pew opens to allow access. The benches are flat planks with a ramrod-straight board for the back that would be uncomfortable to lean against. Red books lie on the benches, which I assume are Bibles. The inside of the church seems cold and formal. Nothing feels familiar to me.

I walk outside and look at the scattered tombstones and cannot tell which direction the bodies are placed; I feel like I'm walking on the dead and ask for forgiveness.

A large headstone says 1813, and this may be a family because the area is enclosed with a grouping of graves inside. A lot of the tombstones give the years the person was born and died. One reads: *In the memory of James Updike, who departed this last February 20, 1822 in the 51st year of his life.* Another one, for his son, says: *Departed his life August 10, 1800, age 16 years, 10 months and 10 days.* This gives me the creeps—August tenth is the day Travis was born.

Updike seems to be an important name. *Children of Wilkins and Abby Updike, Elizabeth S. Updike, died 18 years, Daniel Updike, died 19 years old, Alice Updike 10 months.* I cannot imagine losing three children and the grief that family must have felt.

I walk behind the church and find a place to sit, armed with M&M's, my comfort food, and a box of Kleenex.

It has been twenty-two years since our baby, Elizabeth, died, and my memories of that time are still vivid and unforgiving. Joe and his friend had driven to Seattle, Washington, some four hours away, for the weekend to attend a model airplane show. There was not any reason for Joe to stay home, since I had recently had a checkup. The doctor thought both the baby and I were perfectly healthy. Aunt Lucille and Debbie lived nearby, and I stayed with them.

Around ten o'clock that night, my water broke, and the three of us headed to the hospital. I wore Lucille's robe over my pajamas and slippers because I thought I would be checked by my doctor and then sent home, since the baby was not due for another six weeks. However, the doctor insisted that I stay—I was in labor. Elizabeth was born four hours later.

Early on, the doctor knew Elizabeth was in trouble. She was struggling to breathe.

Twenty years ago, it was not unusual for premature babies to have breathing problems. These babies were not in the womb long enough for their lungs to mature. When they exhaled, their tiny lung segments would touch and fuse together. The amount of oxygen the babies could inhale was increasingly restricted, and eventually this caused a slow, painful death by suffocation.

Elizabeth was placed in an incubator, and within an hour, they had fitted her with a small oxygen mask. Since she was the only baby in crisis, I quickly learned that when the number forty-three was called out over the loudspeaker, it meant there was an emergency in the nursery. That meant Elizabeth. It was rare, but if I happened to be in bed, I would jump up, rush to the window, and watch them frantically try to help her.

At the start of the night, when a nurse saw me standing there, she would walk over and pull down a blind inside the nursery window so I could not see what was happening. Before long, the number was called more frequently, and after that, I remained standing at the window, hour after hour, until eventually they left the blind open.

Lucille and Debbie had stayed until Elizabeth was born, but it was almost two in the morning, so I told them to go home and that I would see them later in the day. Lucille called Joe to say the baby was born, and he and his friend headed back. Joe told Lucille it was very foggy and the trip back would be slow.

Because I had come to the hospital in my pajamas, I did not have any money. It cost a dime to make a phone call, so I could not call Lucille and tell her Elizabeth was in trouble. I know she and Debbie would have immediately come to the hospital to be with me. It seems irrational to me today that I did not demand to use the hospital phone, dime or no dime, but at the time, with all the stress, it never occurred to me.

The doctor wanted me to stay in bed. Although he had given me something to help me sleep, I could not sleep nor stay in bed. All I could do was stand by the nursery window and stare at my small, beautiful, tiny baby girl with the china-doll face, black hair, and long legs as she pulled at her oxygen mask and cried.

The sound was an agonizing wail, and I was amazed she had the strength to cry for so many hours. As horrifying as it was to listen to her, I felt a sense of relief that at least she was strong enough to cry. I believed if I stayed by the window long enough, I could ease her breathing through the sheer force of my will; then the crying would stop. I did not understand until months later the magnitude of the crisis, or that there was no way to reverse the damage to her lungs, or any possible way to save her.

As time passed, I became more and more panicked and began to pray. Over and over, I begged God to help her. How could he not, when it would take so little effort to ease a tiny baby's suffering?

By early morning, the doctor came and stood by me at the nursery window. "Carolyn, we're giving the baby too much oxygen."

"What does that mean?"

"It means that she may have brain damage from the excess oxygen. We're very concerned about her. I'm going to arrange to have her sent to another hospital where they have a specialized neonatal unit."

I could feel my chest tightening; it was hard to breathe.

"I don't care about the brain damage. I'll take care of her. Just help her." My words were hoarse and odd sounding.

The doctor sighed, reached over, and grabbed my arm to steady me. "Carolyn," he said, his voice tight with stress, "I want you to understand that the outlook is *grim*." I stared at him but did not say anything.

That is when I first understood that the doctor meant Elizabeth was dying. My breathing stopped and then came in constricted pants, and I could only continue to stare at the doctor. I remember thinking how old he looked. Why did I pick a doctor that looked so old?

As we stood there, someone inside the nursery walked over to the window and tugged the blind down.

I waited in the hallway near the emergency doors while they arranged for the transfer. The other hospital was only fifteen minutes away, and soon I heard the distant shriek of a siren that steadily became louder, and then I heard the ambulance arrive outside. At the same time that the ambulance driver turned off the siren, a set of automatic doors opened at the far end of my hospital's hallway.

I watched as a group of people, three or four, burst through the automatic doors and sprinted down the long hallway. They were pushing Elizabeth's incubator on a wheeled cart as they bolted toward the waiting ambulance, the wheels making a high screeching noise. Two men from the ambulance charged through the automatic doors on their end, dashed to the incubator, grabbed the cart, and rushed it back toward the ambulance.

Moments before the ambulance team hustled her out the door, Joe walked in the emergency room door. There was so much commotion happening with Elizabeth's transfer that there was little time for him to see her. I was standing braced against the wall to stay out of the way, but Joe had a chance to hurriedly glance at her in the incubator. The only thing I was aware of was that I could not hear Elizabeth crying. Why was she not crying?

Someone held the button that kept the automatic doors open, and the ambulance team quickly loaded the incubator into the ambulance before the siren wailed again. Then she was gone.

I watched the automatic doors close with a soft swishing sound, and I stood there staring at the closed doors.

I knew I would never see Elizabeth again.

No one spoke to us. Joe and I remained standing in the hall while the hospital staff walked back up the hallway and vanished through their automatic doors. We stood there like total strangers, Joe and I; there were no hugs, no crying, and no questions regarding what happened or whether I was okay. Finally I said, "Joe, the baby's dying. I want you to go to the other hospital and stay with her. I don't want her to die alone."

To this day, I'm not sure if Joe went to the other hospital or not. I do not believe he did, because later I heard him mention to someone that the only time he ever saw Elizabeth was when they were wheeling her out. I know for sure he was not there when she died. I think he went home and went to bed.

Astonishing as it seems to me today, we never discussed Elizabeth's birth or death again.

Joe went back through the swishing doors; I walked back to my room, climbed into bed, curled up into a ball, and drew the sheet up over my head. I did not want to look at anyone or anything. Within a few minutes, the doctor came into my room with a nurse who gave me another shot of something.

I'm not sure when, but sometime later in the night, the doctor came in again, woke me up, and told me that Elizabeth had died. I remember him standing there and reaching over to touch my arm, but that is all I remember. I could not even cry.

Joe called the next morning. "Carolyn, the doctor called and said the baby has died."

"I know, the doctor told me last night." That is when I knew Joe did not stay at the other hospital—if he went at all—because the doctor had to call and tell him she had died.

"Well, I've been talking to the hospital, and if we want to bury her, it will cost a hundred dollars to make the arrangements to send her to a funeral home. I don't see any sense in spending the money. I think since she only lived one day, we should just let the hospital take care of the body."

"Okay, if that's what we're supposed to do." That was the end of our conversation, and I fell back to sleep.

Looking back on our short, abrupt conversation, I now regret I did not have the wherewithal to recognize that most husbands would have had the decency to come to the hospital and tell me in person that our child had died. Even the doctor had come to me personally. But Joe did not come, and somehow at the time—and for years later—I considered that behavior reasonable.

Later, the phone rang again. "Carolyn, it's Gary Buell." Gary was a good friend of ours who owned a mortuary and funeral home. "I'm so sorry to hear about the baby. Let me come and get her. I have a casket and I'll arrange to have her buried in the Springfield cemetery. I know a minister, and he'll be there, too."

"Okay. Thank you, Gary." That was all I could say to him.

Joe called again, and I told him Gary was going to take care of Elizabeth. "Joe, I want you to go to the cemetery with Gary and the minister. One of us should be there."

Later I found out Joe did not go.

By midmorning, the doctor came in and told me he was moving me to a different floor, one away from the nursery, and away from the happy mothers with their healthy newborn babies. I'm sure the sight of me was unsettling to them.

"No, I'm going home." I was adamant.

"You can't go home. I've already lost one patient, and I don't want to lose another." He sounded shocked I would even consider it, as it was standard practice during that time for women to stay in the hospital for three days after having a baby.

"Well, I'm going home anyway. I'll come to your office tomorrow if you want, but either you check me out of the hospital or I'm climbing out the window and walking home in this hospital gown." I had already figured out how to climb out the window on our ground floor and had decided to leave that way if he would not check me out. I'm not sure why it did not occur to me to just walk out the front door.

The doctor released me, and I called Lucille to come get me. Lucille, not Joe. At this point, no one cared if I used their damn phone or not. Lucille came and took me home—it was two miles away. Joe was surprised when we came in the front door. We did not discuss Elizabeth. Without a word, I walked into the bedroom and went to bed.

It would take another twelve years before I realized that Elizabeth and my marriage died on exactly the same day.

There are a number of things that have enraged me about Elizabeth's life and death.

First, and by far the most important, was that I agreed to have her thrown out with the trash, like she had no value. Wrapped up in used sheets and tossed out with other people's body parts. Who agrees to do something like that? What the hell was the matter with me? And what the hell was the matter with Joe for even suggesting such a gruesome end for our beautiful baby daughter?

For a long time, I wanted to exclusively blame Joe and his damn issues with money. Everything was about the money to him. Better to discard her little body than to have to spend a hundred dollars! I hated him for that. And I hated myself for agreeing.

I wanted to forget my part in this decision. I rationalized that I was drugged up and did not know what I was doing, that I did not understand the magnitude of what he was suggesting. I wanted to blame anyone but myself. It was not me, I would tell myself. This was all Joe's fault.

But I was a mother, and I should have screamed and kicked at the mere thought. I should have gone to the other hospital in the ambulance. I should have stayed with Elizabeth while she died. I should have been with her when she was buried.

I should have done all of those things, but I did not do them. Now I have to forever live with that.

Joe and I are both equally guilty. It is on me as much as it is on him, and I cannot escape that. There are some things we do in life that are so egregious, so coldhearted, that we are not entitled to a *pass*. That is how I felt about my part in the decision—I did not have the right to ask for forgiveness.

Gary Buell, God bless him, took Elizabeth to the cemetery. The minister was there, and she had a decent burial, no thanks to her parents. She is buried in a section labeled Miscellaneous. There is no marker for her, not even a small rock.

Year after year, I promised myself that I would take the boys and go to the small cemetery in Springfield, Oregon, locate her burial site, and beg Elizabeth for forgiveness. I promised that I would plant a pink dogwood tree in her memory. I promised and promised, but I never went. I just did not have it in me. I believed that I did not deserve to find peace of mind—that I should suffer. And I did.

Elizabeth's memory was a wound so deep, it pierced my soul and would not heal. My behavior was so unconscionable that I believed I did not have the right to ask for forgiveness.

After Elizabeth's death, anytime I thought of her—or even if I was trying not to think of her—I could hear her crying her painful, agonizing wail. I would try to shut it out, as if distancing myself would ease my suffering and my participation in the decision, but it was always there, waiting to draw me back in time.

Eventually, I visualized a long, dark hallway with open doors on both sides, reminding me of what a reflection looks like if you hold one mirror up to another. The image in the mirror appears to go on forever. That is what the hallway looked like, open door after open door as far as I could see, until they blended into infinity. Behind the doors, I could hear Elizabeth crying.

I would start down the hallway closing the doors, first on one side of the hallway and then turning to close the doors on the other side of the hallway. The doors opened inward, so I would reach into the dark room, take hold of the doorknob, and pull it toward me until the door closed with a dull thud. I continued, door after door, until eventually, I was so exhausted from closing them that I would fall asleep.

Now, I'm here at this cemetery that has so oddly called to me. I take a deep breath and ask Elizabeth to forgive Joe and me for our compassionless behavior, for our total lack of sensitivity. I ask her to forgive her mother for not fighting for her, and for not being with her when she died, or when she was buried. I tell her I will always love her, and I will never forget her.

I forgive Joe, and then I forgive myself.

An unexpected flood of relief rushes through me. For the first time in twenty-two years, I feel like I can breathe, and my chest does not feel so tight. I take a few minutes, then gather up my things and begin walking back to Jan's house.

I stop. Oh my God! I do not believe this. Tears begin to stream down my face. In the distance, I can hear a church bell softly tolling. I stand there listening to the pealing before I realize that something is different. I do not hear another sound—it is Elizabeth. Her crying has stopped.

And then I sob.

Chapter 19

THE PREDATOR

After I leave the old church in Rhode Island, I continue north, sustained by an overwhelming sense of peace; the piercing wound in my heart has healed.

I asked for forgiveness—even though I believed I did not deserve it—and I feel it was granted. It was Elizabeth's forgiveness that has finally set me free, removing the heavy guilt, shame, and sadness that had consumed me for many years. I now know there is infinite power in the act of forgiveness, whether we are the one asking for it, or the one granting it to others. It is a rare gift to be cherished and appreciated, and I will always feel blessed.

As I leave Portland, Maine, I see the first highway sign that points me toward home. West 25!

After forty-four days on the road, I cannot stop smiling at a simple road sign. Flipping up the visor of my helmet, I yell out for all to hear: "I'm headed *west!*"

The last couple days I have been visiting with my sister-in-law, Lorraine's, relatives in Hudson, Massachusetts. Lorraine's brother, Paul, and his wife welcome me into their home. They have two active little boys who remind me of Brian and Travis when they were that age, and it is a heaven-sent joy to watch them wrestle like bear cubs.

Paul is a talented artist and has a business, Sign Logics. His tagline, *We Sell Striking Signs*, is painted on his truck. Surrounding the words are lightning bolts that give the painting a dazzling impact. When Paul sees my plain black half helmet, he offers to make it more interesting. He paints the outline of the United States on it with *50/50* written inside the map—fifty states at fifty. I love it!

I have met Lorraine's parents, Flo and Alvin, a number of times when they've flown out to Oregon, and we now have a chance to visit and catch up. Paul's brother, Michael, and his family come by so I can meet their children. It is good to be surrounded by family again.

I cannot get over how happy I am to be heading toward home.

* * *

I'm overwhelmed with sorrow.

The landscape I'm riding through reminds me of the sloping wheat fields of my parents' ranch, except unthinkable numbers of young men did not fight and die there.

The beauty and peacefulness of the gentle rolling hills of Gettysburg, Pennsylvania, belie the massive carnage that took place there over a three-day period in July 1863. That clash of the Union and Confederate forces during the American Civil War left some fifty thousand soldiers from both armies dead, wounded, missing, or captured. Gettysburg is the site of one of the bloodiest battles of the Civil War and is one of the most visited places in the United States.

I remember going to a football stadium once that held twenty-five thousand fans, a tremendous number of people in a relatively small space. I cannot begin to visualize nearly twice that many soldiers lying dead or dying in the pleasant rural vicinity of Gettysburg. How did doctors help the wounded? How could anybody begin to bury so many bodies?

As I walk near aged cannons, other visitors are talking quietly. This is sacred ground, and a respectful demeanor seems to come instinctively to visitors. The magnitude of loss on these fields overwhelms my desire to speak.

A tour bus is loaded with people. They will travel from one battlefield site to another with a guide who explains the war strategies of the various generals. Even though I could go with them, I prefer to take a handheld audio player offered by the staff and travel alone. I want to try and grasp the enormity of this war.

Soon I find myself on a knoll overlooking a lifeless green field. It is quiet and serene up here, and it is difficult to imagine the chaos that took place a century and a half ago. The noise would have been ear shattering: cannons exploding, horses shrieking, and tens of thousands of handguns, rifled muskets, breechloaders, and repeating weapons continually discharging. The agonizing screams of men dying are unimaginable.

I visit the medical museum. I'm shocked to see its rusted, crude artifacts—handsaws and hatchets—used to quickly remove injured arms and legs before infection could spread throughout the body. It must have been brutal for the thousands of wounded and for those who had to treat them. Saving lives was the goal, not saving limbs. Medical supplies were quickly in short supply, and sawdust was packed into body parts to stop bleeding. It saps my strength to simply read the literature and view the rudimentary tools used to try to save lives.

I cannot image what the families of these young men went through. Wives, mothers, fathers, grandparents, sisters, and brothers, many who would never know what became of their loved ones. How can we begin to understand the enormity of this kind of loss?

While I know this war is an important part of American history and necessary to remember, after two depressing days I'm grateful to move on.

* * *

My motorcycle has died.

It is Sunday, and for the last five hours, I have been sitting at a tollbooth in West Virginia. Locating a tow truck able to deal with a motorcycle is a pain, but eventually the answering service tells me someone is on the way. The folks at the tollbooth are kind, giving me coffee and water and offering to help any way they can. Several travelers also offer help, but without a tow truck, there is nothing anyone can do.

The bike makes an odd noise, but I rule out the battery—it is new—and the starter. My best guess is the voltage regulator has fizzled out, which is not something I can fix. There is nothing to do but sit here and watch cars stop and go at the tollbooth. Most people throw coins into a rectangular container attached to the wall. Sometimes they miss, but with so many cars waiting to get through, the agent waves them on anyway. I wonder if they miss deliberately if they do not have enough change. Since I do not have anything better to do, I keep track of the hits and misses, thinking it might be an interesting statistic for someone. But, before long, here comes the tow truck.

Once loaded and tied down with bright yellow straps, my bike sits on the back of the tow truck. I'm astonished by how much stuff is stacked on the rear fender. It is higher than the windshield. My bags do not look so imposing when the bike is parked on the ground, and it makes me wonder how some men travel with only a blanket rolled up near the windshield of their motorcycle.

As it turns out, the Harley dealership is closed on Sundays, which means I will have to hire another truck in the morning to tow it over to their service department. In the meantime, we have been dropped off at a motel. Since I previously purchased an extended warranty in case of a breakdown, this forced delay is actually an unplanned-for luxury.

If I'm more than a hundred miles from home, my warranty will pay for my room for three days and for a rental car. I pass on the car because I want to rest for a few days, and I enjoy walking for a change. This is great—a real bed, a hot shower, and a TV.

Life does not get any better than this.

* * *

On Monday, I arrange to have the bike towed to the shop later in the day.

I have extra time, want to color my hair, and decide to walk down to a small store about a half mile away. It is only seven in the morning, but already the weather is warm and pleasant outside. I slick my hair into a ponytail, slip on a pair of tights and a baggy sweatshirt, grab my sunglasses, and head out. There is no reason to wear my heavy leather coat, so I leave it hanging in the closet.

It never occurs to me to take my gun.

The walk to the store is uneventful. I follow a narrow, potholed street with repair equipment sitting on both sides of the road. No workmen are around and I'm the only one on this quiet and peaceful road. I buy my hair coloring and head back toward the motel.

I'm about halfway back to the motel when I hear a car approach from the rear. The car is scarcely moving, the tires thumping softly into the potholes. As the car creeps past me, I briefly look at the driver, a young man, maybe thirty, with disheveled bleached-blond hair. He is driving an older black GTO and deliberately sits so low in the seat, I'm surprised he can see over the dashboard. Neither of us acknowledges the other as he passes; this is not a friendly encounter. Instantly, my nerves tingle and I'm on guard. I have seen his type before in my law office. This man has the look of a predator.

The man drives slowly toward the end of the road, and I can tell by the way his head is tilted he is watching me in the rear-view mirror. I straighten up and continue walking, but I do not run. It is important not to show fear, but the hairs on the back of my neck prickle.

The road is narrow, and with the heavy equipment in the way, he cannot turn around on this narrow street. Cement barriers obstruct the end. He has no choice but to drive to the barriers, turn left, go around the block, and come up from behind me again. I see the motel in the distance and start walking faster.

Shit. I hear the car slowly start up the street again. I glance around for a rock or something threatening, but there is only hard dirt. I have the small package in my hand, but it is not a weapon. I take several deep breaths to calm myself.

He is methodically closing the gap between us.

Once, when Steve and I were sitting in a booth at a bar, a guy standing somewhere behind us started yelling at Steve. Steve gently pushed me into the corner of the booth and told me to stay there. He got up and turned to face the man. I could tell by the look on Steve's face there was going to be trouble. I expected

Steve to take a fighting stance, put his hands up, double his fists, and get ready to fight.

Instead, I watched the most amazing transformation take place. Steve slowly positioned himself with his legs slightly apart. His shoulders relaxed and dropped, his arms hanging loose at his sides. This happened in one smooth movement as he leaned slightly forward. There was no tension revealed by his body language. The astounding result was one very dangerous-looking and frightening individual.

For the first time since Steve and I had been going together, I saw the man that my father had warned me about.

Steve gradually lifted his right hand, tipped his head slightly, cupped his ear, and never took his eyes off the other guy.

"What's that?" His voice was soft; his two words low and menacing.

The stranger froze and started apologizing. He thought Steve was someone else, or at least that is what he said. That image of Steve's physical conversion has always stayed with me.

This time the predator creeps up and stops his car beside me. He does not move from his slumped position, only his head turns toward me. I stop, straighten up, and turn and square myself to face him while relaxing my shoulders and arms. Slowly I reach up with one hand and push my sunglasses onto my head.

I want him to see my eyes.

He needs to understand this is not going to go down easily for either of us. Neither of us moves, speaks, nor blinks. It seems like forever as we stare at one another, then almost imperceptibly, the car begins to edge forward. I watch him drive to the barrier and turn the corner.

When he is out of sight, I take off at a dead run toward the motel. I know I will not get away with stares a second time. I reach the motel, run up the stairs, and lock the door to my room. My heart is racing as I crack the curtain and watch his black car pull into the motel parking lot. He circles the motel a couple of times and then leaves.

Later, when I have time to think about it, I decide he must have seen me at the store. Otherwise, it does not make sense why someone would be on that deserted road this early in the morning, unless they worked there. I probably looked younger than I am, with my sunglasses on and my hair in a ponytail.

That dangerous encounter ends my relaxing three days. Now I check every black car I see.

And my gun is always with me.

* * *

I cannot lift my motorcycle up off the kickstand.

The bike is packed, I'm ready to leave, and the bike leans to the left, immobile. I straighten the front wheel, turn it hard to the right, and then shift my weight to the right while pulling up on the left handlebar. Nothing. Finally, I ask a man who stands nearby and witnesses this fiasco if he could shove the bike upright. He does, and, once upright, I thank him, start the engine and drive out of the KOA.

For the past several days, I have solicited help from men, women, and teenagers. They are good sports and sympathetic to my predicament. I explain that the muscles across the small of my back were injured, and now I'm unable to lift the bike off the kickstand. Everyone willingly helps, but this is a serious problem. I must make sure someone is around when I park to eat, get gas, ask for directions, or get off the bike for any reason. In addition to the crisis of not being able to lift the bike's weight off the kickstand, it is impossible to push the bike backward by myself.

I'm in constant pain.

My injury occurred when the dealer replaced the voltage regulator. I needed new tires and a ten-thousand-mile checkup, and when the mechanics went through the bike, someone must have inadvertently readjusted the foot pegs. Since my feet rest on the foot pegs all day, any modification affects the way I sit on the bike. Several hours pass before a dull, stabbing pain in the small of my back gets my attention. Kicking the foot pegs forward with my boots, the pressure on my back is immediately relieved, but, unfortunately, it is too late.

I spend a couple days resting and applying massive amounts of BenGay to my back. The recovery is slow, and I stink. If I'm in a grocery store or gas station, I smile innocently and ask, "Who smells like BenGay?" They are onto me, though, because everyone around me moves away.

An injury is the kiss of death on this trip. So far I have been relatively lucky. A continual series of mild aches and pains in my shoulders, neck, arms, hands, fingers, thighs, and legs is always there. However, this constant, shooting pain in the small of my back is a serious setback, and it will limit how far I can travel each day. This stresses me, because my plan was to make better time while heading west. At best, it will be September before I reach the Rockies, and there is a strong possibility that it will be snowing by then.

The vibration from the engine persistently jars my back, making it impossible to relax. I must get my mind right, or the trip will end. There are at least fifteen or so states remaining, which means another three or four thousand miles to ride. I shift my position on the motorcycle seat and a debilitating shock of pain radiates across the small of my back.

I grasp the handlebars, slump forward, and try to breathe.

* * *

This is all Max's fault.

I was riding along the southern border of Ohio, minding my own business, when a guy pulled up beside me on a Honda motorcycle and wanted to talk. He had seen my picture in some newspaper and was interested in my trip. It was impossible to hear each other over the roar of our motorcycles, so we decided to stop for a cup of coffee. I was ready to give my back a rest, anyway.

When Max and I had our midnight chats, he told me I "owe it to my public" to flirt with men. Gentle flirting, he informed me, gives men a sense of excitement. This happy feeling then translates into the fantasy they could have some very fine specimen of a woman, much like myself, for their very own.

Oh, yeah, and at the end of our tête-à-tête, if I'm not interested, I must tell them, "The idea that I would be buck-ass naked with you is a total turnoff," and that "the vision of us together makes me feel like I have vomit in my throat." Well, Max did not go quite as far as that last one, but that was the idea.

Billy Bob and I visited over a cup of coffee, and I discovered he was a Louisiana businessman traveling north to visit his mother in Michigan. How sweet. I liked the idea that my sons might travel the width of the United States to see their ol' mom. We had a pleasant conversation, and I mentioned I was staying at the KOAs. This disclosure did not concern me because I was headed south and he was headed north. I was amiable and perhaps *casually* flirty as duty demanded. He was definitely not my type, even though he was a nice guy. I skipped the buck-ass naked speech.

Almost a week later, here I am in a Kentucky KOA Kamping Kabin slathered down with BenGay. My back is killing me and

I have returned from the shower—no makeup, wet hair—and I'm hunched over in pain. I hear a motorcycle outside and its distinctive sound tells me it is a Honda. The rider stops and parks in front of my cabin. There is a knock on the door. You have got to be kidding me. Sure enough, it is Billy Bob.

I have no idea how he found me with all the KOAs in these multiple states. It is so unbelievable that I do not bother to ask. I learn he has cut his trip short, no doubt in a desperate attempt to unearth me. I do not invite him inside; instead we sit on the porch and talk. He gives me his card and asks if I want to have dinner at his hotel. I pass. He hints at more intimacy in case I'm too dense to pick up on this breathtaking opportunity. After an hour or so, he seems to finally understand that I'm not interested and leaves.

Thanks, Max. That tidbit about flirting was very helpful.

* * *

Kentucky, the state that is well known for bluegrass, racehorses, and miles and miles of white fences, has a dilemma; most of the white fences have vanished.

When I was five, my parents bought me a horse, probably because I whined incessantly day and night about my desperate need, until I finally wore them both down. Trigger, a palomino, was about twenty-five when my parents bought her. She was slow and gentle, and I named her after movie star Roy Rogers's steed—Trigger was the perfect horse for a little girl. Later, when we moved to my parent's ranch, I had several horses.

On this trip, Kentucky was near the top of my list for states to visit. As much as anything, I wanted to see the horse farms, green fields, and sparkling white fences. As it turns out, though, the majority of the fences on the smaller farms are painted black.

A local rancher tells me that black paint wears better and the dark fences look great for about five years, while white fences show chips and need to be repainted every two years. The difference in cost is substantial.

I travel down Interstate 75 and head into the Kentucky Horse Park, a working horse farm and educational theme park. Opened in 1978, the park is "dedicated to man's relationship with the horse." There are numerous special events and horse shows, and I'm pleased to see beautiful white fences everywhere.

It is late in the day, so my time here is limited. However, I want to visit the statue of Man o' War, considered one of the greatest thoroughbred racehorses of all time. He won twenty of twenty-one major races. The impressive statue is life size, and the animal was huge, but what fascinates me most are his hoof prints stamped in cement. The brochure says the hoof prints are spaced to match Man o' War's twenty-five- to twenty-eight-foot racing stride! I pace it off. The distance is astonishing and I figure it is almost the length of a small school bus. It is unbelievable to imagine the blazing speed and the power needed to cover this expanse.

Man o' War competed for two years and revived a struggling sport. He was a national hero, joining the ranks of Babe Ruth in the 1920s. The brochure tells me Man o' War brought international recognition to Kentucky breeders and made the United States the racing center of the world during those years. When he retired, he held five American records at different distances and had earned more money than any thoroughbred.

It would have been wonderful to see the magnificent Man o' War race and be given the chance to rub his soft nose.

I return to my steed and we roar off to the KOA.

* * *

"Would you like to sit on my motorcycle?"

Three young girls, twelve to fourteen, stand nearby and watch while a woman from a local television station in Bowling Green, Kentucky, interviews me. The TV folks leave and enough time has passed that the engine has cooled—important because it is hot outside and the girls are in shorts.

"You'll need to ask your mom if it's okay." Away they charge and then quickly return, cameras in hand. Each girl takes a turn sitting on the bike while the other two snap pictures. They are giggly and happy. Many times there are children of all ages, boys and girls, hanging around during the interviews, so I have started carrying a small notebook in my pocket. I like to give them something positive to think about.

I ask each girl her name and write a message. It is usually a quote that my mother used to tell me: "You can do anything you want to do" or "You can be anything you want to be." I sign it and hand one to each of them. The young girls read their notes, carefully fold them, stick their notes in their pockets, and then they are off.

Several hours pass before it occurs to me that the typical pain of anxiety or longing I usually feel around young girls is gone.

The next morning, I begin to backtrack and will make a large loop that takes me five hundred miles out of my way. This is okay, because I promised to visit an elderly man. My next stop is Martinsville, Missouri.

Population: 44.

Chapter 20

COUSIN SHIRLEY'S OLD DOG

This gravel road is a killer.

The treacherous gravel is thick, coarse, and jagged. It shifts without warning under my tires every time the front wheel is slightly adjusted. I have been on the road for two months, and the last thing I need to do is dump the bike, injure myself, and have to cancel the rest of my trip.

My back aches from trying to manhandle the bike. My nerves are shot as I follow in J.D.'s tire tracks where the gravel is more solidly packed. We head toward his farm in the country.

I have arrived in Martinsville to visit J.D., my cousin Shirley's widower husband. J.D. was seriously injured in a tractor accident a year ago and almost died. Neither of us would be able to lift the motorcycle if it suddenly crashed. His house is in sight, but I will not be able to relax until I'm off this dangerous road. His is the only house for miles around.

These are relatives I hardly know. In 1945, when Shirley was eighteen, she traveled from Oregon to Missouri to visit her grandparents for the summer. There she met a tall, handsome young farmer, and they fell in love. By the end of summer, Shirley chose not to return to the comforts of city life and the security of her family. The young couple married and began the task of farming eighty acres of rural land given to J.D. by his father.

Life was ruthless; summer scorched the crops, and winter brought with it long months of freezing cold, snow, and isolation. Indoor plumbing was a luxury they could not afford. They knew it would be years, if ever, before they had a bathroom in the house. A strong-willed couple, they hung on, raised two children, and became one—a formidable force against the odds.

It was diabetes that finally claimed Shirley. Her illness was long and painful; she was in and out of the hospital and almost blind. It was a year ago when J.D. came home from the fields to find that his only love had died in her favorite chair. Now, after forty-eight years of married life, J.D., seventy-one, is alone for the first time.

We turn off the gravel road onto a long dirt driveway that leads to an old, dilapidated house and a weathered, detached garage. In a field, there are a couple of horses and a white colt born four days ago.

The house was built in 1932. Even from a distance, I can tell that it was past its prime many years ago. As we pull up to the house, the paint is peeling, the structure rotting. Although it is summer, the windows are covered with blue plastic tarps to keep out the wind and rain. J.D. tells me there "ain't a reason to take 'em down 'cause I live here alone."

As I get off my motorcycle, a shabby, older dog rises from under a tree. He hobbles toward me, barking. His voice is fragile and cracked.

"Shut up!" J.D. yells. The dog continues toward me and croaks out a warning.

I do not like it when dogs charge like that, threatening with their ferocity and potential violence. Although he is a big dog, he seems harmless enough, however; he is old, weak with age, and crippled. What is left of his coat is matted with dirt. Pieces of leaves and grass cling to his hair.

His coat shows the ravages of a severe case of mange. Clumps of hair are missing, and I can see his skin is red from continually scratching at fleas or parasitic mites. He has been resting under the shade of a tree but has risen to protect the only home he has ever known.

The dog comes straight toward me and pokes his nose in my crotch.

I do not like that either; it is embarrassing. However, unless I intend to make a scene over the incident, there is not much to do about it. After smelling me, the old dog backs up, looks up at me, and begins to wag his tail.

"You're the first woman who's been here since Shirley died," J.D. explains in an effort to excuse the old dog's behavior. Then J.D. just stands there looking at the old dog and sighs.

"Ya know, I never did like that dog, and that dog never did like me. But he was Shirley's dog, so I just sorta leave him be."

As we head toward the house, the old dog moves to my side, occasionally brushing my leather pants as I walk. I find myself slowing my steps so he can keep up.

Once indoors, I see the inside of the house is starting to deteriorate. The faded, stained wallpaper is peeling from the walls; the place smells stale, stagnant. Still, there is evidence of Shirley's touch: handmade afghans drape over chairs and the couch, pictures of children are placed in homemade frames made of lace and fabric. A small plaster rocking chair with a little old man and woman sits on a shelf. Both figurines peer over half-rimmed reading glasses.

Some of J.D.'s clothes are lying where he left them this morning. His socks are on the floor, his worn bib overalls thrown across a chair. He says, "It don't matter where I leave my clothes because no one comes around here anyway." The only living plants in the house sit by his chair. They were given to him when Shirley died. He says he keeps them close so he can water them.

Walking downstairs to the basement, I see shelves and shelves of fruit jars, now mostly empty. J.D. says canning, baking, and freezing food were a necessity so the family could survive the winters, and that was Shirley's job. A fairly new washer and dryer sit in the corner, the water flowing into a hole in the ground.

As I go outside to walk around, the old dog limps over and follows close beside me. I reach down, speak softly to him, and pat his head. When I brush the hair from my face, my hand smells the way it does when you pet an old animal. I do not mind and reach down to pet him again. His tail slowly wags.

"Come on, old dog. Let's go take a look at that colt."

It is strange how I came to be here. Somehow, J.D. heard about my trip, called my mother, and asked her if I would stop to see him. The last time I saw either of my cousins was thirty-five years ago. However, Mom said J.D. sounded so lonely and eager about the idea of company that I promised to visit.

We decide to take the car so J.D. can show me Martinsville and the countryside. As we leave, the old dog shuffles back and lies down under the tree. I mention the gravel, and J.D. explains that heavy gravel is common and necessary because of the deep snow, pervasive ice, and heavy rainfall in winter. He says if anyone became trapped on one of these remote farms, it could be deadly.

I'm struck by the simplicity and beauty of the area. Soft, rolling hills stretch for miles. The land is flat overall, but when we crest the small hills, I can see far into the distance. The clouds float and move across the horizon like soft, puffy, cotton balls. This is farming country and I can appreciate how Shirley fell in love with the land.

J.D. tells me the story about how he and Shirley met. He says the locals immediately told her that J.D. was "retarded" and "not good enough for her." However, Shirley saw past J.D.'s physical problem, which was an acute hearing loss. He says Shirley loved him just the way he was.

We walk into the cemetery where Shirley is buried. He says that the funeral home was packed with people at her funeral. J.D. leans down to smooth the ground where her new headstone will be placed. He points out his plot next to hers.

Later, he tells me about her last visit to the hospital. Evidently, the diabetes had left her weak and with little control over her body.

"She'd dirty herself and that embarrassed her, 'cause she was a proud woman. She didn't want the nurses to see her soiled underpants. So every day I would take'm home in a plastic bag, wash'm, and dry'm, and bring the clean ones back to her. One day she asked me if I minded. I told her no, I didn't. And ya' know, I didn't, cause I knowed she'd a did it for me."

That evening J.D. offers me one of the remaining pieces of apple pie that Shirley had made. He has kept the pieces in the freezer for a special occasion. We sit and talk about loneliness and death. I think the realization that he might spend the next ten or more years alone is on his mind.

"Do ya think we ever get over the death of someone we love?"

"No, J.D., I don't think we do. I believe that in time we accommodate death because there's no other choice. I've tried to move the death experience into the back of my mind, because I've found that's the only way I can move forward with life. I keep the memories."

"But it's been a year, and I still feel awful and miss Shirley so much. Sometimes people tell me I need to get over it."

"Of course you miss Shirley. You two married when you were kids and have lived together almost fifty years. You know, J.D., there's not a timeline for grief. You don't have to feel like you should 'get over it'—because you don't. It's okay to feel miserable and sad." He stares at his empty pie plate.

"I'm a tough old buzzard."

"I know you are."

In the morning, J.D. apologetically tells me he had a bad night. He says it has been a long time since he broke down. He believes he is supposed to be strong and not let his emotions show. I hug J.D. and tell him it is okay for tough old buzzards to cry. At first, I think it is my visit that has upset him, but really, I believe it is the finality of eating the last of Shirley's pies.

The next day we decide to visit J.D.'s son, Veryl, and his family. I feel the tightness in my neck and shoulders as we drive on the gravel road. I'm leaving the next morning and realize I'm anxious about riding on this hazardous road again.

Veryl lives several hours away and, like his father, is a farmer. Life has not been easy for his family either. J.D.'s daughter, Janine—a schoolteacher—also lives hours from him. It is rare for all of them to get together, but J.D. does not want to leave his farm.

It is dark when we head back to J.D.'s house, and again my thoughts return to that damn gravel road. Early on, I decided to trust my intuition and to thank Ada, my guardian angel, each night for a safe journey. We are on the back roads when I silently ask Ada to give me a sign if everything will be all right in the morning.

It has been pitch black outside for the past several hours. Only the headlights and the stars light our way. We wind through the sparse, rural countryside and then enter a tiny borough. Three or four houses line each side of the street. Ahead, the only streetlight glows on a solitary green street sign. From a distance I can tell the writing is small. As we pass the isolated light, I glance at the street sign and see the lone word: ADA. All my tension dissolves.

When we arrive back at J.D.'s house and I open the car door, the old dog is there. He immediately rests his big head on my thigh. He looks at me with his watery eyes and I pet him and scratch his ears. I'm sure Shirley must have done this a thousand times.

The next morning as I pack my motorcycle, the old dog never leaves my side. He follows me back and forth from the house to the bike, staring intently at me. He knows I'm leaving.

J.D. and I hug each other. He is crying. He will lead me to the highway, and we will wave goodbye. He leaves first in his car. I stop, kneel down to talk to and pet the old dog one last time, and then wait for him to go back to his spot under the tree. He never moves.

It happens when I start the engine.

The dog lets out a long, low, mournful wail, the sound an animal makes when it is in pain. As I pull out of the driveway, he begins to follow me, hobbling faster in an effort to keep up. I think he will stop when he reaches the end of the long dirt driveway, but he continues on, howling that heart-wrenching sound.

Tears stream down my face as I turn onto the gravel road that will lead to town. As I crest the first rise, I look in my rearview mirror and see the old dog has finally stopped, no doubt exhausted from the effort. I ride down the backside of the rolling hill and crest the next. Each time I crest the following rise, I can see him growing smaller and smaller in my mirror as he stands there and watches me go.

After leaving Missouri, I'm upset for days. It breaks my heart that life has to be so difficult, so unfair. That people must settle for loneliness when all they really want is love. However, I believe my cousin Shirley was blessed. She had what few people ever know: the love of a good man, family, and the companionship of a devoted dog.

But, I must tell you, that as I ride on the lonely, quiet back-country roads, my thoughts drift.

I am haunted by the sound of that old dog.

Chapter 21

BREAKING FREE

I pass a group of happy-looking campers, wave, and head to a secluded area in the back of the KOA campground.

The Des Moines, Iowa, KOA is packed with families and travelers enjoying the last weeks of summer. Soon my odyssey will end and I want to take advantage of any opportunity to be alone. Nevertheless, before the bike is unloaded, six campers—couples, I presume—walk across the field and introduce themselves. They ask the standard questions about where I'm from and how long I have been on the road.

"We saw you pull in and wanted to invite you to join us. You don't have to be out here in this field by yourself."

"Thanks, that's really thoughtful of you, but I prefer to camp alone." Most find the idea of a woman traveling alone on a motorcycle unbelievable, but fascinating. These campers look at one another with surprise that I chose to be out in this field by myself.

I explain that the purpose of this trip was to address and over-come my fear of loneliness. What I have noticed throughout this journey is after I admit to a fear of living alone, the focus of the conversation changes and people want to talk about it. The fear of personal loneliness is a concern for far more people than I initially believed. This group is no exception.

A man in the group asks, "Are you still lonely?"

"No, I'm not. I was lonely and overwhelmed, though, when I started this trip several months ago. The idea that I'd be spending so much time by myself was unnerving, and sleeping alone in my tent freaked me out." A couple of the campers agree. "But as the weeks passed, I became more comfortable and the fear started to subside. Initially, it reminded me of getting into a river when the water's too cold. I didn't like the sensation and wanted to get out." I remove my tent and other items off my bike as we talk.

A tall, handsome man standing near a beautiful woman with long blonde hair chimes in, "I've felt like that before in the water, and I didn't like it either."

"Me neither. But then I discovered if I stayed in the water long enough, my body slowly adjusted to the temperature." I unhook a bungee cord to let loose my sleeping bag. "Eventually, I came to enjoy my time in the cold water. I didn't think that would be true, but it was."

A woman about twenty years old snickers. "I think I'd rather stay out of the cold water and get a tan on the beach." She is dressed in a hot-pink coordinated outfit that matches her nail polish. She reminds me of myself not that long ago, when how I looked was so important to me. I feel differently today.

"That's what I used to think, too, before I started this trip. Now I know if I buck up and take the plunge, the uncomfortable feeling will pass." The woman who would rather stay on the beach does not agree, but the blonde woman is interested, so I continue. "I'm not sure why doing what I didn't want to do ends up making me want to do it more. I'm as surprised as you are that I like being alone."

"When did it change for you?" The blonde woman steps closer to me.

"Not all at once, that's for sure." I pause to think about it a little more. "It happened so gradually that I can't pinpoint any particular time. If I can use the water analogy again, it's like I waded in up to my knees. Then I stood there freezing and shivering, trying to decide whether to move deeper into the water or return to shore." I open one of my saddlebags but decide to wait to pull out clothes until the group leaves. "There were many times I thought I must be out of my mind to be doing this."

"I'd have to agree with you on that," the beach woman adds, her lips curled in disgust.

"You're not the first one to tell me that," I say laughing.

"Tell me what you did next." The blonde woman has quietly been watching me. She discounts the beach lady with a wave of her hand, her wedding ring flashing in the sun.

"Well, in time I forced myself to walk in up to my waist. Inch by inch, I adjusted to the cold until I was submerged. It was being totally submerged that made me realize how happy I was in the deep water, even though it was cold. That's my best explanation."

"I'm afraid of ending up alone. It's always in the back of my mind." The blonde woman's face is serious, and her tall, handsome husband is dumbfounded. "I didn't know that," he adds softly and reaches for her hand. She continues.

"I might give wading a try, but I'd have to start with my toes."

"Toes are a great place to start. It's the starting that's important. It doesn't matter how long it takes to finish."

She walks over and gives me a tight hug, and the group heads back toward their tents. As I finish unloading the bike, my thoughts return to J.D.

J.D. has chosen to live his last years alone. When I asked him if he would consider remarriage, he was adamant that he would not live with another woman. He joked that he and Shirley were both "mean enough for each other." I have the sense, though, that J.D. believes it would be disrespectful to Shirley if he met someone he liked. It is a double-edged sword for him: his happiness verses Shirley's memory.

I think the fear of loneliness chips away at the spirit. It seems to me that the reality of loneliness is more difficult as people age. Perhaps that is why many older people are more inclined to look to God for solace within themselves.

The opportunity to discuss loneliness has occurred many times with both men and women on this journey. Some of them have said that they would rather have any companion because that is better than being alone. They believe that settling for a less-than-ideal partner insulates them from loneliness and can shield them from themselves. I empathize with their point of view because that is where I was not that long ago when deciding to settle for Robert.

I wish life were easier for everyone, but I believe each of us must find our own way in our own time. My road has been bumpy, but hope and optimism elbow me forward. When I think about relationships, I realize I'm still aggravated and angry with Robert because he abandoned me in Florida.

Tomorrow, while heading to Wisconsin, I'm going to try to figure out why this is still on my mind.

* * *

Relationships that end . . . are often not that easy to forget.

This morning I talked to Joy and she gave me the latest update on Robert. He bought a house in Portland and plans to stay in the area. I find that remarkable after his whining about Oregon's rain and cold weather. He has made it clear to his family that he will not be responsible for his mother's care. He is also spending time with a nice woman whom I know. He has moved on, and rather quickly.

When it comes to letting go of the relationship, I'm the problem. I need to figure out why I cannot let go of these feelings of anger when it is perfectly clear the relationship is over. More importantly, why am I still irritated, when the truth is, I'm relieved to be done with it?

One of the things I love about riding is it clears my mind. Hours of riding with the wind in my face helps me see things more sensibly, and my anger toward Robert wanes. Common sense prevails, and I begin to look at my problem from another perspective.

Over the years, I have met a number of nice men, any one of whom could have been a practical match for me. We usually had similar interests, they liked my sons, and we enjoyed each other's company. These men were interested in a committed relationship with me, but I did not have any romantic thoughts about them; they were like brothers to me.

Never once did I damn myself for the way I felt. It was impossible to snap my fingers and manufacture passionate feelings. So why be aggravated with Robert when his feelings changed? He is certainly entitled to choose whom he wants to spend his time with, as am I. This is just the way life is, and it is unreasonable to take it personally.

J.D.'s comments about Shirley's last few days in the hospital have stayed with me. He was devoted to her and did his best to help her because "she'd a did it for me." When Shirley was old and sick, her body betraying her, she could count on J.D. to help her through the unpleasant times without him complaining or resenting her. This is the true measure of love. Robert is not there for his mother, and I know when the time comes, he would not be there for me.

This is not the man I want to grow old with.

I want the type of love that Shirley and J.D. had, or nothing at all. If true love does not happen, so be it. My life will be full and joyful regardless of what destiny brings. One way or the other, though, I will not settle for less.

Taking a deep breath, I exhale and serenely release all my anger and frustration toward Robert into the wind.

* * *

I'm heading to Madison, Wisconsin, to meet Buzz Buzzelli, the editor of *American Rider* magazine, and to see if I can write some articles for his publication.

American Rider is a popular, nationally published magazine. Its focal points are articles about motorcycles, enthusiastic riders, rallies, and maintenance tips. Buzz and his wife have graciously invited me to spend the night at their home. This gives Buzz and me a chance to get to know one another, and we have a long talk.

"Carolyn, would you consider writing an article about your trip for *American Rider*?" We are sitting at the kitchen table drinking cups of steaming coffee. Buzz walks over to a coffee table, picks up the latest copy, and places it in front of me.

"I would love to. Actually, Buzz, I was hoping to write *several* articles for your magazine."

Buzz sets his coffee mug on the table and leans toward me. "Well, I'm looking for a woman to write a column that addresses the needs and goals of women riders. Today only about seven percent of women ride, but that statistic is increasing." I pick up the magazine and glance through it.

"I believe the time has come to give women riders more coverage in our magazine, and I think you would be perfect for the job. What do you think?"

I had read their magazine before, and Buzz is right. There are very few articles written by women. "I'm flattered you would think of me, Buzz, but the person who's truly knowledgeable about motorcycles and the industry is Joy. Joy has been an integral part of the motorcycle community for over twenty years. Plus, she is a good friend, and I don't feel comfortable taking a potential job away from her." I smile. "You know, Joy is very supportive of women riders. In fact, she was my mentor when I started riding about three years ago. I was a terrible rider, and without Joy's help, I probably would've killed myself." I take a sip of coffee. "I think you know Joy."

Buzz walks over, picks up the coffee pot, and refills our coffee cups.

"Yes, I do, and you're right that she has a wealth of information about the motorcycle industry. How about this? I'll publish a women's column and the two of you can alternate writing articles."

"Well, that sounds perfect! It will be fun, and I know Joy will be a big asset to your magazine."

I spend the night with the Buzz and his wife. The next morning, I head to Milwaukee, Wisconsin, home of the Harley-Davidson motorcycle plant.

I'm anxious to see the new Harleys coming off the assembly line.

* * *

The H-D parking lot is full of rows and rows of Harleys.

A television crew and a Harley-Davidson public relations man are there to meet me. As we walk toward the plant, we pass a long line of motorcycles on either side of the entrance. I think these are the new motorcycles because they are so clean and shiny. However, the public relations man tells me they belong to some of the men and women who work at the plant. My motorcycle is a muddy mess, but I park it beside the shiny bikes anyway.

Before my trip, I contacted H-D in the hope they might sponsor me, but I learned their policy is not to sponsor individuals. I expect to get the standard short tour given to tourists, but unbelievably, I'm treated like royalty and given a VIP tour.

Handed a hard hat and safety glasses by an employee, the three of us walk into the plant near an assembly line. A continuously moving pulley system transfers pieces from one end of the assembly line to the other. Each man or woman attaches a specific part provided at his or her work station. What starts out to be an odd collection of unique pieces ends up becoming a beautiful motorcycle. It is amazing to watch the coordinated interaction between the various people and witness the transformation. It reminds me of musicians playing a symphony.

After leaving the factory I head north to Upper Michigan and stop after a couple hours to stay in a motel; the muscles in the small of my back are an ongoing aggravation. I sound like a broken record with this endless complaining, and I am glad the same people are not around to hear me whine. I have made some progress, though, because I can finally lift the bike off the kickstand by myself.

The room is nice, and I have a chance to see today's television interview. This is rare since I'm always on the move and usually not near a TV. I'm about to change the channel when the weatherman mentions a cold front that is moving south across the Great Lakes into Upper Michigan and Wisconsin. However, the weather up north does not concern me—it is still summer—and I switch channels.

How cold could it possibly be?

* * *

It is freezing-ass cold up here!

The wind screams across Lake Superior and blasts into the right side of my motorcycle. The bike veers into the fast lane, and cars scramble to get out of my way. It is nerve-racking. The air is so cold, each time I exhale it fogs up the inside of my visor, and it is difficult to see. I flip up my visor for a couple seconds and the icy air dives into my lungs, hoping to warm itself, making it even harder to breathe. The muscles across the small of my back tighten. Inside my thin leather gloves, my fingers are frozen and numb. It is awkward to bend them when I need to pull in the clutch to shift gears with my left hand or brake with my right hand.

It would be wonderful to have my warm winter gloves, boots, heavy sweaters, neck warmers, silk underwear, and extra jacket. Unfortunately, these things are packed securely away in the box I sent home to Travis.

That moment of bravado, when I unloaded Robert and emotionally cleaned house by sending the bulk of my warm clothes home, made sense while basking in the sweltering sun in the Florida Keys, but not now. That lapse in judgment was a mammoth and dangerous mistake.

I left Iron River, Michigan, this morning expecting to cross upper Wisconsin on my way to Duluth, Minnesota, without any problems. However, the icy, aggressive wind dissipates my energy and after an hour of riding, I'm forced to find a place to stop. It takes another hour of drinking hot coffee to warm up before I can con myself into getting back on the bike. Fortunately, I still have my electric vest and face muff. Without these two items, there is no way I could cross Michigan, Wisconsin, or Minnesota.

The bitter wind increases near the bottom of Lake Superior. Once again it slams the bike into the fast lane. I struggle to maintain control, but I am unsuccessful. The bike continues to veer, forcing nearby cars to swerve. My body aches, but there is nothing to do except to continue on until I can find an exit.

Dear God!

In front of me, I see a gigantic, towering bridge jutting skyward. It is enormous. I have never seen or been on a bridge this high before. There is no way I can cross that bridge, because the wind's velocity will increase the higher I climb. It is impossible; the wind will knock the bike and me over.

I was so focused on the highway and the cars around me that I forgot to look up. Frantically searching for an exit sign, I discover they are all behind me. There is no choice but to cross the damn thing. As I climb higher, the wind's power increases and smashes into the side of the bike again, the crosswind almost shoving me over before I regain control. I check my rearview mirror and bless the drivers behind me; they are slowing to give me room to maneuver.

This is a very treacherous situation, and I force myself to control my breathing and concentrate. There is no margin for error here—I could easily be killed on this bridge. I pray and promise God all the good things I will do if I can get off this bridge safely. After an agonizing amount of time, I reach the top of the bridge and start down the other side. Still, the wind rages on.

I finally exit the bridge. I survived, barely.

Ragged, I somehow manage to locate the campground where I plan to spend the night. After checking into the KOA, the manager tells me about the terrible weather they are having. The campground is full, but they arrange for me to sleep in one of their small trailers on the property. It is too cold to sleep in the tent, and I need to get warm and relax my back.

"This is a historic cold spell for this time of year. We've broken all kinds of records. This storm has surprised all of us." I agree and mention the bridge, and he is shocked that I rode over it. He says the locals call it the *High Bridge*.

"It's over ten stories tall. They built it that high to accommodate the large ships coming and going from the Great Lakes. If I were you, I wouldn't go over it again in this wind. It's really dangerous for cars. Seems to me it would be nearly impossible on a motorcycle." He doesn't have to worry about that happening again.

Once settled, and after checking the map, I figure I have covered over ten thousand miles since leaving home. I have been on the road for sixty-six days. Oregon is still several thousand miles away. I groan and wish I were home.

I honestly do not know if I can ride that far.

Chapter 22

THE WINDS OF CHANGE

The coffee is hot and I warm my hands around the outside of my coffee cup.

I'm sitting at the counter in a small café in Duluth waiting for breakfast and feeling extremely sorry for myself. While looking at the map last night, I figured it would be another three hundred miles before reaching Fargo, North Dakota. That will take a minimum of six hours, but probably eight or nine in this weather. Outside the café, an American flag is flapping frantically, the treetops yielding to the wind.

The perky waitress brings my breakfast, leans forward, and whispers to me. "See that man sitting over there at the end of the counter?" I check out a guy who is about fifty, in a heavy plaid coat, wearing a wool cap, and nod. "He saw you ride in on your motorcycle, and he thinks you're Wynonna Judd."

"He thinks I'm Wynonna Judd? That's funny. I've heard she rides a motorcycle and has red hair, but seriously, I'm not Wynonna. If I sang, people would run screaming from the room."

She walks over to break the bad news to him and then comes back. "He doesn't believe you. He insists that you're Wynonna."

"You're kidding! Well, I'd tell him he could have my autograph for a hundred bucks, but I don't know how to spell Wynonna."

"I do." We are both giggling, highly amused with ourselves.

"That's perfect. I'll split the money with you." Back she goes, chats with him for a moment, and returns.

"Now he doesn't think you're Wynonna." Darn.

I finish my breakfast, thank the man for the compliment, and head for the bike. The interaction between the three of us has been entertaining and I feel much better as I head west. One way or another, I must reach Fargo before nightfall.

As expected, the ride to Fargo is grueling. I'm so tired after reaching the KOA, I feel like crying. The TV folks are scheduled to meet with me shortly, so I drink coffee to perk up. In the last couple of days, Annette Murray, my KOA contact, has arranged three interviews. My back is killing me, and I'm losing my gusto. Ever the show-woman, however, I put on my game face and actually enjoy the interview.

After the TV crew leaves, I notice everyone is watching the weather channel. This time I pay attention. It looks like there is a severe electrical thunderstorm headed our way. The television shows pictures of people an hour north of here holding hail almost the size of baseballs. We do not get storms like this in Oregon, and I am awed by the size of the hail.

The manager suggests I put the bike in the KOA garage and says it would be safer if I slept upstairs above the office, instead of outside in my tent. I opt for the garage and pass on the room.

Later it occurs to me that I must have a death wish.

A few of us walk outside and stand with our backs tight against the office wall. The electrical storm passes overhead and treats us to a dramatic light show. I have never seen anything like this. The storm is beautiful, dangerous, and captivating to watch. A jagged burst of lightning startles the black sky and is then followed by a resounding *boom*. We jump and laugh. Rain comes down in dark, harsh sheets, but the overhanging roof protects us. It is about nine o'clock at night when the storm finally wears itself out, and the locals tell me it has moved on. I trudge through a wet field to my tent. A man and his young daughter join me—their tent is near mine—but we are the only ones out here in this saturated field.

Earlier, I had pitched my tent under the only tree in this field. Burrowing into my sleeping bag and drained from the past few days, I quickly fall asleep. Sometime later in the night, the noise from a stunning detonation of thunder jars me awake. My heart is pounding and it is raining so hard, I fear the fragile tent might collapse. If the rain does not take this rickety thing down, surely the wind will. The storm has not moved on, it only paused for a while. Now it passes directly overhead with intermittent outbursts of lightning and thunder blasts.

I lie flat in my sleeping bag and weigh my options. Lightning flashes again, illuminating the inside of my tent. I'm concerned about that tree. My dad used to say, "Never stand under a lone tree in a lightning storm." I wonder if he meant tents, too. The storm continues in waves, each wave more violent than the one before. The little girl screams and her dad yells at me.

"Hey, lady, we're going to make a run for it and see if we can find someone from the store to help us. Do you want to come with us?" This is a dangerous decision; if lightning hits the soaked ground, they could be electrocuted. The pad under my sleeping bag protects me as long as it stays dry.

"Thanks, I'm going to stay here." I hear them running and the little girl screaming, but thank God no lightning strikes the ground.

The lightning and thunder continue throughout the night and I'm exhausted by morning. I should have been in the garage with my motorcycle or in the safety of the office. What the hell is the matter with me?

If I do not stop taking these unreasonable risks, I'm going to be killed.

* * *

Nebraska has been on my mind for the past week.

After leaving J.D.'s house, I swung west and meant to ride through the eastern part of that state. Somehow I missed my turnoff and ended up riding along a river on the Iowa side instead of Nebraska. Eventually, I crossed a bridge into Omaha, Nebraska, turned around, and headed back into Iowa. It was a quick trip and I was in Nebraska for mere minutes, probably riding less than a mile in that state.

When I started this adventure, one of my self-imposed rules was that the motorcycle wheels had to turn in each state before that state could be crossed off. The wheels turned in Nebraska, but it continues to bug me I shortchanged that state.

I leave Fargo, North Dakota, exhausted from last night's storm, and head south, back to Nebraska. The wind is now at my back and no longer blasts into the side of my bike. Immediately, I relax, and the tension leaves my body.

When I reach South Dakota, the sky clears and the weather warms. The rural countryside is beautiful and flat, and the view is unrestricted. Once in a while, there are remnants of a shack or an old barn, perhaps a hundred years old. It is desolate out here and I wonder how early families living on the plains managed. Where did they get water? Did they have neighbors? How did they deal with loneliness? Like J.D., these people must have been "tough old buzzards." I like to think that if these pioneers reconciled themselves to loneliness, then they could adapt to any adverse situation.

Finally, I understand that lonely people are not cowards.

I thought I was a coward when my fear of living alone consumed me. Now I know lonely people are brave to deal with this unsettling fear, and I am proud of anyone who admits they are afraid. I want to tell others it is okay to feel fear, any fear. If they will confront it, whatever fear they have will fade, and their apprehension will ease. I want to encourage people to be bold, to take a chance on life, to step outside themselves, and to let them know that they can do this.

The other thing I did not understand prior to this trip was *why* I feared living alone.

That fear never made logical sense to me, because overall I am not a fearful person. I have never had a fear of dying or even dying alone. However, I think because Elizabeth did die alone, the circumstances of her tragic death and the horrible aftermath remained locked in my mind, and then somehow manifested itself into my fear of being left alone in old age.

I'm not sure whether it is Elizabeth's forgiveness, this time alone on my bike, or both, but whatever it is—my fear of loneliness is gone—and I will forever be grateful.

I think about the past couple of days and my struggles with the wind. As long as I continue west, the northern wind pounds the bike and me, which is exhausting and frightening. However, the minute I change direction and head south, with the wind at my back, riding is enjoyable. This is a lesson I need to apply to my life. I need to remember it is okay to choose different options if life becomes complex. It is not necessary to stick with one direction. It is okay to be flexible with relationships, work situations, or my children.

As I ride south, my back is not hurting as much and I relax. Tomorrow, I will be in Nebraska.

Unbeknownst to me, a decision made in that state will impact the course of my life—though surviving the state is not easy.

* * *

I cross into Nebraska and head west again.

The crosswind increases, but it is not as strong as it was in Upper Michigan. The land is flat and the view is unobstructed for miles. The sky is blue with white, scattered clouds. As I ride on the backcountry roads, I unexpectedly come across miles and miles of sunflowers growing on both sides of the highway. Occasionally, someone plants one or two sunflowers in their Oregon yards, but nothing compares to the beauty of these fields.

Yellow petals frame the sunflowers' big brown faces. Each plant has large green leaves and a thick green stalk that must be six feet tall. They gently sway in unison. In the distance, it is a palette of yellow. The sunflowers look like happy faces swaying and seeming to sing, "Have a nice day."

I exit the road, park my motorcycle, and walk to the edge of a field to touch the solid, scratchy stalks that tower over me. It is quiet and peaceful out here, and the serenity reminds me of my parents' ranch.

Many years ago, I promised myself that if my parents ever needed help, I would move back to Roseburg, Oregon, to care for them. Mom and Dad have always been there for me, and I will not abandon them in their old age. Dad is in his eighties and Mom is close behind him; both have major health issues. Brian and Travis are independent, enrolled in college, have girl-friends and jobs, and are moving forward with their lives. The time has come for me to return home and care for my parents. The decision made, an inner calm courses through me.

I head north and for the first time that day, I notice dark, ominous clouds gathering near the top of the mountain I must cross.

Those clouds look ugly.

* * *

Leaving the highway, I shut down the engine and study the menacing weather ahead of me.

If I'm to arrive in Billings, Montana, in three days, I must cross that mountain today. Annette Murray has arranged a party in Billings in my honor, saying that everyone is excited to meet me. Annette tells me the KOA executives have been extremely pleased with the positive advertising generated from my trip. At some point, the United Press picked up the story, and many articles were published in cities I never visited.

But here I sit staring at threatening black clouds. By now, I'm a good judge of the weather, and I know it is best to get off the road. I passed a couple of small towns earlier, and it would be easy enough to return to one of them and wait out the storm. If I continue on, it is highly unlikely there will be any safe place to stay before the other side of the pass.

Damn. I take a deep breath, start the engine, and head into the storm.

Halfway up the mountain, the storm's fury strikes. The road is narrow with tight curves, the rain increases, and it is hard to see through my visor and windshield. My raingear is in my saddlebags and it was stupid to not put it on before I started up the mountain.

I stop on the shoulder so I can get out my raingear, but I discover the shoulder of the highway is thick sand. If I put the kickstand down, it will sink into the sand, and the bike might topple over. I carefully ease back onto the highway. My leathers quickly become soaked and heavy, and my body temperature drops.

Just when I think things cannot get any worse, the thunder and lightning starts. I'm acutely aware that the metal on the bike would make a great lightning rod, but there is no turning back now. There is nothing to do but to continue on through the hellish storm until I'm over the pass. After another couple of exhausting hours, I find a motel near the Badlands National Park, check in, and attempt to dry my drenched leathers. Looks like common sense still is not my strong suit.

I have made a decision, though. I'm absolutely, positively done with extreme winds and death-defying storms. Never again will I deliberately ride into another storm.

Not when I'm this close to home.

* * *

Badlands National Park, which encompasses about 244,000 acres in South Dakota, is a dichotomy.

On one side of the highway, brown and gray eroded buttes, pinnacles, and spires thrust up out of the earth. Little vegetation grows near the peaks of these misshaped mounds. This desolate area goes on for miles with no civilization in sight.

On the other side of the highway is one of the largest protected mixed-grass prairies in the United States. The tall grasses feed a variety of wildlife, including bison, bighorn sheep, and prairie dogs that chirp if I walk near them. It is a strange sight and I visualize two dissimilar worlds colliding.

The park brochure says the Lakota Indians gave this area its name, *mako sica*, which means "land bad," to describe the uninhabitable side. Native Americans have used the prairie side for their hunting grounds for eleven thousand years, and many Lakota still reside in this area.

The fossilized remains of the rhino, horse, and saber-toothed tiger can be found here. People from around the world come here to study the geologic deposits, hoping to find rare fossils.

I leave the Badlands and head west to one of the places I have always wanted to visit: Mount Rushmore. For a change, the weather is warm and dry with little wind.

Surely the mild weather will last for two more days so I can arrive in Billings, Montana, on time.

* * *

Mount Rushmore, near Keystone, South Dakota, takes my breath away.

The heads of four famous presidents are carved into the granite stone of an imposing mountain. Presidents George Washington, Thomas Jefferson, Theodore Roosevelt, and Abraham Lincoln stare majestically toward some unknown vista. Each face is somber, and their chins are pointed upward. A pamphlet explains the sculpted heads measure ". . . sixty feet, as tall as a six-story building. The width of each eye is nearly eleven feet, each mouth, approximately eighteen feet."

Originally, the project of carving Mount Rushmore was undertaken simply to increase tourism in the Black Hills region of South Dakota, but later it received congressional approval. The project started in 1927 and ended in 1941. Amazingly, there were no fatalities during construction, which is hard to imagine as workman hung from ropes to drill holes for the dynamite used to carve the heads.

Walking around the visitor center, I'm captivated with the vision and tenacity required to create this sculpture in only fourteen years. This must have been a demanding undertaking for all involved. I read about how each man was chosen as a representative of America's history. I come across a quote by Theodore Roosevelt: *Far better it is to dare mighty things, to win glorious triumphs, even though checkered by failure, than to take rank with those poor spirits who neither enjoy much nor suffer much, because they live in the gray twilight that knows neither victory nor defeat.*

This is a marvelous quote and I think it is a superb way to live my life. Success comes with the risk of failure, but I believe there is no disgrace in being knocked to my knees. For me, the disgrace comes from not getting up again. It is a good thing I believe this, because over the years I have had my share of setbacks. I copy the quote down in my notebook.

The camping area is crowded, but eventually I locate a small, vacant spot to pitch my tent. Mount Rushmore is a popular tourist attraction, summer is ending, and everyone is scrambling for tent space. My new neighbor, Stan, is also traveling alone on a motorcycle.

Once settled, Stan walks over and we discuss where we have been and why we are traveling alone. It is not unusual for men to travel alone, but Stan's ride is extraordinary, and he explains what brought him here.

"Last year I had my heart replaced. In the beginning, I was so panicked my body would reject my new heart that I rarely moved out of my chair." I motion to Stan and we head to an empty picnic table and sit down.

"Eventually, I became as much a cripple with my new heart as I was with my old one. That's when I decided that this summer I was going to take a trip on my motorcycle." Three young boys dart past us and then slow to check out the motorcycles. They discuss the bikes for a brief moment, and then they are off again.

"What did your family think of your decision?"

"My wife was totally freaked out, and my kids were upset. No one wanted me to go. I have several biking buddies who offered to go with me, but I turned them down. I knew I had to go alone, or I'd never get over my fear." Stan leans on his elbows and looks past me in the direction of Mount Rushmore.

"How long have you been on the road?" I turn and glance toward the mountain.

"A couple of weeks. Each day gets easier. I wanted to be brave in the beginning, but to be honest, I was as scared as my family. I had to force myself to move forward each day. I'm making a loop, and I should be home in another couple of weeks." He looks relaxed, but his voice betrays a quiet anxiety.

"Are you glad you made the decision to travel alone?"

"It's been a godsend. I finally feel like I'm free. I miss being home, though." A whisper of a sigh escapes him.

"You know, Stan, it sounds like you've accomplished what you set out to do. Whenever you're ready, it's okay if you want to go home." I reach into my pocket and take out my notebook. "I want to give you a quote by Teddy Roosevelt that I copied." I tear out the page and hand it to him. He reads the quote and says, "That's a good one, all right."

"Would you mind if I had your address? I'd like to send you a note and tell you I made it."

"Of course you can have it." I write down my address, tear out the sheet, and hand it to him.

The next morning, Stan tells me he has decided to go home and start his life as a healthy man who is not afraid to take a chance on life. We take down our tents, load the bikes, and hug one another goodbye. I tell him how proud I am of him and how much I admire his courage.

This will be a good day. I should be in Billings by four o'clock. That is plenty of time to get myself together for the party this evening.

The weather is so nice that I do not bother with my heavy leather pants and jacket and stuff them in the bottom of my duffle bag. Wearing only my jeans and a light shirt and jacket, I pack my raingear in the top of the saddlebag, even though I'm not concerned about the weather.

This decision to skip wearing my protective leathers will prove to be a horrific mistake.

Chapter 23

DEADLY STORM
ON THE HIGH PLAINS

The ride across eastern Montana is relaxing and warm, a welcome reprieve to finally have the storms behind me.

I'm about a hundred miles from Billings when I see an odd-looking cloud shaped like a *V*, which reminds me of what pictures of tornados look like. However, I cannot imagine that they have tornados in Montana.

The cloud funnels down and looks like it touches the earth somewhere north of me. I'm in the westbound lane and ease off the highway. I see a small group of people in the eastbound lane gathered beside their cars, and we all take pictures of the cloud. I do not walk over to ask anyone about it, thinking the cloud just has an unusual shape.

Although it is not raining, I slip on my raingear over my light jacket and jeans. The wind is picking up and dark storm clouds rapidly gather in the north. This would be a good time to get off the road, but I'm only a couple of hours from Billings. I increase my speed, convinced I can outrun any storms.

The swiftness of the approaching storm shocks me; the sky darkens and the black, heavy clouds drop to the earth. I'm on a two-lane highway heading west. However, no cars are traveling in the eastbound lanes. This is a bad sign.

One method I use to analyze potential turbulent weather is to watch the approaching cars. If three cars in a row have their headlights on and the windshield wipers are swishing at a high speed, at minimum, I am in for heavy rain. But this is the first time that I do not see any cars at all, either approaching, or on the highway in front or behind me. Everyone seems to know something I do not. I check my rearview mirror and see that the storm is closing in behind me. It is pointless to turn around. There is no outrunning the storm now—my race is futile.

I'm screwed.

The storm is an onslaught from the north, and it attacks me with a sudden, terrifying vengeance, slamming into the right side of the bike. Its power is so forceful that I'm momentarily stunned. Then my heart pounds, one frantic beat colliding with the next. I try to compose myself: *Breathe, Carolyn, breathe. Focus. Do not panic.* It is no use; I'm not calm, my breathing is labored, my chest muscles constrict, my shoulders tighten.

That vicious blast effortlessly muscles my 750-pound motorcycle away from the fog line and across the centerline into the oncoming lane. I'm not concerned about the location because there are no cars on the road. However, another blast of aggressive wind could dump me in the ditch on the opposite side of the road.

Dropping my right shoulder and hip, I forcefully throw my body sideways and downward to the right. Simultaneously, I strain to pull up on the left side of the handlebars and then twist the throttle with my right hand to increase the speed. Gradually, the bike moves toward the fog line while inclining dangerously to the right. If there is an abrupt drop in the wind's velocity the bike will crash to the ground. But riding upright is equally dangerous since the wind can easily pitch the bike over in the opposite direction.

I quickly glance down and see my right foot peg barely miss the pavement. If the foot peg scrapes the highway, it will jerk my motorcycle off-balance and slam it and me to the ground. Without my heavy leathers on, the impact could easily kill me or break a number of my bones. Now I have to consider that risk and my muscles tense even more.

For the past hour, thunder, lightning, and heavy, coarse rain have accompanied this ferocious storm screaming southward off the high plains. The rain and wind are so exhausting that it is a struggle to continually concentrate on the danger. My mind drifts, and that funnel cloud worries me—maybe they do have tornados in Montana.

I look down at the sand on the side of the road's shoulder. Could I chance driving onto the wet sand and staying put while I sit out the storm? If the sand is deep and the kickstand sinks into the sand, the wind will topple the bike over, and I could be trapped under it. Even if I'm able to jump off the bike, I will have to spend the night out here, whether I want to or not. And I will not be able to unload the bike when it is on its side.

That means I cannot get to my tent, warm clothes, or my dry leathers that are in the bottom of the duffle bag. Parking on the highway is not an option either, because with my weak back, I doubt if I can lift the bike off the kickstand since I would have to push it upright into the force of the wind. Neither option is a good one. There is no choice but to ride on.

Without my heavy leathers to protect me, my body temperature drops. My fingers are stiff from the cold, and my body aches. Although my raingear is watertight, my light shirt is drenched. The stress has me sweating profusely. It runs from my neck down my spine, into the crack of my butt, and soaks my jeans. Exhaustion and fatigue overwhelm me. As my energy drains, the immediacy of this dangerous situation increases.

How did this happen? Only days ago, I promised myself I would never ride into another storm. I have been on the road almost two and a half months, traveled over thirteen thousand miles, and now I may be killed in a freak storm on an isolated highway in Montana. *I am such an idiot!* I knew a storm loomed, but my sense of obligation to my corporate sponsors in Billings overrode my good sense.

I must concentrate, yet my focus slips away. Taking slow, deep breaths, I try to compose myself. My heavy breathing fogs up the inside of my face shield. I try to look through it, but everything is a haze. It is critical that I relax. I try to relax my grip on the handlebars so the bike's movements are not as erratic; relax my shoulders so I can conserve my strength; relax so I can focus on what I'm doing. But I cannot relax, I cannot. This inability to get myself under control is what will finally kill me.

My luck has finally run out.

And to think I'm only three days from home.

Home. When I die, Brian and Travis will grow up without their mother. Who will take care of my parents in their old age? I sense these are important questions, but I do not have the energy to think them through. Hammered by the wind and rain, my energy recedes, my focus fails, and my will weakens.

Ada help me! Help me!

I am listening to the rhythmic sound of the Harley's engine when an unexpected surge of tranquility flashes throughout my body—my tension vanishes—and I'm overcome with a strange, overwhelming sensation of peace.

Is this what people experience right before they die?

* * *

Guardian angels appear in the most unusual places.

Just when I cannot ride another moment, when I'm convinced that I'm going to die, a rest area appears. Pulling in, I park alongside a large idling semi-truck, push down the kickstand, shut the engine off, and sit there in the pouring rain and screaming wind. I'm ready to collapse, but I'm too exhausted to even get off the bike.

Twenty minutes later, another Harley rider streaks into the rest area and parks his motorcycle near a picnic table and some trees. He is obviously concerned with that location, so he moves the bike inside the men's restroom. I continue to sit by the semi, too fatigued and weak to try to lift the bike off the kickstand or attempt to move it.

Eventually, the trucker beside me braves the storm to tell me I would be better off moving my bike to the other side of his truck. It is true—I would be out of the wind—but unfortunately, I'm unable to move this bike anywhere. I explain about my back and ask him if he would mind asking the biker I saw earlier if he could move my bike. The biker graciously agrees and parks my bike beneath the women's restroom overhang. The three of us line up against the rest room with our backs to the front wall, which protects us from the wind and rain.

We exchange war stories. The trucker starts first.

"I thought I could make it to Billings, but the wind was pushing me all over the road. I came around a tight corner, checked my side mirror, and saw the back wheels of my semi lift off the ground. That's when I pulled in here." We are amazed the wind could lift the rear of his heavy truck.

The biker continues, "I ride my motorcycle back and forth on this road every day to go to work. I've been in some bad storms. Once I was hit by hail so large, I had to have stitches in my head. But I've never seen anything like this."

He went on, "I was hugging the white fog line on my side of the road and took a corner too fast. The wind caught me and shoved my motorcycle across both lanes into the soft sand on the other side of the road. I almost dumped the bike. That got my attention, so here I am."

I tell my miserable tale and then go to dig my leathers and dry clothes out of the bottom of my duffle bag, grab some snacks to share, and head into the bathroom to change. I try to call Annette several times to let her know I'm okay and that I will not be there tonight. There is no answer, so I leave messages on the answering machine. The biker tells me the cell service out here is poor, almost nonexistent.

The three of us stand and watch the freeway. No cars pass from either direction. I guess everyone else has more sense than the three of us. After an hour or so, a yellow Volkswagen pulls in and parks directly in front of us. A young woman remains in her car, crying.

After a few minutes, I walk over and tell her that even though we are a sorry-looking bunch, we are not dangerous—she is welcome to join us. She is relieved and lines up on the wall beside us. She says her car was being pushed all over the highway. She could not keep it in her lane and was terrified she was going to crash.

Hours later, the storm subsides somewhat. The biker suggests we make a dash for Billings. It is getting dark, though, and he says there may be deer on the road, and that they are most active at this time of night. Hitting one could be as hazardous as the storm. We decide to form a caravan, first the trucker, then the small car. The biker and I will bring up the rear.

The wind is still screaming and the rain is vicious, but by the grace of God, all of us make it safely to Billings. I pull into the first motel I see, too exhausted to hunt for the KOA. I need to spend a couple of days in a bed and rest. Besides, practically everything I own is soaked.

Checking for messages, I hear several from Annette. She had left messages earlier, but I did not hear them before heading into the storm.

"Carolyn, please stop and get off the road. There's a very dangerous storm out there and numerous accidents. We had to cancel the party. We'll catch up with you tomorrow or the next day." I can hear the stress in her voice. A man in the background is yelling.

"Tell her to get off the road! Tell her to get off the road!"

I turn up the heat, get out of my wet leathers, and hang my sopping clothes around the room so they can dry. After a hot shower, I go to bed.

I'm done for today.

* * *

Later the next day I'm rested and meet with Annette Murray, a petite, curly brown-haired spitfire.

We immediately hit it off and plan to spend the next three days together so she can show me around. First, she introduces me to the corporate folks. Laughing, the executives tell me it was Annette who convinced them to sponsor me.

"She was persistent and determined, insisting this type of advertising would encourage women to stay at KOAs. Frankly, we didn't think you could manage this undertaking. But Annette's pushy." One of the execs in a gray suit gives Annette a playful nudge with his elbow.

Another suit chimes in. "That's right. Finally, we gave up and said, 'Okay, Annette, let's give it a try and see how far she gets.'"

"We hated to admit it, but Annette was right." Everyone laughs. "We've received a tremendous amount of positive feedback not only from the press but also from the KOA personnel."

Another man steps forward and shakes my hand. "Thank you for being such an excellent and entertaining spokesperson for us. We would like to work with you again."

"It was my pleasure, but Annette gets all the credit. She's been wonderful to work with, with just the right balance of assertiveness and kindness. She tried to keep tabs on me, which wasn't an easy thing to do."

Annette's smile widens, but she does not disagree with me.

"I really appreciate the groundwork that went into organizing the media events. I just had to show up and chat. That's always fun for me." Annette and I say our goodbyes and head to her office.

Over the next three days, Annette gives me the grand tour of Billings. She has recently purchased a reconditioned, older red Cadillac convertible and she chauffeurs me around town in style. Ever the organizer, she arranges a jet boat tour up one of the local rivers and a radio interview.

The next morning, I join the *Breakfast Flakes*, an early morning talk show. Both guys are quick and funny, and the conversation flows easily. Lately, the media questions have changed once again. Earlier questions focused on why and how I was able to make this trip, then fears, and then they asked about loneliness. Now one of the Breakfast Flakes asks, "Your trip will be over in a few days. What have you learned?"

"When I started this trip, my purpose was to overcome my fear of being left alone after my sons grew up and moved out. I like the quote by Ralph Waldo Emerson that says 'Do the thing you fear and the death of fear is certain.' I decided to take his advice and attack my fear by traveling alone."

One of the Flakes looks startled. "Let me get this straight. You decided to travel alone so you wouldn't be lonely? I have to tell you, that sounds like a weird way to combat loneliness."

"I know it does, but I found that doing what I was afraid to do, being alone, caused my fear of loneliness to vanish."

"That's really amazing. What would you tell lonely people about your experience?" The other Flake slides the microphone closer to me.

"I want to tell lonely people that it's okay to admit they are lonely. I think it takes great courage to admit it. I wouldn't admit my feelings for a long time, but after I did, I found a lot of people felt the same way. Now I try to be the first to say 'hello,' and I have found that people are really open and want to talk about it."

"That's cool. What was the most important thing you learned?"

"On a personal note, when I started this journey I felt guilty over a horrible decision I made twenty-two years ago. It was only after I asked for forgiveness that I found peace of mind, and it was that serenity that finally set me free. So I guess I would say to people that seeking forgiveness is empowering, and if they ask for it, perhaps it will help them, too." Both Flakes are quiet for a moment. "This has been fun, guys, thanks for having me."

The three days pass quickly. Tomorrow, I head to Missoula, Montana.

The plains are behind me, the Rocky Mountains ahead.

* * *

I find the Missoula KOA and opt for a Kamping Kabin.

My neighbors are a nice family with two little bouncy girls, around five or six years old. When the engine cools, the girls climb on my motorcycle, and I take a picture of their family. I give each girl an inspirational note for their mom to read to them, and they thank me.

Again, the feelings of longing I used to have are gone. I wonder if I will feel this way with younger girls. Missing who Elizabeth would have become was always the hardest for me when I was around young girls. Now, I'm at peace with myself and can just enjoy the delightful nature of the children.

Another neighbor, Doug, is hauling his Harley in the back of a pickup and visiting friends. Doug was a pilot for the Air Force and flew B-52s. Our conversation is easy, and he invites me to have dinner with him at a local restaurant. We sit for hours and talk about philosophies, interests, and goals. I enjoy hearing his remarkable perspective on a range of subjects.

I tell him about my initial reservations about taking this trip: the fear of loneliness, my guilt over my daughter's death and the power of forgiveness, the hardships and storms. Doug is an introspective man and asks what made me keep going. Why did I not just give up and go home?

"Many times I did feel like quitting, but I knew nothing was going to change if I turned around and went home. I was lost and filled with guilt, and the only direction I knew to go was forward."

Doug has some thoughts on my growth.

"Carolyn, I think you're like a fine antique piece of furniture that has been painted. It isn't that the paint isn't pretty, because it is. But underneath the paint is where the wood's true richness lies: its fine grain, quality, and sturdiness. You've chosen to strip away the layers of paint. What remains is the beauty of your true inner self."

"Thank you, Doug. That is a lovely analogy and a very sweet thing to say." Doug is such a nice man, and I reach over and squeeze his forearm.

Prior to this journey, I had lost sight of the great men out there. I decide to put the past behind me, drop my guard, and see what happens. However, I'm so content to be by myself now that I'm no longer interested in pursuing a relationship. I do not feel compelled to be half of a couple anymore. Somewhere on this voyage, the frantic fear of being alone vanished in the wind.

That does not mean that if I were to meet the right man and fall in love, I would not consider marriage. The difference is that now marriage will not be a crutch for my loneliness, but rather the joining of two, strong, independent people who choose to walk hand-in-hand through life.

As amazing as it seems, tomorrow afternoon I'll be in Oregon. I have not told anyone about my arrival date. I plan to stop in The Dalles and get a room.

I want to take advantage of these last few days to be alone.

Chapter 24

MY SOLITARY SHADOW

I'm nearing the Idaho border when a car passes and then brakes.

The car pulls forward again, the red brake lights come on, and then the driver slows until I draw up alongside his car. The occupants stare at me. I check them out, but they do not appear threatening. In the front seat sit a man and a woman, a teenage boy sits in the back. I nod with a chin-up motion. They move ahead, brake, drop back behind me, and then pull forward again. This has happened before if someone recognizes me from a television interview or if my picture is in a local newspaper, so I'm not concerned.

I'm ready for breakfast, spot a small café, and take the next exit. I'm settling in when I see the same car that passed me earlier drive into the parking lot. The man walks into the restaurant and asks me if I'm Carolyn Fox and if I went to Douglas High School in Winston, Oregon. I tell him I am. I realize it is Larry and we went to high school together about thirty years ago. Our graduating class consisted of sixty-two people.

Larry, who now lives in a different state, says that in June his mother sent him the *News-Review* article and picture of me riding in downtown Roseburg. He says that for the past several months, he and his wife have looked at every rider in case I might be one of them. They were returning home from a wedding in Wyoming when they spotted me. They were not sure it was me, because in high school I had short, bleached blonde hair, and now I'm a redhead. They had already passed the exit when I turned off, but his wife made him come back and check. We have breakfast together and a wonderful visit.

My past seems so far away now, but it is important to remember my roots. I believe it is this mixture of our past and present experiences that makes us who we are today.

Many years ago, when I was a little girl in rural Winston, I attended a Sunday school class, and the teacher would repeat a quote from the Bible that said, "And it came to pass." I always thought this meant something was going to take place in the present or the future.

Now I have to wonder if during all those centuries of transcribing the Bible, a period in the sentence was inadvertently lost. Perhaps the sentence was really supposed to read, "And it came. To pass." Meaning our life experiences come to us for a reason—even if extremely difficult—so that we can learn and grow from them. After the experience has passed we are stronger, wiser for the lesson, and better people.

What I learned from Elizabeth's death was that the power of forgiveness can set us free.

That was Elizabeth's gift to me. And there was another positive gift that came from her death: it changed the way I felt about children. I became a better mother to my sons because of Elizabeth. I was more loving, kind, and patient than I might have been otherwise. I fought for my sons, protected them, and loved them unconditionally. This is still true today.

For me, this is the true meaning of the quote, and it speaks to my life's journey.

* * *

It is early September; the ride over the Rockies is cool, but uneventful, with no snow on the highway.

As I travel from Spokane, Washington, to The Dalles, Oregon, it is warm and pleasant. This is perfect riding weather that offers me time to reflect on my trip. Before I left Portland, I was concerned that the woman who left would not be the same woman who returned. I was right to think that, but wrong to be concerned.

I am not the same woman, but I like this woman better. She is calm, collected, seasoned, and grounded. I have changed, and my new serenity has instilled a confidence that I did not think was possible only a few short months ago. All fear of loneliness or living alone has disappeared, whisked away by the wind.

Ever since leaving the old church in Rhode Island, I no longer have feelings of remorse or longing for Elizabeth when I see little girls or young women. I'm at peace with myself; the piercing ache in my heart has healed; and I am no longer drawn to that dark hallway with the agonizing cries. Finally, I found the courage to ask for forgiveness, and by the grace of God, it was granted. I owe that to Elizabeth and will always remember and love her.

The important decision was made to move back to Roseburg and care for my parents. They live in an apartment building that they own. I talked to my mother the other night, and she told me an apartment directly across from theirs is vacant; I will move into that one. I'm anxious to spend time with my brothers and their families, returning to the people I love. My parents are excited and relieved that I will be there for them in their old age.

After checking into one of The Dalles' motels, I unload my things and call Joy. She and some friends will meet me in a couple of days so we can ride back to Portland together. I have been on the road for seventy-seven days and traveled over 14,000 miles. I cannot wait to see everyone again, especially my sons. After I'm home, I plan to fly to Alaska and Hawaii, rent a Harley in each state, and complete my journey prior to the end of the year.

I ride out to The Dalles Dam, park my bike, and walk over and lean against a rock overlook. The Columbia River Gorge is beautiful and I'm struck by the contrast of the massive dam and a small, weathered wooden structure that is probably a hundred years old. Flocks of seagulls sit on rocks, others glide gracefully on the updrafts. It is quiet and peaceful here.

Indians used to fish at this location, and portions of an old Indian village remain. An aged Shaker church with a simple cross on the peak of its wooden frame looks to be on the verge of collapse. With time, all things change, and I believe this is as it should be.

Silently, I thank those who made this trip possible. My parents for their financial and emotional support, Brian and Travis who have always had faith in me, loved me, and unselfishly encouraged me to "Do what makes you happy." I thank Elizabeth for her gift of forgiveness. And I thank God and Ada for looking after me.

Across the river, a train heads toward me, traveling along the base of a low, flat hill. It is a long train, a hundred cars or more, and the throaty blast of the whistle echoes across the water as I recall my first night in my tent, when I was alone and scared.

The train's whistle sounds again, more intense as it comes closer. The train cars pass one by one and move out of sight, and then the whistle fades, a reminder that all journeys have a beginning and an end.

I get on my bike and ride along the same highway that Steve and I traveled several years ago. On that first apprehensive ride on a Harley, I remember being a tentative and uncomfortable passenger. Now I'm a seasoned traveler who values and protects my time spent alone.

As the warm, balmy wind massages my face, I glance down and smile as my solitary shadow dances along the highway.

I close my eyes for a moment, hearing only the Harley's steady, peaceful rhythm.

Epilogue

THE YEAR I TURNED FIFTY

T he year I turned fifty was a roller coaster of emotions.

My 50/50 trip was a soul journey packed with exhilarating highs and heart-wrenching lows. My personal growth and happiness materialized when I ultimately asked for forgiveness and made peace with myself.

In mid-September, I flew to Alaska, borrowed a friend's Harley, and rode in that rugged, awe-inspiring state. In November, I flew to Hawaii, again rented a Harley, and completed my fifty-state odyssey, calmed by the ocean's tranquil cadence.

Tragedy struck our family in late September of that year when my handsome, loving brother, Gary, whose great smile and charismatic personality charmed all who knew him, died from a massive heart attack. Gary was fifty-one.

Prior to the end of the year, and while living near my parents in Roseburg, Oregon, I met Dennis Foster, a handsome Harley rider, and we fell in love. This time, the reasons were right; we married six months later. In 2015, we will celebrate our twentieth wedding anniversary.

Both Brian and Travis have been happily married for many years. Brian has three children, and Travis has two. Both boys are successful; we all live near one another and visit often.

Between us, Dennis and I have five children and eleven grandchildren (seven boys and four girls). We take our local grandchildren on adventures—a hike behind a waterfall, a helicopter ride, the coast, museums, and outings with the metal detectors.

Several years ago Dennis and I sold our Harleys. We replaced them with a Jeep Wrangler, and today we RV and rock crawl in the Arizona desert for a portion of each year. I have to admit, it is nice to have an air conditioner when it is hot and a roof when it rains.

Joe and I put the past behind us many years ago. Today we come together for family events. George Orwell said "Time heals all things," and for me, this is true.

My life has been an incredible journey; my blessings are many.

In July 2014, I turned seventy. As always, I look forward to life's next adventure.

* * *

Each spring—when the pink dogwoods bloom—I recall a sweet, china-doll face and I am renewed with the gift of forgiveness.

About the Author

Carolyn Fox was admitted to the Oregon State Bar in 1989 and successfully owned and operated two private law practices. She started law school at forty-one, learned to ride a motorcycle at age forty-six, and obtained her private pilot license at sixty. She has also worked as a private investigator and served as a grant writer to help fund nonprofit organizations.

In 2015, Carolyn published *69 Explosive Divorce Tips: The Divorcee's Guide for Surviving Emotional Landmines*. She writes for national and international magazines, and has been published in *Science of Mind*, *American Rider*, *The Enthusiast*, *Hog Tales*, and more. She had a story featured in Kay Allenbaugh's national bestselling anthology *Chocolate for a Woman's Soul*, and she has contributed numerous articles to *Thunder Press* newspaper.

The author resides with her husband, Dennis Foster, in West Linn, Oregon. She is represented by MacGregor Literary Inc. Find her online at carolynfox.us.